Radio Journalism

Guy Starkey and Andrew Crisell

Los Angeles • London • New Delhi • Singapore • Washington DC

SAGE Publications Ltd
1 Oliver's Yard
55 City Road
London EC1Y 1SP

SAGE Publications Inc.
2455 Teller Road
Thousand Oaks, California 91320

SAGE Publications India Pvt Ltd
B 1/I 1 Mohan Cooperative Industrial Area
Mathura Road
New Delhi 110 044

SAGE Publications Asia-Pacific Pte Ltd
33 Pekin Street #02-01
Far East Square
Singapore 048763

British Library Cataloguing in Publication data

A catalogue record for this book is available from
the British Library

ISBN 978-1-4129-3014-7
ISBN 978-1-4129-3015-4 (pbk)

Library of Congress Control Number Available

Typeset by C&M Digitals (P) Ltd., Chennai, India
Printed in India at Replika Press Pvt Ltd
Printed on paper from sustainable resources

Journalism Studies: Key Texts is a new textbook series that systematically maps the crucial connections between theory and practice in journalism. It provides the solid grounding students need in the history, theory, 'real-life' practice and future directions of journalism, while further engaging them in key critical debates. Drawing directly from how journalism is studied and understood today, the series is a full-service resource for students and lecturers alike.

Series Editors: Martin Conboy, David Finkelstein, Bob Franklin

Alternative Journalism   Chris Atton and James F Hamilton

CONTENTS

To our loved ones. They know who they are.

ACKNOWLEDGEMENTS

We wish to express our grateful thanks to all those who have in one way or another enabled us to write this book – our families, our many good friends and colleagues, both past and present, as well as our interviewees. In particular we must mention Kate Arkless Gray, a freelance broadcast journalist now working for the BBC, Julia Barthram of ITV News, Louise Bell and Katy McDonald of the University of Sunderland, Richard Evans of BBC Radio Wales, Professor Stanisław Jędrzejewski of the Leon Koźmiński Academy of Entrepreneurship and Management in Warsaw, Raina Konstantinova of the European Broadcasting Union, Bao Li for additional research, Brian Lister, an independent radio management consultant, and of course the editor of this series, Professor Bob Franklin of Cardiff University, for some very sound advice and guidance along the way.

1

THE TRAVELLER WHO CAME CALLING: A SHORT HISTORY OF RADIO JOURNALISM

The importance of radio journalism

Journalism is an activity that we primarily associate with newspapers, magazines and television. Indeed, among the many who turn to sound broadcasting as a source of background music, few may be aware that *radio* journalism exists. Hearing an occasional 'capsule' of news within the sequence of records, they perhaps assume that compiling it is about as challenging and glamorous as Cinderella's day job.

In this book we are going to be making some rather large claims for the importance of radio journalism. But we should begin by pointing out that it requires skills which, even in the preparation of capsule news, are additional to the investigative and literary abilities that every journalist should possess. On radio, the drafting and delivery of news copy is not a simple matter. Like television's, but unlike those of the newspapers, its words are constantly dissolving or *evanescent*: but unlike television's, they are wholly invisible, as are the people who utter them. Consequently, its listeners seldom give radio their undivided attention. Its news copy needs to be written and presented with these factors constantly in mind – to adopt an easy and intelligible speech idiom even as it strives to do justice to the often complex and detailed character of events.

Yet the case for the importance of radio journalism rests on something other than the fact that it is more demanding and skilful than might be supposed. Most of us accept that journalism – the reporting and analysis not simply of 'the news' but of current affairs in their broadest sense – is at the heart of the BBC's public service endeavour, and since television commands much larger audiences than radio, this is often taken to be 'television' journalism. However, we will suggest in this book that it is often on *radio*, with its ability to handle facts, issues and ideas without visual distraction, that this endeavour is most effectively performed.

The origins of journalism

A career in radio journalism is thus highly worthwhile, but to make the case for its current and future importance we need to know something of its past. Its origins lie in the natural human desire to know more about what is going on in the world that lies beyond the compass of our horizons and our own experience. Even that information which the early travellers brought to a community, recounting what they had seen or been told by someone else, could not wholly satisfy this desire. So the development of the printing press by Johann Gutenburg around 1450, with its ability to disseminate news, information and comment on a mass scale, first demonstrated the potential of humankind to produce and consume something that would become recognisable as journalism.

The print medium firmly established itself as a conduit through which a discourse could elaborate the results of journalistic activity. On the audience's behalf, someone could find, collate and digest a considerable amount of information and then synthesise from it an account which was presented in such a way as to satisfy the audience's natural curiosity, amuse, entertain it and even call it to action. Today, print still performs this important role, but because technological advance tends to be exponential, the last century produced increasingly rapid developments in distribution technology. This resulted in new mass media that would provide other popular platforms for the practice of journalism. The cinema newsreel, pioneered in 1910 by *Pathé's Animated Gazette*, offered audiences new experiences in the form of moving images to accompany text and eventually a *spoken* narrative. Yet, because newspapers and newsreels required both mechanical processing and distribution over land, even today print and film lack a compelling advantage possessed by the news-bearing travellers of old: immediacy (Starkey 2007: 115–16).

The development of radio

The invention of the first of the electronic media, the telegraph, provided that immediacy. It allowed point-to-point communication over long distances in real time, although a direct connection by wire was required, and rather than being a medium of mass communication it, like the telephone a little later, offered only person-to-person transmission. It was the development of radio (initially known as 'the wireless') that brought the benefits of mass distribution which were previously confined to the printing press. Radio broadcast over wide areas by sending electro-magnetic waves into the air. Its messages were available to anyone within range who had a suitable receiver, to large, real-time audiences who could hear of events quite literally within milliseconds of their occurrence.

Among the early pioneers were Guglielmo Marconi, who first demonstrated transmission and reception but was slow to spot radio's potential as a mass medium, and Reginald Fessenden, who in 1906 broadcast the first programme of voice and music, but who failed to capitalise on his idea, so is merely a footnote in the history of broadcasting. These early delays in the exploitation of the medium tempt one to the conclusion that new media technologies are introduced into society only in so far as their potential for disrupting the *status quo* is limited (Winston 1998). Certainly, in various hands radio could be a powerful force in a number of different ways, a point we shall return to later. However, it was destined to become as important a medium as print – durable, as its hundred-year history attests, and, as the popularity of podcasts demonstrates, capable of exploitation through twenty-first-century distribution technologies. By today's standards it took a remarkably long time for Fessenden's pioneering broadcast to be imitated on any grand scale, but over the following two decades sporadic experimental broadcasting gradually gave way to regular services – in Britain under Marconi, in the United States under Fessenden's successors, and even in communist Russia, where in 1917 revolutionaries had used wireless telegraphy rather than speech transmissions to proclaim their victory and try to foment a worldwide uprising.

The power of radio as a means of entertainment and propaganda was swiftly demonstrated, yet it did not immediately produce radio *journalism*. In compiling his first programme, Fessenden omitted all news, even though the concept of news reporting was well established in the press. He played recordings of music and read a passage from the Bible, but had he thought of it he could have included the world's first news bulletin and quite legitimately led on the historic significance of his own actions. Alas, radio's great potential as a platform for journalistic activity was yet to be perceived: this great inventor of dozens of patented devices missed a golden opportunity and, as we shall see, it fell to others to perceive and exploit radio's potential to bring immediacy to the task of reporting the world to mass audiences.

The distinctiveness of radio journalism

What, though, is *radio* journalism, and how does it differ from other types of journalism? What do they have in common, and what are the reasons for the differences and similarities? How do these different traditions in presenting factual narratives coexist, and where radio journalism is distinct, why is it so? Just as print journalism is more than the front and back pages and includes reviews, in-depth analyses and comment which also solicit the attention of the reader, so radio journalism is much more than 'the news'. It is to be found in factual output of many kinds: in programming as much as in bulletins. It is also expensive to produce, requiring more effort to source and to evidence, to illustrate and to communicate, than does the playing of pre-recorded music or the relaying of spontaneous conversation. The many forms in which radio journalism exists today could no more be invented overnight than Fessenden could conceive of a news bulletin in his first broadcast. They developed slowly, often beginning as the spark of an idea, always a product of the institutional context from which they emerged, and, once established, mimicked and extended by rival radio stations.

Some institutional contexts were more conducive to the development of radio journalism than others, and in different countries radio industries developed in different ways. The Marconi Company was a private business (Crisell 1994: 18), but in the United Kingdom the private ownership of radio stations was short-lived. This was because the governmental Crawford Committee of Inquiry – the second of many – recommended that broadcasting should be publicly owned (Crawford Committee 1926). In the United States, radio remained largely in the hands of commercial operators and these two sharply contrasting models of institutional ownership influenced the development of radio journalism in different ways in different countries. This distinction between the public and private sectors of the radio industry, one larger or smaller than the other depending on the country one cares to examine, is an important one. We consider it important enough to provide a framework for our analysis, and it is a theme that will run through this book.

Journalism, news and the development of the BBC

Today, the British Broadcasting Corporation (BBC) is the United Kingdom's oldest and, by common consent, pre-eminent broadcasting institution. Its role has always been to provide a comprehensive 'public service' that transcends the mere market, and we are used to the idea that news and current affairs are at the heart of this public service provision. As relatively recently as 1992, it published a policy document, *Extending Choice*, in which it posed the question: 'What, then, are the defining characteristics of the BBC's public purpose?' And it replied: 'Firstly, the BBC should aim to provide the comprehensive, in-depth and impartial news and information coverage across a range of broadcasting outlets that is needed to support a fair and informed national debate' (Franklin 2001: 103).

This aim is nowhere more apparent than in radio. Over its networks and stations as a whole, that which is not music is overwhelmingly journalism: news and what we might term 'contemporary information' – current affairs, sport, and other matters of perennial public interest, such as health, consumerist and lifestyle issues. There are exceptions, drama, light entertainment and phone-in conversation among them, but with the exception of the latter they are also expensive to produce, which explains why they are almost entirely the preserve of a public service broadcaster. But all the other genres fall within the province of journalism. Music is the main concern of Radios 1, 2 and 3 (although Radio 2's flagship midday show, presented by Jeremy Vine, has a current affairs theme), but Five Live is wholly given over to news and sport, while news, sport, 'factual' and current affairs make up just over two-thirds of the output of Radio 4 (BBC 2004: 143). Finally, the extensive provision of news and information is the means by which BBC local radio seeks to distinguish itself from its commercial rivals (Crisell and Starkey 2006: 18). There have been periods during which these provincial outposts of the corporation have broadcast nothing but speech, but more recently they have favoured a diet of speech punctuated by music.

It may therefore come as a surprise to learn that news and current affairs were not always at the heart of the BBC's public service endeavour. In the early years of broadcasting they formed a marginal, derivative and rather meagre component of its programming. This was partly due to factors outside its control and partly a matter of perceptions and values. A body that saw more clearly than many into radio's potential as a rapid news medium was the Newspaper Proprietors' Association. Noting the threat that it would pose to the press, the Association lobbied the government to place a news embargo on the British Broadcasting Company. Launched in 1922, the company was prohibited from transmitting bulletins until the evening and obliged to take all its news from the press agencies. Moreover, the governments of the 1920s and 1930s feared that the new medium could be used to win public opinion to seditious views. While in the United States and elsewhere radio was left to commercial companies to develop (Starkey 2007: 23–4), the prevailing view in the United Kingdom was that it was too important to be left to the private sector. When, on 1 January 1927, the BBC was transformed from a private company into a public body, the British Broadcasting Corporation, its charter forbade it to editorialise and restricted the kinds of political content it could carry. Among governments, the fear that broadcasting can promote sedition, first articulated by Crawford (Crawford Committee 1926: 14–15), persists to this day.

Finally, John Reith, who was the Managing Director of the company and then the first Director General of the corporation, took little interest in news and politics (Boyle 1972: 173, 222) – and in this, he was not wholly untypical of his time. In the great scheme of things, news did not always rate highly. This was partly because people were less bombarded by news and information than they are today. News provision, almost entirely in the hands of the press, was intermittent – daily rather than continuous – and thus recognised as 'old' even as it was being consumed. In its infancy, the BBC sometimes broadcast no news on certain days because, in its view, no news had occurred (Scannell 1996: 160).

The impact of radio on the character of the news

Yet radio itself would soon transform the character of the news and thus help to change the perception of it. This began with the General Strike in 1926, a major confrontation between millions of workers and their employers. The government had armed troops at its disposal in case any physical outbreak of class war were to threaten the nation's security. Because much of the press was shut down by striking print workers, the news embargo on the BBC was lifted for the duration of the strike, and its five daily bulletins provided information of a topicality that could not be matched even by those newspapers that were still appearing. To the now rapidly growing body of listeners, it must have seemed as if a traveller had, indeed, come calling, with stories to tell of what was happening elsewhere. Families would gather round the wireless, enthralled by what they heard. This was the consumer electronics revolution of its time – and the first in history.

The sensation of immediacy prompted a new habit of tuning in to the radio to find out what was going on in the world, and the 1930s were marked by improvements in the production of radio news. Bulletins were drafted in language that was less 'literary' and rather more suited to the ear. Magnetic – hence instant – recording technology arrived, and the BBC gradually freed itself from some of the restrictions that the government and newspaper industry had imposed. Certain major stories broke that radio could cover more contemporaneously and more vividly than the press. Among these were the great fire at the iconic Crystal Palace in London, the last illness of George V in 1936 and the Munich crisis of 1938, which seemed to pull Europe back from the brink of all-out war. Eye-witness accounts were not just factual in content, like those of the press, but emotively coloured by the voices in which they were heard.

During the Second World War (1939–1945), radio journalism achieved a certain level of maturity. In times of war the public hunger for news is insatiable, and for the first time in history a technology existed to feed it. The BBC's war reporters were given the same battle training as the troops, equipped with portable disc recorders and despatched to the front line, whence they were able to send back detailed descriptions combined with a modest amount of actuality. The volume of material they produced was such that, for the first time, extended news programmes could be broadcast. *Radio Newsreel*, which began in 1940, and *War Report*, launched in 1944, contained not merely a bald recitation of events, but eye-witness accounts of them and recordings of the sounds they made. The very word 'newsreel', which was borrowed from the cinema, affirms the BBC's confidence that radio could now match some of the iconism of film (Crisell 2002: 61). Finally, in 1944, the BBC acknowledged the enhanced status that broadcasting had helped to confer on the news by ceasing to rely on second-hand and often print-focused accounts of foreign affairs and appointing its own over-seas correspondents.

For ten years or so after the war, radio news enjoyed relatively plain sail-ing; although the march of communication technology was quickening, the fledgling television service posed no threat since it, too, was a BBC monop-oly, and all broadcast news was in the hands of a single controller (Briggs 1995c: 63). Moreover, such is human conservatism, that just as radio news had initially been thought of in terms of the press, so now television news was being thought of in terms of radio. Apart from a 10-minute newsreel which was shown on five evenings a week and aped that of the cinema, tele-vision news between 1946 and 1954 consisted only of re-broadcast radio bulletins accompanied by a still photograph of Big Ben. Even after 1954, when a slightly more pictorial bulletin was introduced, the newsreaders remained invisible, declaring themselves only as 'voice-overs' behind pho-tographs, film clips and caption cards.

Hence, in the United Kingdom radio journalism developed at a pace that today would be considered rather leisurely. Since the absence of real com-petition encouraged complacency rather than innovation and influences from overseas were slight, the institutional context provided little impetus for change until the mid-1950s. Reith's BBC had been short on fun and long on moralising, serious in its musical programming rather than popular in its outlook (Crisell 1994: 22), so the attempts made during the 1930s to break the BBC's monopoly had focused on entertainment rather than factual con-tent. They had been mounted by privately-owned broadcasters such as Radio Luxembourg, Radio Normandy and Radio Eiffel Tower, which used transmitters on the continent to beam signals across the English Channel.

The impact of television on radio news

Hence, if the Corporation was being challenged by rivals in those pre-war years, it was not in respect of its news coverage. What changed everything was the launch of Independent Television (ITV) in 1955, and particularly of ITV's networked news provider, Independent Television News (ITN). Both BBC television and BBC radio were hit hard – radio irreversibly so – but competition had the unforeseen, longer-term effect of moving the provision of news and current affairs nearer to the heart of the BBC's public service philosophy. Indeed, it is arguable that the Corporation comes closest to performing a public service in the *radio* provision of these things. To demonstrate this, we need to look at broadcasting developments over the last half-century.

Unblinkered by a radiogenic past, ITN brought a new and televisual per-spective to news reportage and in so doing, took large numbers of viewers away from the BBC. But by the end of the 1950s, the latter had emulated its rival and lured many of them back. What television did in general was to devastate the audience for radio and it has been suggested that the fast-moving Cuban missile crisis of 1962, with its images of weapons on the decks of freighters, was the story that would establish television's lasting dominance as a news medium not only over radio but the press (Hood and O'Leary 1990: 35–6).

Suddenly it seemed as if radio – with journalism now at its core – had been sidelined. Unrelenting technological advance had created a monster that would bring about radio's destruction. Just as the discovery of electro-magnetic radio waves had created a platform for a new and immediate journalism of sound that was able to trump both print and film, an even newer technology, offering immediate images as well as sounds, now threatened to kill off radio. From the middle of the 1950s there was therefore an urgent need to rediscover radio's core strengths. With the fortuitous arrival of transistor technology, which enhanced the mobility and portability of receivers, music above all, but also news and information, emerged as forms of content that audiences were eager to consume as a background to their other activities. The first radio sets had been bulky objects that took up a considerable amount of space in the living room and required power from large rechargeable batteries. These were replaced by mains-powered receivers which of course remained in a fixed location where they could be plugged into a socket in the wall. Then, in the 1950s an attractive range of transistor radios appeared: compact by comparison to the old valve wireless set, they could run off batteries similar in size to those used today and, most important, they were *portable*. Now listeners could experience radio in different rooms, they could buy multiple sets, take the radio with them on holiday, even enjoy listening on the beach. The 'tranny' quickly became a 1960s icon and even, in London's fashionable Carnaby Street, a style accessory.

The revival of radio – and of radio news

Radio's technological renaissance was fuelled by social change. In the late 1950s and early 1960s, a whole generation of 'teenagers' (the word dates from about this time) began to assert themselves culturally, economically and politically. What they craved from their radios was American 'rock 'n' roll' music, to be played round the clock and not just in the miserly doses supplied by the BBC's Light Programme. A burgeoning music scene, a desire to access American hit records and a real sense that the BBC was ignoring youthful tastes led to an invasion of the airwaves by 'pirate' broadcasters, such as Radio Caroline, Radio London and Swinging Radio England. This new challenge to the monopoly of radio that the BBC still enjoyed also came from across the sea. But this time the commercial operators, as keen as their predecessors to make money from paid-for advertising, were broadcasting from converted ships and disused military forts situated just outside British territorial waters.

These were primarily music stations, whose commitment to journalism extended no further than relaying the news they had lifted from the BBC networks, but they demonstrated the demand for a kind of programming within which news would play a vital role. The impression that the pirate presenters were marooned on the high seas and divorced from the lives of their onshore listeners could be mitigated by the inclusion of almost up-to-date news. The listeners, who were mostly unaware of its source, felt that these stations had their finger on the pulse of the nation: that they were musically more advanced than the BBC, but also just as capable of satisfying that universal human need for news and information.

With radio rescued from extinction by a new generation of listeners whose tastes and interests would grow and change with age, new uses were found for the medium. While television steadily colonised people's evening leisure time, radio was able to find large audiences during the day, when people were less free to abandon other activities in order to indulge their sense of sight. Breakfast time soon became radio's peak period and it still commands a larger share of the audience until early afternoon (Radio Advertising Bureau 2007).

Among the first to see that there was still a place on radio for a substantial treatment of news and current affairs was Robin Day, one of the original ITN newsreaders and later a formidable political interviewer. In 1955 and while still employed by the BBC, Day proposed a daily 'Morning Review' that would eventually take shape as the *Today* programme. His rationale was a shrewd one:

> ... there is a steadily increasing audience to car radios. This element must be particularly large first thing in the morning when people are motoring to work. These people cannot read while driving. Why should we not offer them comment and description that the rail or 'bus traveller can read in his newspaper?

> (quoted in Donovan 1997: 3)

The *Today* programme launched in 1957, at first carrying mainly apolitical features but soon becoming 'harder' and newsier (Donovan 1997). Indeed, as part of its plans to reorganise sound broadcasting in 1970, the BBC thought of turning Radio 4 into an all-news network, while news and current affairs were also seen as the key strength of its local radio stations, which had begun to open in 1967. Moreover, with programmes like *Analysis* from 1970 and *File on Four* from 1977 (both Radio 4), the notion of radio journalism broadened to cover all forms of current affairs that could be effectively presented through speech and sounds – not just breaking stories but ongoing and background issues, and not merely through straight reportage but in interviews, actuality, debate and commentary.

The importance of *Analysis* and *File on Four* cannot be overstated, and we will return to them later. In essence, they are extended speech programmes which focus on single issues and explore them in sufficient depth to allow a range of views to be considered and analysed, reinforced by expert comment and even summed up by the drawing of appropriate conclusions. This approach contrasts with the magazine format typified by such programmes as *Today* and *Radio Newsreel*, which cover a range of topical items within a single edition. Indeed, topicality is not a prerequisite for *Analysis* and *File on Four*, since their in-depth reporting requires an extended period of investigation and post-production before they can be broadcast.

See it happen: the ascendancy of television news

Nevertheless, there can be no doubt that by 1970 television was the major medium for 'news' in its primary, minimal sense of important events that have only just occurred, permit some visual treatment and have not been greatly moderated by backgrounding, analysis or commentary. Radio and newspapers could only *tell* what had happened, between them offering a limited actuality of sounds and fixed images: television could *show* it, and the number of things it could show was growing all the time. From 1963, satellite feeds brought to its bulletins images of what was occurring half a world away, and during the 1980s the replacement of film by magnetic tape and a general miniaturisation of components enabled cameras to become portable and thus capture things that had once been beyond them. Now, instead of merely telling about other lands, unusual events and remarkable experiences, the visiting traveller could *display* them.

Over the last 25 years the number of television outlets has also multiplied: two more terrestrials have launched – Channel 4 in 1982 and Channel 5 in 1997; the first cable and satellite stations appeared in 1983; and since 1996, digital television has triggered a further huge expansion on all three platforms. Television is now so abundant that a miscellany of content on any one channel is beginning to seem old-fashioned; enough channels exist to permit 'themed' or specialised content, and the prime candidate for theming is news. The sheer quantity of, and demand for, news; the reduction – often to zero – of the gap between the point at which it occurs and the point at which it can be shown; the improvements in picture quality and the growing sophistication of on-screen graphics all prompted the growth of 'rolling news' channels like Sky News (1989), BBC World Service Television News (1991), CNN (1992) and BBC News 24 (1997).

News and the concept of public service broadcasting

Yet at about the same time an extraordinary paradox was emerging. The BBC's public service endeavour depends, and has always depended, on its ability to provide what the market cannot. Why, then, should the BBC speak increasingly of news being at the heart of its public service provision at the very moment when news was available on a wider range of broadcasting outlets than ever before?

Part of the reason was historical and political. In the primordial days of broadcasting scarcity, news was not high on the BBC's agenda, and by today's standards it was relatively uncritical of the government's conduct during both the General Strike and the Second World War (Thompson 1990: 258; Starkey 2007: 128–30). Yet because it never acted merely as the government's mouth-piece, the Corporation acquired a reputation for the balance and integrity of its reportage during both. In recent years it has come to seem only reasonable that a body which is publicly funded and seeks to serve the nation as a whole should stake its reputation on an ability to tell the truth about the world in as impartial and authoritative a way as possible. It has generally sought to do so by offering more *perspective* – more context and analysis – than its televisual rivals, who are primarily preoccupied with news *actuality*, with the sight and sound of events. This is the 'mission to explain' that was formulated by John Birt, who coordinated the BBC's news and current affairs departments from 1987. He 'emphasised the need to give news stories a methodically researched analytical context in order to provide more journalistic depth and superior understanding' (Born 2005: 57).

Because of the attacks on the BBC by the Conservative government during the 1980s, this is sometimes characterised as a retreat into self-justification and a timorousness about interpreting political events as news. Moreover, Birt's centralisation of news and current affairs was seen as making the BBC more, not less, vulnerable (McNair 2003: 105–10). Particularly after he became Director General in 1993, Birt acquired numerous critics, and his successor, Greg Dyke, found he had inherited 'a deeply unhappy organisation' (Dyke 2004: 139). One of the most frequent charges against Birt was that in the form of a new internal accounting system called 'producer choice', he hugely increased bureaucracy at the expense of programme making. Dyke managed to reduce some of the bureaucracy and left office in 2004, riding a wave of support from the staff. Without doubt, though, the most influential Director General of all has been the BBC's first and longest-serving, John Reith, whose job was to establish an arm's length relationship between the Corporation and successive governments, a feat he managed through 11 turbulent years until 1938.

A combustible relationship: the BBC, the government and reportage of the news

Crucial to this relationship is a need to be independent of government yet avoid antagonising it so much that the next licence fee is set at a punitively low level. It is arguable that in 1926, the year before incorporation, Reith was too supportive of the government, siding with them against the strikers (Thompson 1990: 258). He asserted that since both the government and the BBC were 'for the people' the BBC should be 'for' the government too. The Second World War presented the BBC with few qualms about the ethics of supporting the war effort, and Prime Minister Winston Churchill's radio broadcasts were important motivators for a public under siege from Hitler's Germany – particularly at the time of the evacuation of British troops from Dunkirk in occupied France. Many historians consider them to have been crucial in influencing the United States to enter the war as our ally. (We will consider the development of international radio journalism in a later chapter, but it is worth noting here that once war was declared a number of American correspondents in Europe, among them Egbert (Ed) Roscoe Murrow, vividly described the build-up of the German war machine and the aerial bombard-ments of London. Their reports for the American networks also helped con-vince a reticent American public that they should abandon their neutrality and join in the fight against the Nazis (Crook 1998: 91–2).)

It was through the BBC that the future French President, General Charles de Gaulle, was able to broadcast rallying calls to his occupied compatriots (Kuhn 1995: 86–9). However, institutional contexts and people's expecta-tions change over time, and nearly 40 years later Margaret Thatcher com-plained that the BBC's coverage of the Falklands War was insufficiently 'patriotic' (MacGregor 1997: 134). The path between patriotism and neu-trality is a difficult one to tread, as Greg Dyke found out in 2003, yet most broadcast journalists identify the ability to be impartial as essential to their survival – and their credibility (Sheridan Burns 2002: 11–12). The path is as difficult to tread in radio as in television, but there are some fundamental differences between the two.

How radio's news coverage is better than television's

One problem for television is that it is not the most efficient or effective medium for practising journalism, and it was inevitable that it should have developed in different ways over its own, briefer history. Because, like radio, it operates in time, it is able to communicate much less information, and of a rather less complex nature, than newspapers and books, which operate in space. A newspaper is capable of carrying many more words than can be uttered in a conventional radio or television bulletin. But television's pictures create a further difficulty. Contextualisation – the attempt to explain and analyse – is a verbal process that deals largely in abstractions, and the pictures it accompanies, even if of little more than the newsreader or reporter, have a tendency to distract the viewer. Moreover, if it qualifies or conflicts with the pictures, the viewer is tempted to ignore it and credit the pictures: we tend to trust what we can see rather more than what we hear (Crisell 2006: 60–4). Yet not only must contextualisation support the pictures: it must be slowed down in order to give us the opportunity to view them, thus further reducing the amount of detail and degree of complexity it can carry.

The limitations of television news can be circumvented in one of two ways. The first is to run extended bulletins, a solution favoured by Channel 4. These allow individual items to be more fully explained and analysed, even if not to the extent that is possible in a newspaper. But such bulletins demand a considerable commitment from the viewer. There are, of course, specialist channels which in theory allow the viewer to watch news round the clock, but their content consists of repeated and only slowly evolving bulletins – the 'rolling news' that presupposes the brief, often intermittent viewing that is much more typical of our time.

The second possibility is to minimise the distracting and protracting effect of the pictures by, in a sense, carrying fewer of them. Television must always show pictures, of course, but bulletins could carry much less footage of the news events themselves and instead show 'talking heads' – those who report, analyse and discuss them. This would, in effect, make *what is seen* subordinate to *what is said*, and in the old days of unwieldy cameras and relative broadcasting scarcity, this is what television often did. But at a time when scores of channels are competing for the fragile attention of the viewer, this is no longer a realistic option. Television must increasingly fall back on what sales folk would describe as its 'unique selling proposition': the provision of interesting – and if possible exciting – pictures (Crisell 2006: 166–9). Even though the BBC is obliged to provide material that the market will not provide, and so to that extent is relieved of the need to compete, its discursive news and current affairs programmes, such as *Newsnight* and *Panorama*, have been pushed to the edges of the schedule. Moreover, *Panorama*, once the flagship of BBC's television current affairs output, has in recent years become much more pictorial and rather less discursive and analytical.

We therefore arrive at a remarkable fact. If an in-depth coverage of news and current affairs is at the heart of the BBC's public service endeavour – if the contextualisation, discussion and analysis that are collectively described as its 'mission to explain' are what distinguishes it from other broadcasters – then this endeavour is performed not so much by television as by the less popular medium of *radio*. It is perhaps no accident that for the radio provision of such things, the BBC has no serious rival.

Why should words alone be able to do more justice to news and current affairs than words combined with pictures? Words can describe both the physical, visible events that pictures show (indeed they often have to describe what the pictures refer to, since pictures are not always self-explanatory) and the context and significance of these events. But in their latter function, words benefit from the *absence* of pictures, since pictures introduce an irrelevant and distracting concreteness into what is in essence an abstract discourse. It is, of course, true that we are mostly seeing *something* while we are listening to the radio: we do not necessarily listen with our eyes closed. But the unrelatedness of what we are seeing to what we are hearing makes it much easier for us to focus on abstractions and concepts when they are aired on the radio than when we encounter them on television (Crisell 2004b: 7–10).

How radio became central to the BBC's public service mission

At the very time that TV channels began to multiply, it was recognised within the BBC that news and current affairs are at least as much a matter of issues, ideas and significances as of visible occurrences, and that radio is better equipped to deal with them than television. From the 1980s the corporation renewed its attempts to convert Radio 4 into an all-news network, and during the 1991 Gulf War provided a continuous if temporary news service on the station's FM frequencies (Starkey 2004a: 26). Then in 1994 it launched the populist news and sport network, Radio 5 Live. Even as a mixed programming station, Radio 4's daily output includes the *Today* programme from 0600 to 0900, *The World at One* from 1300 to 1330, *PM* from 1700 to 1800, an extended news bulletin from 1800 to 1830 and *The World Tonight* from 2200 to 2245. Moreover, its weekly output embraces a range of specialised current affairs in such programmes as *Farming Today*, *Money Box*, *File on Four*, *Analysis*, *From Our Own Correspondent*, *In Business* and *Law in Action*. There is nothing like this quantity of news and current affairs in the mainstream television networks, and even in the all-news channels, nothing like the amount of commentary, explanation and discussion that these programmes afford. It is precisely because they would make dull viewing that they are so effective on radio. Moreover, they help to ensure that the BBC enjoys the continuing protection of those arbiters of the licence fee, the politicians. It gives them considerable publicity, whether by reporting them or allowing them frequent opportunities to be heard, and although in the late afternoon and evening radio commands much smaller audiences than television, it is popular with the professional middle classes whom politicians need to reach because they are the nation's opinion formers.

Some historical erosions of the public service ideal

This was as important in past decades as it is today, for if the BBC is to survive, it must have a critical mass of support behind it. Reith firmly established public service broadcasting as aloof from commercial pressures and, thanks largely to its position as a monopoly, untroubled by audience ratings. By at first not challenging the press over the provision of news, he bought some time during which the BBC was able to become better established. However, in the 1930s the popularity of the continental stations, particularly on Sundays, was unsettling for the BBC since it prompted some criticism from the press but not enough to cause a change in direction. Perhaps it was at this time that Reith formed the opinion that commercial broadcasting is akin to 'dog racing, smallpox and the bubonic plague' (Crisell 2002: 86). He was largely right in perceiving it as popular, downmarket, potentially lucrative and 'infectious' among audiences. Yet even without commercial radio, the BBC would have to change and with Reith's departure, the process began.

The Second World War killed off the continental commercial stations, but among the tens of thousands of young soldiers stationed away from home it also created a craving for entertainment, and the launch of the Forces Programme in 1940 at the government's request was an early post-Reithian concession to populism. It was not to be the only one. Successive Director Generals had their own views on audience ratings, and in answer to the challenge of the 1960s offshore pirates, the Light Programme that had replaced the Forces Programme was renamed Radio 2 in 1967 and was joined by a new pop music service for youth, Radio 1.

There also followed a period of considerable ratings success for BBC television, which seemed to suggest that audience figures had assumed greater importance in the corporation's thinking. In 1985, press attacks on the BBC, led by withering editorials in *The Times*, resulted in the setting up of an inquiry into the corporation's funding by the Peacock Committee. Its definition of public service broadcasting (PSB) identified eight key principles:

- availability to the whole population
- relevance to all tastes and interests
- provision for minorities, especially those who are disadvantaged
- a special relationship to the national identity
- distance from vested interests
- licence fee funding

- aiming for quality rather than large audiences
- ‘a set of guidelines within which to work

(Harrison 2006: 227–8).

Despite the definitive terms in which the Peacock Committee reported to government (Peacock Committe 1986), its legacy lasted only a short while. During his period as Director General, it allowed John Birt to be relatively resistant to populism and his diversion of funds into news and current affairs bolstered the practice of journalism within the corporation. However, Greg Dyke's instincts were rather different, and he was criticised for taking some of the BBC's television output downmarket. So the debate reignited early in the new millennium. Even during the recent period in which the BBC Charter was being reviewed (before being extended for another ten years from 2007), there were loud calls for Radio 1 to be privatised, funded from advertising and even to be run by the state-owned television broadcaster Channel 4. Radio 1, it was claimed, was one service that the market certainly *could* provide. Meanwhile, what had 'the market' – that is, the commercial sector – been doing?

The development of commercial radio in Britain

Despite the success of commercial radio in the United States and elsewhere, it was not until 1973 that 'independent' radio, as it was called, launched in the United Kingdom, and even then only as a local operation. This was the culmination of a long-fought campaign by those on the political right and a small number of entrepreneurs keen to profit from sound advertising on a relatively modest investment. Since 1927, the latter had been denied the chance to make money out of radio, even though the medium proved to be big business in the United States. They were constantly reminded of the opportunity they were missing by the 7,000 or so commercial stations which were thriving on the far side of the Atlantic. Today's talk of 'spectrum pricing', which means that every frequency on the broadcast radio bands has a value that someone could realise, contrasts sharply with the twentieth-century notion of those frequencies as a scarce public resource. The continental stations of the 1930s and some of the offshore pirates of the 1960s had made considerable amounts of money out of radio. The logistical difficulties of broadcasting from foreign countries or the high seas had limited their profitability, but legal transmissions from British soil seemed to promise easier profits, perhaps even matching those that had been made by the companies that had launched 'independent' television.

Some of the 1960s pirates had campaigned against the 1967 Marine Broadcasting (Offences) Act, which was introduced to starve them of advertising, make it illegal to supply them from the mainland and prevent British citizens from working for them, but they failed to mobilise enough public support to defeat the legislation and most of the stations closed down just before the Act came into force. However, in 1970 a new Swiss-owned station, Radio Northsea International, ran a vigorous on-air campaign against the Labour government of the time. Broadcasting during a closely-fought general election under the name Radio Caroline International, it is thought to have swung some key marginal constituencies in southeast England to the Conservatives because it was the first time that under 21s had a vote (Street 2002: 112). The Conservative Party's manifesto included a clear commitment to introduce legal commercial radio (up to 60 stations), and its accession to power was a key moment in the history of radio in the United Kingdom – a victory for ideologues and entrepreneurs alike.

'Public service' and news in the commercial context

Under the Sound Broadcasting Act 1972, Independent Local Radio (ILR) was given a public service duty analogous to that of the BBC to provide 'material of range and balance', including adequate news (Barnard 1989: 74–5). The first two stations, Capital Radio and the London Broadcasting Company (LBC), opened in London, but while the former followed the prescription of the Act, the latter, whose full title was LBC News Radio, was exceptionally required to supply the metropolis with an all-news and information service. For the other local stations that would follow, LBC also operated a networked news service, Independent Radio News (IRN), which was conceived along the lines of Independent Television News and which the stations were required to fund through an annual subsidy. The first commercial radio regulator, the Independent Broadcasting Authority (IBA), would allow only the best resourced of the local stations to produce their own news; the others were obliged to broadcast a live three-minute bulletin from IRN, followed by their own local bulletins (Crisell and Starkey 2006: 19).

The public service duty that was imposed on commercial radio soon proved insupportable. Local stations lacked the money to provide 'material of range and balance' that was of adequate quality. Moreover, such a duty was archaically premised on an era in which radio, and not television, was the primary supplier of the public's informational and cultural needs. By forcing the stations to offer a range of material, the IBA also reduced their income because they could not deliver audiences that advertisers could clearly identify. There were other reasons why those great expectations of instant profits failed to materialise; national brands were slow to perceive the potential of advertising on a purely local medium. Its coverage was at first limited to the larger conurbations – London, Birmingham, Manchester,

Glasgow and Liverpool – and a handful of smaller cities and towns, such as Sheffield, Portsmouth and Swansea. In another ideological tussle, the Conservatives ceded power to Labour in 1974. The incoming government, though disinclined to close down those ILR stations that had begun broadcasting and proved popular in their own areas, prevented the fledgling network from expanding beyond 19 stations and thus delayed by several years the development of national coverage.

Farewell to public service: the dawn of deregulation

The one thing that the stations could profitably broadcast was pop music, and for the next ten years or more this was the element that was used to package all the other prescribed material – 'meaningful speech', news, religious output and items of community interest. Merely to enable the stations to survive, the IBA was gradually obliged to relax its grip. Against increasing competition from pirate operators, it allowed them to stream more of their output and take programme sponsorship. Then at the end of the 1980s they were encouraged to yield identifiable audiences to prospective advertisers by splitting their frequencies, transmitting chart music on FM and, in most cases, golden oldies on AM. This was a reaction to the IBA's 'use it or lose it' decree, a hasty attempt to ensure that their previously simulcast services became alternatives to each other. Only one, Liverpool's Radio City, chose to assign its AM frequency to speech.

As well as authorising the launch of stations at national and regional level, the Broadcasting Act of 1990 at last relieved independent radio of its residual public service duty and allowed it to 'chase the market': local stations were no longer obliged even to carry local news (Radio Authority 1995: 13). Yet in practice many of the stations continued to broadcast news or some form of current affairs and still do. Between 1973 and 1991 Independent Radio News remained in the hands of LBC, but during the 1990s their connection was severed and IRN incurred competition from Network News and Reuters Radio News, whose clients included its own London stations and the national Virgin Radio. IRN's next competitor was Sky News Radio, later taken not only by Virgin but, ironically, by LBC on both its frequencies.

The survival of news and current affairs on commercial radio

If the general supply of broadcast news is more than equal to demand, and if the 1990 Broadcasting Act imposed no specific obligation on the independent stations to do so, why do most of them continue to carry news and current affairs in one form or another? One answer is that since the staple diet of these stations is recorded music and recorded adverts, news and current affairs provide, along with the presenters' voices, a salutary reminder that radio is fundamentally a *live* medium – that it differs from CDs and similar media in its potential for spontaneity, novelty and unpredictability. Moreover, not only is the music broadcast by these stations not live, it is not local. Hence news and current affairs are also a means of affirming the localness – and at network level even the 'nationalness' – of stations that otherwise carry little other than music of a deracinated, international character.

The challenge for independent radio is how to distinguish such output from the strong and traditional news and current affairs agenda of the BBC – and, indeed, how to make it as entertaining as the music for which most of its listeners have tuned in. The tendency of its news coverage has been to give more prominence to 'human interest' stories and to expand into the associated areas of show business and leisure. Classic FM, for instance, whose main aim is to adapt classical music to the norms of popular culture (Crisell 1994: 76–9), focuses on news of what is happening in the world of the arts and entertainment, while the news bulletins of Virgin Radio (which was rebranded Absolute Radio in 2008) contain a large admixture of music and sports items.

In independent radio's coverage of current affairs two trends are discernible. One is a shift from 'political' to softer issues. The other is a move away from the 'broadcasterly' modes of reportage and documentary to more audience-focused discussions. One of the first of the national licences that were permitted by the 1990 Broadcasting Act was for an all-speech station, perhaps on the assumption that the speech would consist of informed narrative and debate about political and cultural matters. In the event, the licence was awarded to Talk Radio UK, which launched in February 1995. After an early and unsuccessful experiment with 'shock jocks', it later became Talk Radio and, from January 2000, talkSPORT. But talkSPORT and stations that mix music with a relatively high speech content, such as the regional chain branded as 'Century FM', tend to offer demotic argument and gossip about current issues rather than informed commentary and explanation. Studio guests who have a measure of knowledge or expertise are sometimes present, but while requiring research into the issues that might be discussed and those controversial aspects that will move the discussion along, the journalism needed for such content does not involve much straight reportage, analysis or actuality. Century FM in northeast England, for instance, offers what it terms 'the Century Issue', which is described on its website as:

An in-depth news feature focusing on topical issues facing people across the North East. Tune in three times a day for a full round up of listener reaction, opinions, texts and calls as the Century FM News Team takes you through all the day's headlines.

(www.100centuryfm.com)

The primary focus here is on *listeners* – on what preoccupies them – rather than on the informers, who, it is promised, merely 'take you through the headlines' rather than descend into dry and detailed backgrounding. And the listeners have a double stake in the content because they cannot only hear others like themselves expressing the enthusiasms, anxieties and aversions that they share, but also have a multi-media opportunity to make their own contribution to the discussion. Hence for independent radio, news is packaged not so much as a 'mission to explain' but as another form of gratification that will capture and hold audiences, and thus advertisers.

Other ways to skin the cat: radio, news and propaganda

The differences between the BBC and the independent sector are important, but fortunately not matters of life and death. The ideological battle fought on British soil over what institutional form radio should take contrasts sharply with the way the medium was treated in a number of other countries. Since the first telegraphic messages of the Russian communists, radio's potential as a propaganda tool has been widely perceived. De Gaulle's broadcasts across the English Channel to France were countered by misinformation transmitted back to Britain by the Nazis. This featured the voice of William Joyce, who became popularly characterised as 'Lord Haw Haw'. But examples abound even in peacetime. During the 'Cold War', which lasted from 1945 to 1990 and followed the division of Europe into two armed camps, one supported by the USA and the other by the Soviet Union, radio was used as a propaganda tool on both sides of the divide (Starkey 2007: 119–20). Propaganda is the antithesis of good journalism: it masquerades as disinterested fact but is intended to serve a particular ideological purpose and we shall consider later under what circumstances, if any, it might be acceptable.

Radio journalism under the British broadcasting divide

We have seen that radio journalism has exploited technological advance in order to fulfil a human need. Yet despite the ubiquity of print journalism at the beginning of the last century, its development has been relatively slow. A combination of newspaper interests and establishment conservatism delayed the integration of journalism with the new medium of radio, but once 'radio journalism' became established it proved more than capable of responding to our need for news and information about the world that lies beyond our own experience. We have also noted how institutional factors and competing ideologies have ensured that contemporary radio broadcasting is underpinned by two philosophies that are not simply different but fundamentally incompatible (Crisell 2006: 42). The first is the 'public service' philosophy, which regards broadcasting as a common cultural resource that should be as widely accessible as possible and paid for by a tax on all owners of broadcast receivers (in the United Kingdom, of television sets not radios). This philosophy is embodied in the BBC and its aim is to provide the broadest range of content, even that which might not be economically justified in terms of the numbers who want it or could not otherwise afford it. The second philosophy, that of independent radio (and television), is that broadcasting is primarily a market whose products are bought and sold – sold by broadcasters and bought either by audiences or advertisers. As we explore in greater depth the nature and practice of radio journalism, this philosophical divide will underpin our discussion.

2

CONSTRAINING THE BROADCASTERS AND TRAINING THE JOURNALISTS: POLITICAL ECONOMY AND SOCIAL DEMOGRAPHY

How 'reporting the facts' is affected by other matters

We have been exploring the combined effects on radio journalism of developing technology and a number of institutional factors, but there are many other influences that contribute to its production and consumption. At the heart of all journalism lies a potential conflict that goes back to the early print era and the very beginnings of the profession. To report the world beyond the audience's own experience is an activity that cannot be value-free. Someone has to make choices about what is reported and how it is represented, for 'reality', in the sense of a set of absolute truths that are accepted by everyone, is non-existent, or at any rate unknowable. Hence, what is reported is often controversial (Starkey 2007: xvi–xx, 1–20). In radio, journalism is heard from the mouths of its practitioners: they do not write it down for consumption by readers. Its audiences cannot see for themselves what is being reported, nor even those who are reporting it. Neither can they know very much about the reporters or those who employ them. Finally, they cannot be very sure, even if they have a suspicion, about any constraints that affect that work.

Yet in terms of what is described as 'political economy', a range of influences are brought to bear on radio journalism that affect the nature of its content. When journalists make selective representations of the world, what role is played by their backgrounds, upbringing, education and the social groups within which they feel most at ease? How do their formative experiences and attitudes compare with those of their audiences, and if they were to think about it, would the listeners believe the journalist to be 'one of them' or someone with a very different view of the world? Since the production and consumption of journalism are shaped by the nature of both journalists and audiences, social demography is clearly an important consideration.

The balance of power between news reporters and news consumers

In pre-journalistic times the news-bearing traveller might sometimes have been treated with suspicion; before the development of the mass media intelligent audiences may well have asked who this person was, and how accurate his or her stories were. Such a face-to-face encounter offered the chance to test their plausibility and draw out themes and issues of particular interest. By asking questions, listeners could attempt to resolve any doubts they may have had about the truthfulness of what they were hearing, and they could ask to hear more of certain aspects of an account that particularly interested them. However, the development of newspapers and the arrival of *mass* media distanced audiences from their primary sources of information, and required them to place more trust in those who reported it.

Although they encounter them from a distance and cannot subject their claims to direct scrutiny, audiences expect journalists to tell the truth, to report as honestly and accurately as possible the facts and events of what Habermas (1989) identifies as the 'public sphere'. Within this sphere is articulated a wide discourse, consisting of a mix of general and specialised topics of current debate, each of which may be of interest to greater or smaller groups of people. By raising issues and spreading knowledge through bulletins, or by confirming certain opinions and perspectives in discussion programmes, radio journalism contributes to the public sphere in several ways. People who phone in or gain other access to broadcasting can participate directly in a wide political debate, albeit one which is mediated and distanced from the actual events it is discussing (Campbell 2004: 190, 193–4). The relationship between those located within this public sphere is, of course, unequal. Some are purely audiences, consumers of the discourse spoken by others who have the ability to articulate their own perspectives. The latter are the producers: in news and current affairs programming, the journalists. Indeed, in the course of their history journalists have earned – or bestowed on themselves – some rather grand and disinterested titles: custodians of truth, watchdogs of democracy, tribunes of the people. But these obscure the fact that most journalists are also employees of businesses that exist to make money. Truth may be the priority, but in the case of the commercial sector, profits are the *sine qua non*.

The political economy of the mass media and of journalism in particular has been scrutinised since theorists first invoked Karl Marx's identification of corrosive implications in the dominance of capitalist influences in society.

Later analyses updated Marx's assessment for more modern contexts (Golding and Murdock 1973: 205–34; 2000) but still considered the profit motive to be pivotal. The effects of political economy on journalism are, however, controversial. The 'revisionists' have perceived only a limited influence of the media on the audience's knowledge and understanding of the world, while others maintain that their influence is decisive (Curran 1990). We will reflect in Chapter 6 on audiences and the wealth of debate surrounding their reactions to media messages, but merely note at this stage that political economy affects the *process* of radio journalism, just as it is implicated in the production of media messages of all kinds.

Why, though, should conflict arise between journalism and the contexts in which it is practised, within organisations which produce journalism for others to consume, and even within journalists themselves, who mainly work for organisations and only rarely for themselves? To these questions there are a number of answers. One is that truth and fact, though needful for the public to know, are sometimes not very interesting (McManus 2002: 273). Another is that certain truths may relate to the newspaper itself or its proprietor or those who place advertising with it, and reflect discredit on any or all of them. And a third is that if a newspaper reports disreputable truths about certain individuals, they may bring a costly legal action against it.

How newspapers became editorially slanted ...

The first newspapers were little more than noticeboards, but as they multiplied during the eighteenth and nineteenth centuries, there was a further sense in which the 'straight' reportage of the facts could threaten profitability. In the public sphere there existed a single pool of information that was available to all the newspapers: if they were to report it in the same objective or disinterested way, what was there to recommend one paper over another?

In practice, of course, differences between newspapers rapidly emerged and have grown ever more apparent. First, some papers might manage to gain a monopoly of certain sources of information and publish 'exclusives', or print the facts ahead of their rivals in the form of 'scoops'. Second, and as we suggested above, it is a truism that no two individuals will report 'the facts' in an identical way. Facts are almost invariably multifaceted, often disputable, and with uncertain relationships to a myriad of other facts. A report is always coloured, deliberately or otherwise, by the powers of expression and predisposition of the reporter – and the question of what quintessential fact or truth lies beyond the reports of it is one that journalists happily resign to philosophers. We return here to the point that 'reality' is often controversial, as is the way it is represented. For print journalists, differences in style, content and editorial viewpoint are to be exploited in order to enable their newspapers to compete for a profitable share of the market. Not only could the reportage of facts and events be tailored to the socio-educational levels of a particular readership, but the predispositions and reactions that were implicit in the reportage could be made explicit in the form of *comment* on those facts and events. This was the role of the newspaper editor, whose *editorials* were deliberately opinionated. Hence newspapers could compete with one another not simply by offering different *versions* of the facts but different *attitudes* to the facts – attitudes that could be set out in an overtly rhetorical way in order to influence or confirm the views of the reader. It is hardly surprising that most of the national and metropolitan newspapers tended to support one or other of the main political parties (Seymour-Ure 1974: 157–9).

...and how broadcasting was different

However, in the case of the other major news medium – broadcasting – the potential conflict between the need to be truthful and accurate on the one hand, and to make money on the other, did not arise. Why? In the United Kingdom, the British Broadcasting Company, which later became a public corporation, was not established as a conventional business: it had an assured income from receiving licences and was allowed to operate as a monopoly. This meant, on the face of it, that it could report the truth in as objective and disinterested a way as possible without the need to indulge in editorialising. Indeed, the government forbade the BBC to editorialise for this and several other reasons. One was that as a scarce medium whose aim was to serve the public as a whole, radio should not expound views that would appeal to only a section of it. Another was to do with the particular character of radio. In a paradoxical way, editorial opinion expressed in the print medium can combine a sense of authority and impersonality: unlike handwriting, it does not appear to originate from a private individual and carries a kind of generalising weightiness. But views expressed through the human voice sound singular and idiosyncratic and are as likely to provoke strong reactions as thoughts expressed in an informal conversation. In this respect, governments have always felt that broadcasting has a much more incendiary potential than the press and have been loath to allow any of its institutions, whether public or commercial, to editorialise.

The editorial pressures on public service broadcasting

Free from the need to operate as part of a business, could journalists therefore use broadcasting to report the full facts and in a wholly disinterested way? Alas no, for the old conflict between the need to tell the truth and the need to make a profit was replaced by a new one – between the need to tell the truth and the need to appease the government. It was the latter who provided the BBC with its renewable charter and fixed the level of its licence income. Every ten years, as the charter comes up for renewal, the BBC is plunged into uncertainty as the government of the day publicly and privately considers the terms of the new document – or even whether to renew it at all. Other interested parties contribute to the debate, some protective of the BBC but others predatory, calling for it to be wholly or partly privatised, or forced to fund itself through advertising, or to cede part of its licence income to another body, such as Channel 4 Television or community radio. Inflation requires that the licence fee itself must be regularly renegotiated, and a generous settlement from the government ensures a period of relative prosperity, while parsimony results in a downsizing of programmes and staff.

Hence, from the beginning the corporation was not only obliged by its constitution to refrain from editorialising, but often found it impolitic to report those facts that might embarrass its paymaster. The Gilligan Affair of 2003, in which a BBC journalist claimed that the government had sought to exaggerate the military threat posed by Iraq in order to justify Britain's invasion of that country, vividly illustrates that this conflict persists. When a public inquiry conducted by a former High Court judge, Lord Hutton, exonerated the government and described the BBC's journalism as flawed (Hutton 2004), many people found the verdict unpalatable. It did, however, demonstrate the controversial character of the BBC's journalism, to such an extent that the corporation launched a thorough review of its practices (Neil et al. 2004). The gravity of the affair was underlined by the fact that soon after Hutton's findings became known, the Chairman and the Director General both tendered their resignation.

The BBC's news operation is now subject to other pressures. Though the corporation remains licence-funded and, in its essential function, free from the need to make a profit, it lost its domestic monopoly in 1955, and in being obliged ever since to compete for audience share has thus had to behave in a 'businesslike' way. Until the early 1980s the competition was restrained because ITV was required, like the BBC, to operate as a public service broadcaster. But since the arrival of other commercial operators on terrestrial, cable and satellite platforms, the competition has become cut-throat. Unsurprisingly, this has produced some heart-searching within the BBC about what principles should now shape the corporation's news provision:

> The PSR [programme strategy review] enabled executives to air the dilemma at the heart of the BBC's democratic self-conception: to what extent was the BBC's role to lead public opinion by supplying information that it judged to be of universal value for citizens? To what extent did it mean listening to consumers' ideas of what they want from news?

> (Born 2005: 410)

How broadcasters set the news agenda

We saw in the previous chapter that the primary way in which the BBC has sought to distinguish itself from its rivals, and so appeal to a significant sector of the audience, is by pursuing a 'mission to explain' – to provide news in depth and with a sufficient analytical context. In practice, however, this is not so very different from the editorialising that characterises the newspapers. Analysis often includes speculation and comment, and these in turn reveal something of the opinions and values of the analyst. They may be rather more subtle than those declared in a newspaper editorial or leading article, but they are discernible nonetheless. Moreover, as well as merely reporting public affairs, BBC journalists often influence the way they will develop – and nowhere more than in radio. For instance, on Radio 4's *Today* programme, or anywhere within the output of Five Live, journalists form their own views of what should constitute the news agenda and effectively impose it in the kinds of on-air questions they put to the politicians and the other public figures they interview.

This activity is known as agenda setting. Whereas in ancient times it was the audience who set the agenda by putting questions to the news-bearing traveller, it is now the journalists who, through the media they 'control', decide what the public needs to know and discuss (McCombs and Shaw 1993). It is true that journalism tends to provide large amounts of what it perceives its audiences to be interested in: the public sphere is not a constant cacophony of unfocused chatter about every aspect of human knowledge. Subjects of particular concern rise and fall in their importance according to a range of factors: topicality through relevance to some recent event; a regularly occurring phenomenon or an anniversary; relevance to some human need, such as survival in the face of global warming; entertainment value because they conform to some current trend; or curiosity value because they intrigue, amuse or titillate in some unexpected way. Since certain audiences will have particular interests at particular times, some explanations of journalism rationalise it as 'market driven' (Koch 1990: 23; Underwood 1993: 163).

However, just as a supermarket exerts some control over public demand by deciding what products or brands it will stock, producers in the public sphere wield considerable influence over consumers by limiting the range of alternatives from which they are able to make a choice (Lewis et al. 2005: 9–11). If they find the range on offer too limiting, some consumers may go elsewhere, but others will settle for what is most easily available.

What we are suggesting, then, is threefold. First, broadcast journalism is in certain ways more effective at setting the news agenda than newspaper journalism. Second, this ability, as well as the ability to offer a kind of implicit editorialising through commentary and analysis, has at least as much impact as the overt editorialising of the newspapers. Third, and as argued in the previous chapter, BBC radio plays a bigger part in these things than television and commercial radio do. The launch of commercial television in 1955 and commercial radio in 1973 introduced into broadcasting the potential conflict between reporting the facts and running a business that has always existed in the newspapers. But, again partly because of what governments see as the 'incendiary' potential of the human voice, the independent sector, like the BBC, is prohibited from editorialising. It has therefore sought to distinguish itself from its public sector rival by supplementing mainstream political journalism with a greater focus on 'human interest'. This can be more closely defined as news from the realms of entertainment – sport, the arts, show business – and, especially in radio, issues of immediate concern to 'the man in the street'. The aim of these is to stimulate audience-centred debate, much of it on-air, and we might note that it was the BBC, not the independent sector, that fought a bitter dispute with the government in 2003 over Iraq, and that it is a BBC programme, *Today*, that is widely considered to set the nation's political agenda. This is despite the huge growth in the commercial sector since its faltering beginnings in the 1970s. Table 2.1 shows how rapidly the commercial sector grew in the 1990s and early 2000s, while during the same period the BBC's provision of analogue radio stations remained fairly static.

Table 2.1   Comparison of commercial and public sector provision of licensed FM and AM radio stations on the United Kingdom mainland, 1972–2007

In Q1	All commercial analogue stations	All BBC analogue stations (national/regional/local)
1972	0	4/3/20
1982	40	4/3/22
1991	115	5/4/39
2001	255	5/6/40
2007	300	5/6/40

How British broadcasting is regulated

This growth in the number of services provided by the commercial sector did not occur in a vacuum, and we will continue our discussion of the political economy of radio journalism with a closer look at the regulatory framework that exists for both the BBC and the independent sector. In both radio and television, the BBC must operate according to its Charter and Agreement, and since 2003 independent radio has been supervised by the Office of Communications, known as 'Ofcom'. Under the terms of the current charter, as under the previous one, the provision of news on the BBC's domestic services is an explicit requirement. They must provide 'comprehensive, authoritative and impartial coverage of news and current affairs in the United Kingdom and throughout the world to support fair and informed debate at local, regional and national levels' (BBC 1996: 6). Moreover, '[t]he Corporation shall transmit an impartial account day by day prepared by professional reporters of the proceedings in both Houses of Parliament' (BBC 1996: 7). The regulators stress that the news must be reported and presented with due accuracy and impartiality (BBC 1996: 8; Ofcom 2005: 25), but they also concede that 'balance' does not have to be achieved by a continuous and bewildering alternation of contrasting points of view within a single programme: it may be achieved over a series of programmes (BBC 1996: 10; Ofcom 2005: 27).

In choosing this approach, the regulators have rejected such awkward compromises as have allowed partisan broadcasting in other countries. One is enshrined in a system called *lottizzazione* in Italy (Roncarolo 2002: 72, 86–7), which during the 1970s allowed television channels to be allied with different political parties. This meant that Italian viewers could pick and choose between different perspectives as easily as British newspaper readers can decide to read the *Guardian* rather than the *Daily Telegraph* (Starkey 2007: 27–8). In France, the current regulator, the Conseil Supérieur de l'Audiovisuel (CSA), attempts to ensure a plurality of views by licensing local *radios associatives* which support a range of politically affiliated stations in a particular area. In effect, these both complement and counterbalance one another.

The regulatory framework in the United Kingdom is rather less straightforward than its language implies, for it contains paradoxes that are designed to reassure the public. On the one hand, the stress on balance and the general expectation that it shall be 'fair' place broadcast news in dramatic contrast to an opinionated and partisan press. On the other hand, the framework treats the issues of balance and impartiality in a subtle and flexible way, acknowledging that the former does not imply absolute neutrality (BBC 1996: 10). Broadcasters may not be allowed to mount soap boxes, but neither are they obliged to be insipidly non-committal for, as we noted earlier, BBC news contains a fair amount of implicit editorialising that is bound up with its 'mission to explain'. However, there are certain ideological positions that may not be factored into any attempt to be editorially even-handed. For instance, because they are banned by legislation, racist material and child pornography are not given the same airtime or degree of credence as other topics. There are also 'common sense' discourses which tend to exclude other perspectives on controversial issues, such as the wisdom of preserving the environment rather than destroying it, although 'common sense' can be used to exclude ideological positions which, though unpopular, may still be defensible. Journalists rarely give scope to calls for the return of capital punishment, even though public opinion polls suggest that it would be popular. There are other perspectives that tend to be excluded from the public sphere simply because they are perceived to be unpopular. One such is republicanism, the notion that Britain should dispense with its monarchy and elect a president instead.

Issues of ownership in commercial radio

Another concern of Ofcom and the commercial regulators that preceded it (the IBA and the Radio Authority) is ownership. Newspaper proprietors have always been notorious for seeking to wield political influence by dictating the editorial policies of their publications (Curran and Seaton 1997: 42, 48, 76). As long as they are broadly palatable to their readers, a newspaper's politics might be determined by the owner's own political ambitions or even on a whim. Provided that such intervention does not damage profits, many proprietors regard their newspapers as personal megaphones, a means of imposing their opinions on others (Allan 2005a: 11–13). Hence the more newspapers they control, the louder their voices.

Thanks, however, to the regulation of content that exists in British broadcasting, there is no Rupert Murdoch in radio to threaten such pluralism as remains in the press. But because there is no *bête noir* to worry independent commentators or listeners about undue influences over commercial radio journalism, little attention is paid to what is the seemingly unstoppable concentration of ownership in the sector. In 2007, the largest group of stations was controlled by GCap Media representing 13.1 per cent of listening, and the second largest by EMAP (10.1 per cent) (RAJAR 2007). The strength of the BBC's ratings mitigates the effect of such concentration, but a weakened corporation would be less of a guarantor of pluralism. In 2003, when the Communications Act allowed a greater consolidation of ownership and Ofcom had only just come into being, GCap was formed from what were the two largest groups at the time, GWR and Capital. Since most of the GCap stations carried very little 'journalistic' speech beyond the short, hourly news bulletin, it would be an exaggeration to suggest that this has produced some great challenge to democratic pluralism and freedom of expression. But there may be implications for the future, both within large groups and the wider industrial context. The consolidation of ownership is of particular concern when foreign buyers are allowed access to the market and a chance to swallow large groups of stations. In 2008 GCap was taken over by Global Radio (formerly Chrysalis Radio) and EMAP's radio business was bought by the German publisher, Bauer. Moreover, future governments may be less inclined to use stronger regulation in order to ensure that pluralism survives.

In the United Kingdom, *The Times*, the *Sun*, *The Sunday Times* and the *News of the World* are owned by Australian-born Rupert Murdoch's News

International, which is in turn controlled by News Corporation. Through it, Murdoch's interests in Australia extend to the country's only national broadsheet, *The Australian*, and dozens of other titles, giving him control of 68 per cent of the capital city and national newspaper market, 77 per cent of the Sunday newspaper market and 62 per cent of the suburban newspaper market (Jackson 2003). In the United States, where he assumed US citizenship in order to circumvent restrictions on foreign ownership, his newspaper holdings are limited to the *New York Post*. However, Murdoch's worldwide media empire extends to book publishing, magazines and various terrestrial and satellite broadcasting companies, such as Star in Asia, Sky in Europe, and Fox in the United States and Australia (Allan 2004: 49–51). Other globalising forces in the media include Time Warner and Disney, which, along with News Corporation, make up McChesney's 'Holy Trinity' (2000: 91–100). CNN, for example, with its numerous rolling news services on TV and radio, is situated within Time Warner's multi-million dollar portfolio of film, publishing, cable systems, television networks and interactive services.

We will return to the issue of globalisation in Chapter 5, but just observe for now that all this is quite contrary to the founding principles of ILR. In the 1970s and 1980s the IBA carefully monitored ownership, prevented the transfer of licences between owners, and awarded them only to groups that could demonstrate their 'worthiness' through links with the local community. Happily, British commercial radio has so far managed to avoid being swallowed up by the global giants, although this was a possibility even under previous and tighter regulators. In the 1970s, when some of the stations were in financial difficulties, the IBA allowed limited foreign ownership, and both Selkirk Communications of Canada and Darling Downs Television of Australia invested in a handful of the original stations, including LBC. But there was no question then of the *cross*-media ownership that would have appealed to a Murdoch or a Time Warner, whose domination across a number of media might easily threaten pluralism and democratic expression. Far from it. In order to prevent any market domination of local news provision, local newspapers were prevented from involvement in local radio. The idea of a local newspaper controlling the local radio station was unthinkable.

The growth of cross-media ownership

However, times change, and with them attitudes. As the number of commercial stations increased in all but the smallest and least populous of markets, both governments and regulators perceived cross-media ownership to be less of a threat. Whereas in any one locality there had once been three national television channels, four national radio networks and perhaps a BBC and an 'independent' local radio station, services in both broadcast media were now proliferating at an extraordinary rate and bringing a growth in consumer choice. In the 1990s both television and newspaper companies began to accumulate sizeable holdings in commercial radio, even where there was an overlap in the editorial areas of the media they owned. Century Radio, the collective name of the first regional stations, was set up by Border Television, which was later to fall prey to the rampant consolidation of the originally federal network of ITV companies, and the Wireless Group, including talkSPORT, was bought up by UTV, formerly Ulster Television. But the most blatant exploitation of synergies between overlapping print and radio outlets was achieved by the East Midlands Allied Press (EMAP). EMAP named a number of its digital-only stations after popular niche magazines such as *Smash Hits*, *Heat*, *Mojo* and Q, yet because the content of these stations is much less closely regulated by Ofcom than that of their analogue rivals, the news forms only a tiny part of their schedules.

Ownership is particularly difficult to detail in a book, because an account can be rendered obsolete by only a few weeks of corporate machinations and capitalist chicanery. Some stations change hands simply because a group prefers to concentrate its interests within a single region rather than manage operations over a wide area. However, Table 2.2 offers a comparison of the largest groups in 2001 and 2007. Whereas the original ILR network was made up of companies that were locally based and truly independent of each other, few retain that independence today, even when they survive as the ostensible licensee. Most have been bought up by someone else and are controlled from another part of the country. GWR grew out of a modest but ambitious station called Wiltshire Radio, which was launched in 1982 and operated from a small town outside Swindon. Few would have predicted then that it would build an empire large enough to conquer the Capital Radio Group. This happened in 2004 through a 'merger' and then a boardroom coup in which most of Capital's executives were ousted.

Nevertheless, expansion that depends on a finite resource – analogue broadcast spectrum – cannot be infinite. In 2007, after 35 years of growth in the sector, Ofcom allocated the few remaining frequencies to the last group of local and regional FM stations. Among those whose competitive applications were successful were the established groups EMAP, with Liverpool's City Talk, and GMG, with Rock Radio in Scotland, and newcomers Canwest, who have created the 'Original' brand for their stations in the South West and Scotland.

We might conclude our discussion of political economy by asking whether the hotly debated question of ownership actually *matters*. Could it be that regulation is still so tight that globalisation, the consolidation of stations into

Table 2.2 Comparison of the top six UK commercial radio groups in 2001 and 2007 by number of licences owned

Group	AM & FM licences (2001)	Group	AM & FM licences (2007)
GWR	47	GCap Media (formed from 'merger' of GWR and Capital)	73
Capital	20	EMAP (following takeover of SRH)	38
EMAP	18	The Local Radio Company	26
Scottish Radio Holdings	16	UTV	18
The Wireless Radio Group	16	Guardian Media Group	11
UKRD	12	UKRD	10

groups and the growth of cross-media ownership hardly affect radio journalism in any negative way? The idea that mere ownership can create political bias in commercial radio in the way that it does in the press is surely naïve and misleading. Few accusations of proprietorial influence over Sky News have been sustained, even if many people invoke ideological reasons for refusing to subscribe to it. Ofcom regulates the domestic commercial radio channels in the same way that it regulates commercial television (Harrison 2006: 118–26), and the provisions relating to election coverage that are contained in the Political Parties, Elections and Referendums Act 2000 apply to both media. Hence, on the eve of polling day the broadcasting channels will not follow the newspapers in declaring their allegiance to a particular party.

Some have argued that Sky was uncritical in its coverage of the 2003 Iraq war, but it was nowhere near as supportive as was Fox News in the United States (Dyke 2004: 181) – and nuance in coverage is in any case very difficult to measure. The increasing importance of Sky Radio News and a consensus that Murdoch's editors behave according to the expectations of the public rather than the dictates of their proprietor (Allan 2005a: 11–13) might cause us to fear that if regulation is weakened, the potential for mischief will grow. Hence the key role of regulation in promoting democracy: each guarantees the other, for if one is weakened the other will surely suffer.

Sitting on a cushion: radio journalists in the public sector

The political economy of journalism finds practical expression in the environment in which journalists operate. The relative wealth of an organisation impacts on the physical resources on which journalists may draw, and on the rewards they can expect for their efforts. The relative stability of the BBC derives from a licence fee settlement that, while not always satisfactory to the corporation, is often index-linked – or at least includes some allowance for inflation. This enables the BBC to engage confidently in medium-term planning and results in a professionalism that is hard for the commercial sector to match, subject as it is to the rise and fall of advertising and sponsorship revenues, the ebb and flow of the economy, and the demands of shareholders for a return on their investment. Viewed from a loosely Marxist perspective, the socialist model of a corporation funded from taxation and centrally controlled for the benefit of both producers and consumers may well appear more attractive to radio journalists than the capitalist model, where the market determines not only how well funded a company is but also how much cash it can pay its staff. In the commercial sector, forward planning is always more constrained by a volatile market, remuneration is often lower than in the BBC and, since a drop in profits may cause shareholders to demand cutbacks, the risk of redundancy is greater. In 2007, for example, EMAP shed staff in order to rationalise its business, and journalists were among the hardest hit.

The BBC's relative immunity from market forces means that as well as providing more generous rates of pay, it is able to promote career progression, and secondments are common. These allow staff to transfer temporarily to other locations or even to other jobs within the corporation and acquire very different forms of professional experience; radio journalists can 'taste' television journalism or, for a certain period, take on a more senior role. This allows the BBC to develop its in-house talent, provide its staff with fresh challenges and fill gaps in its human resourcing with reliable people who gain new career opportunities. It is inevitable that the BBC is also more unionised than the commercial sector; pay scales and career structures are negotiated with the National Union of Journalists (NUJ), though only rarely does a dispute between the two sides result in industrial action. The NUJ is less well represented in the commercial sector, where journalists are more exposed to the vagaries of the market.

Where do the journalists come from?

Having examined the political economy of radio journalism, let us now 'interrogate' the journalist in the way that their sceptical listeners might have questioned the news-bearing travellers of the past. Now, as then, we might ask who *are* these particular strangers in our midst? Where have they come from and why are they here? Our analogy between the journalists of today and their tale-telling predecessors is not, of course, wholly apt, for the journalists' appearance among their audiences is not a matter of chance. They have arrived not by unmarked roads or uncharted seas, but along a carefully plotted career path beginning with training and then a first job. Unlike those who journey from place to place and chance upon people on the way, journalists have made a conscious decision to become news bearers. Weaver asks 'Who are journalists?' (2005: 45) and concludes from his research that what most inspires them is a 'love of writing'. Others perceive their motivation to be 'an enjoyment of reporting, a desire to be involved in current events and history, an interest in politics, and the enjoyment of telling a story'. The *radio* journalists we have interviewed also cite the immediacy of the medium, its flexibility, and their ability to communicate with an audience in real time. And here lies a problem with the majority of studies such as Weaver's and those he cites: they do not distinguish between radio journalists and journalists who work in other media.

We can identify some common traits, however, and there is a good deal of mobility between one medium and another. As they go about their work, most journalists are informed by a sense of professionalism; they are not amateur raconteurs whose stories are filled with marvels that have been found by chance, but trained and qualified practitioners. They must work to established standards and observe professional and regulatory codes of practice which require the provision of certain standards of evidence for what they report. Yet, despite the professionalism of their approach, there can be no denying that a hermeneutic, or interpretative, element exists in even the most professionally conducted journalism (Giddens 1984: 284). Journalists are mere human beings and reportage is a re-presentation of something observed. It cannot exclude an element of subjectivity and so cannot be entirely value-free.

We therefore find ourselves in the realm of demography. We must ask who journalists are and what made them – and these questions are as pertinent now as when they were first posed. Can audiences consider the radio journalist to be 'one of us', or is she substantially different in her outlook, attitudes and assumptions? If so, the audiences may consider her representations of the world to be flawed, based perhaps on a different perception of 'reality' and thus misleading. Since we are all influenced in some way by our origins and our experiences, let us now attempt a broad demographic analysis of radio journalists within both the public and commercial sectors. We will then consider whether their backgrounds have some bearing on the stories they tell, provide a summary account of the structure of journalism

education and training in the United Kingdom, and conclude with an outline of the issues at its heart.

As is so often the case, we are beset with difficulties of definition. Even the
term 'journalist' is not straightforward. We can probably agree about the person
with a notebook and trench-coat who is the full-time employee of a daily newspaper and sent out to press conferences and crime scenes. Some analyses serve
to reinforce such stereotypes (e.g. Delano 2000: 266–7). But what about the
person who works full-time as a teacher or solicitor and writes an occasional
theatre review or humorous column for a periodical? There is the further problem that within the agreed category of 'journalists', *radio* journalists are seldom
distinguished. The category to which they are normally assigned is *broadcast*
journalism, which might embrace not only TV journalists but those working in
interactive media. On the other hand, the Sector Skills Council for the media
industries, known as Skillset, often prefers to focus on media *workers*, a category
that embraces many professions beside journalism. Nevertheless, much of what
is asserted of journalists in general, and certain things that are asserted of media
workers, will be at least broadly true of radio journalists.

Yet even if we can agree about what constitutes 'a journalist', the question of
whether journalism is a profession is also in doubt. Some commentators think it
is not, but merely a collection of practices (Weaver 2005: 48–9). Others ignore
the emphasis on routines, the requirement to conform to house styles and many
other aspects of contemporary practice that we shall explore in Chapter 4, and
regard it as an art form. We disagree with both positions, and will continue to
adopt as our premise the notion that journalism is a profession – one which is not
always beyond reproach, but of which it is possible to be proud.

Now for some detail. In 2002, the Journalism Training Forum estimated
that between 60,000 and 70,000 journalists were working in the United
Kingdom – a number that is expected to have risen by 20,000 in 2010. Of
these, about 21 per cent were working in broadcasting, 11 per cent in radio
(7 per cent at regional or local level and 4 per cent at national or network
level) (Skillset 2002: 18). The audio visual workforce is a highly educated
one: 66 per cent are graduates, 25 per cent of them with media studies
degrees, and 24 per cent have an additional, postgraduate qualification
(Skillset 2003: 11). To journalism as a whole, access is now almost entirely
restricted to graduates: 98 per cent of entrants have at least a first degree,
and 58 per cent of the journalists who work in radio have a journalistic qualification (Skillset 2002: 4, 34).

Radio journalism: a halfway house between print and television?

There is a perception within the profession that radio journalism is a kind of
halfway house between the press and television – that many people who work

for television began their career in newspapers and reached their destination via an apprenticeship in radio. This perception probably has some basis in fact. Before the 1970s, when the qualifications for a career in broadcast journalism were formally determined, almost all radio journalists had a newspaper background: until then, journalism was virtually synonymous with *print* journalism. As the BBC was setting up its network of local radio stations, beginning with Radio Leicester in 1967, it was to the local newspapers that it turned for recruits. The growth of ILR created further demand, and the medium's renaissance made it attractive to many print journalists who sought an escape from some of the humbler routines of the average local newspaper.

There are many cultural and practical differences between working in a local newspaper and working in radio. Richard Evans left an evening newspaper in South Wales to work for a commercial radio station in Bristol. His career took him to Radio 1's *Newsbeat*, then Radio Five Live and later back to Cardiff to BBC Radio Wales:

> The first culture shock was leaving a team of up to twenty reporters to become a one-person news operation – reporter, editor and broadcaster, often all at the same time. There were many new skills to learn – editing, using sound, operating a radio studio and writing for radio. I'd been taught to write stories that grabbed your attention in the first paragraph and would 'cut from the bottom' – radio is much more about a narrative. I found it useful to imagine telling a story to a man you had met in the pub, a parent, a partner, or a friend who was interested in what had happened but who might have been locked in a cupboard for a couple of days. As far as the BBC is concerned the best advice I had was 'go easy on the adjectives and attribute everything'.
>
> (Personal communication, 8 July 2007)

Even today it is not hard to find radio journalists who began their career in newspapers, and a certain amount of cross-over persists. Indeed, cross-media working is becoming more prevalent, since what were once entirely separate media are now converging in ways that a decade or two ago would have been unimaginable – a process we will return to later in the book. But since the establishment of the Broadcast Journalism Training Council (BJTC),[1] and the development of other formal and informal direct entry routes, the number is much smaller: many journalists now begin their career in radio. On the other hand, there is a modest but steady drift from radio into television (Delano 2000: 263). In 2002, about 18 per cent of journalists working in TV had previously worked in radio (Skillset 2002: 31).

Radio journalists by class, gender, ethnicity and age

The social demography of journalism is interesting. According to the Skillset study, the gender split in the profession as a whole is roughly equal: 51 per cent are male, 49 per cent are female. Only 4 per cent, however, are non-white. Moreover, it is an increasingly middle- and upper-middle-class profession: in 2002, only 3 per cent of entrants came from a family headed by someone in a semi-skilled or unskilled job (Skillset 2002: 4). Such occupational background analyses confirm the view that journalism is an elitist profession, even though the assertion that was made by former US Vice-President Dan Quayle in 1992 that journalists were a 'cultural elite' has often been disputed (Weaver 2005: 46). Nevertheless, manual workers and other listeners in lower paid professions may wonder how relevant to their own lives are the observations made by journalists of unmistakably middle-class backgrounds. Our interpretation of the statistics depends, of course, on what importance one attaches to differences of class, gender and ethnicity, but those that relate to ethnicity are likeliest to catch the eye. Within the higher echelons of named newspaper columnists, radio news correspondents and television news presenters and reporters, both women and ethnic minorities are quite strongly represented, but whereas this seems an accurate reflection of the former, it may imply a certain tokenism in respect of the latter. Lower down the ranks of the profession, journalists from ethnic minorities are rather harder to find.

Let us first consider the question of gender. It seems that whereas their newsrooms are often dominated by women, the presenters of music radio stations are mainly male, with females relegated to such ancillary roles as traffic and travel reporter or even 'sidekick' (Mitchell 2001: 273). This may be due to prejudice on the part of the programmers, as some feminist assessments of the industry maintain. Alternatively, it could simply be that, in line with those differences in academic achievement that have been documented by educationalists, women are more attracted than men to the apparently more cerebral role of journalist. Gender is, of course, a more important issue for female rather than male journalists, and in drawing conclusions from a cross-media survey, Ross (2001: 534) considered those who have not suffered overt sexism to have been 'lucky'. One woman journalist told us:

> In some commercial stations there is an element of 'keeping up with the lads' and putting up with treatment that would be considered inappropriate in other jobs. They avoid giving females sports stories at all costs and put entertainment news our way instead. I don't think it gets in the way of promotion, though, it's just banter. There seem to be lots of female News Editors around. Whether they earn the same as the men, I don't know! There is still a 'jobs for the boys' mentality in places, like one man being hired to cover sport just because he played football with the Editor. He had no NCTJ, no legal experience, no radio background, nothing!

> (Interview with the authors, 17 April 2007)

However, the sheer numbers of women in many radio newsrooms, where they often predominate, may offset any such disadvantage. To assume that all women journalists operate in a mainly male environment is naïve, for many radio stations are managed by women.

Moreover, those studies (such as Ross 2005: 292), which suggest that women journalists are commodities whose looks are used to boost television ratings, tend to overlook the neutralising effect of radio, where only the first name and voice of a female reporter will distinguish her from any male colleagues. Radio has little of the 'leer factor' to be found in television. Nevertheless, when Ross asks why few females are war reporters and compares behaviour at press conferences to that of boys in public schools (2005: 287–98), she makes a point which is of greater relevance, for it is on moving out of the newsroom and into the wider world that the obstacles of gender present themselves.

In both presentation and journalism, though, ethnic minorities are far less prevalent. Whether the ethnic mix of the working population as a whole is fairly represented is another issue, and one that, as Delano suggests (2000: 270), is not entirely straightforward. Surveys inevitably depend on how individuals categorise themselves, and they may not always feel that a predetermined category fits them. In terms of ethnic minorities who seek access to journalism training, Delano's analysis suggests, persuasively, that they are under-represented across the profession. Occasionally this is noticed. Director General, Greg Dyke, told listeners to BBC Radio Scotland that, in under-representing on its staff the ethnic minorities among its audience, the corporation was 'hideously white' (21:00, 07/01/01).

Age is another criterion by which we are all defined and to some extent judged. There are few 'old hands' in local radio journalism, particularly in the commercial sector, and this is largely because salaries seldom keep up with expectations. The lure of better pay in national radio or television means that smaller stations find it hard to retain staff. Even television journalists have a short professional life-span, and Chris Underwood, the then General Secretary of the Institute of Journalists, wrote in the *Press Gazette* on 6 June 1997 that it was usual for a journalist's career at the BBC to end at 50. There are exceptions, the sexagenarian *Today* presenter John Humphrys among them, and even some commercial radio journalists have become so well known that they can command the higher salaries the sector normally reserves for its star presenters. Indeed, Humphrys' pay was famously described by his programme's outgoing editor as 'wheelbarrow loads' of money (Davies 2006). In a typical large urban ILR station, the salary of the breakfast presenter may be four or five times that of its most junior journalist. There are exceptions to this rule: Piccadilly Radio in Manchester, now Key 103, has succeeded in retaining staff over many years.

Promotion to the role of News Editor (called Head of News on some stations) brings better pay and conditions, but many journalists have developed their careers in other directions within the radio industry, becoming programme controllers or managing directors. Ralph Bernard, the founder of Wiltshire Radio and GWR, and until 2008 the Chief Executive of GCap Media, was himself a journalist. We have already noted that the BBC provides second-ments for its staff and clear opportunities for career development, so, while the age profile of radio journalists may suggest a profession mainly for the young, it clearly provides access to other interesting and potentially lucrative occupations.

Are these socio-economic factors of any great consequence? Does the background of radio journalists affect their reporting, or are they so con-strained by official codes of broadcasting practice, management expecta-tions, style guides and their own professional training that their personal autonomy is limited? Perhaps not. The NUJ code is unequivocal on the need for balance in coverage: it affirms that they should 'strive' for fairness and accuracy, avoid confusing 'comment and conjecture [with] established fact' and eschew 'distortion, selection or misrepresentation' (NUJ 2004). Yet newspaper journalists are routinely pressured by their editors and propri-etors to misrepresent politics, and in 2007 the Chartered Institute of Journalists, an alternative trade union in the UK, criticised the NUJ for its official stance towards Israel. Thus, self-regulation may not be as reliable as it seems. Greg Dyke's criticism was prompted by his belief that attitudes among BBC staff are indeed affected by their socio-economic profile, and the BBC, Ofcom and others, such as the Cultural Diversity Network, have developed initiatives to address this issue. One of the charges levelled against the BBC by Channel 4 Radio, and discussed later in this book, is that the output of Radio 4 shows a clear bias towards 'middle-England'.

The structure of journalism training and education

One way to tackle the problem of representation is to make access to the profession as flexible as possible. The structure of journalism training and education in the United Kingdom is based on entry into the profession at one of three levels: non-graduate, graduate and postgraduate. It results largely from the decline of in-house or 'on the job' training in the style of old-fashioned apprenticeships, and universities and colleges have taken on this role with enthusiasm. The distinction between education and training is a contentious one, but it is fair to say that they both reflect the traditional dominance of print within the profession. Most journalists would probably agree that the print medium requires the most exacting skills of all the media and a level of literacy that is not strictly necessary in broadcasting. Hence the body responsible for the training of print journalists, the National Council for the Training of Journalists (NCTJ), is not merely an accreditor of courses taught by other bodies but administers its own exams, which all aspiring entrants to that branch of the profession are required to sit. It is also the sole body that provides a pre-entry course for non-graduates (who are of course dwindling in numbers), and the course has validity for broadcast as well as print journalism. This means, in effect, that an apprenticeship and competence in print journalism are considered to be appropriate for journalism in any medium.

However, at graduate and postgraduate level, broadcast journalism has its own validating body in the form of the BJTC. This, in contrast with the NCTJ, administers none of its own exams but exists purely to accredit courses in broadcast journalism that are taught in various colleges and universities in the United Kingdom. It is an association of all the major employers of broadcast journalists, along with those educational institutions whose courses it accredits. Moreover, it will accredit courses only in their entirety, whether at first degree level or at postgraduate (diploma, master's) level.

The BJTC is not the only validating body. In response to its legal requirement to ensure that broadcasters provide their staff with relevant and inclusive training opportunities, Ofcom launched the Broadcast Training and Skills Regulator (BTSR) in 2005. In turn, the BTSR, Skillset and the trade body representing the commercial radio industry, the RadioCentre, have formed the Radio Skills and Development Forum. Another promising initiative is the Radio Skills Strategy, developed by Skillset and the Radio Academy, one priority of which has been to develop a system of kitemarking for courses in radio practice.

Nevertheless, the BJTC is the main validator for higher education, and in devising the courses for which they seek its accreditation, the colleges and universities are allowed a fair measure of autonomy and flexibility. Some degrees and diplomas are focused on journalism while others embrace the broader fields of media and cultural studies. But to gain accreditation, a course must include a core of practical skills and theoretical knowledge. For the former, the institution must provide such facilities as a functional newsroom with appropriate outside links, a studio unit, one portable sound recorder per student, and an adequate number of editing-/work-stations. Students must also gain work experience through placements or, as they are now often known, 'internships', and in order to offer the full range of abilities implicit in the multi-skilling required by the industry (Delano 2000: 266), they must acquire proficiency in scripting and microphone presentation. In theoretical terms, the students must gain adequate knowledge of the relationship between law and journalism; the workings of public administration, including the operation of the essential services; the anatomy and machinery of local and central government; journalistic ethics; and the structure and underlying philosophies of the British mass media.

Although at the time of writing radio journalists are in relatively short supply, most editors would baulk at recruiting a beginner without either

NCTJ or BJTC credentials, together with the considerable work experience that might be gained through an internship. Even where minded to allow informal, on-the-job learning, editors simply lack the time to teach the legal and civic aspects central to all journalism training and education, and would probably insist that the beginner attends a suitable course.

Radio journalism: academic discipline or a set of techniques?

We might conclude this chapter by suggesting that in allowing entry into the profession at a number of levels, the British system of journalism training and education is designed to accommodate a central philosophical debate. Indeed, the very words *training* and *education* bring that debate into sharper focus. Do aspiring journalists merely need to acquire a set of practical skills and techniques as a kind of appendage to another, more substantial and ideally contrasting, programme of study? Or is journalism – or more broadly, the mass media and popular culture – itself a substantial and challenging programme of study? The advocates of specialised journalism or media/cultural studies degrees insist that their graduates are highly professional and media-literate, yet there is an argument that journalism and media studies are in essence about the forms and structures of communication rather than its content. Lacking an adequate intellectual province of their own, they therefore supplement practical training by stealing, magpie-fashion, from other disciplines; journalism gives its students a smattering of law, government and public administration, while media degrees dabble in politics and social issues like race and gender. Cultural studies, it is further suggested, cannot offer even the practical training of journalism and media courses but merely diluted, incoherent borrowings from literary and film studies, sociology and politics.

In contrast, it is claimed that students who undergo journalism and media training only at postgraduate level are more 'grounded and rounded'. Having studied such subjects as English, History, Classics, Modern Languages and Politics (the authors are even aware of one whose degree was in Pharmacology!), they possess knowledge which even if not of direct relevance to their journalistic activities is substantial and systematic and indicative of analytical skills. But others would assert that this mode of entry produces mere dilettantes, and that the reluctance to regard journalism, media and culture as worthy of sustained undergraduate study amounts to nothing more than old-fashioned snobbery and elitism. It is in any case worth adding that the 'training/education' quandary is not confined to journalism. Most of us would regard law as a serious academic discipline, yet the possession of a law degree is not the prerequisite of entry into the legal professions. Graduates of other disciplines are acceptable, provided they sit and pass a conversion course that qualifies them as solicitors or barristers.

Note

1 The organisation launched in 1981 as the Joint Advisory Council for the Training of Radio Journalists. It then became the National Council for the Training of Broadcast Journalists and finally the BJTC.

3

RIDING THE RADIO RAPIDS: RECENT POLICY DEVELOPMENTS

Should broadcasting be regulated or liberated?

We have seen how, over the last century, governments have been reluctant to leave radio to the broadcasters in the way that the press has been left to regulate itself. Since Crawford first pronounced on the scarcity of radio spectrum and its implications for democracy (Crawford Committee 1926), the BBC has operated strictly within the terms of the Royal Charter that was granted to it and which has subsequently been renewed every ten years. Giving it the freedom to do as it might please has never been an option. But governments, whether Conservative or Labour, were even less likely to expose the commercial sector to the full force of the market: it is subject to that legislation restricting mergers and monopolies that governs most industries. The legislation ensures that even newspapers are subject to controls over ownership. Today's radio industry is the result of a long history of government intervention that belies the original, and honourable, intention that broadcasting should be free from all political influence.

In order to avoid the charge that they seek any influence, successive governments have sought consensus over their dealings with broadcasting institutions, and through Royal Commissions, Green Papers and White Papers have proposed only changes that would win both popular support and the agreement of the Opposition. The minor ideological skirmish that threatened to destabilise ILR in the 1970s was soon forgotten, and the only controversy remaining over commercial radio is not about whether it has the right to exist but about the extent to which it needs to be regulated. Indeed, so great was New Labour's ideological shift to the right that much of the deregulation that has occurred within the sector took place during the ten years that Tony Blair was Prime Minister.

Let us rewind a little further, though, for the past 20 years or so have seen a succession of government interventions in broadcasting, many of them inspired by what Franklin has termed the 'perennial issues' of regulation and funding, and some in response to questionings about the BBC's right to exist. These questionings were to be found in the press, and particularly the Murdoch newspapers, which were envious of the BBC's regular and guaranteed income from the television licence fee. In the mid-1980s Murdoch was developing his first Sky Television channel, which was operated on a very tight budget, highly dependent on re-runs of ancient American comedy and cop shows, and aimed at the fledgling UK cable TV market. Since Murdoch's interests did not at that time extend to radio, television bore the brunt of his attacks, but radio was used in support of the argument that the corporation was a bloated, over-extended enterprise, ever-growing, ever-encroaching on the natural territory of the free market, and stuffed with left-liberal and often inept programme makers (Franklin 2001: 23–5). Beneath all the editorial bluster there may have been a germ of truth, but a ruling Conservative Party that still resented what it saw as unsupportive coverage of the Falklands War was only too ready to reconsider the nature and role of the BBC. To this end it appointed a committee under Professor Alan Peacock (Peacock Committee 1986).

The Peacock Report and the broadcasting acts of the 1990s

The expectations that Peacock would savage the BBC's claim to public finance, recommend the abolition of the licence fee, and force it to compete for advertising with the commercial sector turned out to be unfounded (Franklin 2001: 25–7). Instead, the committee rejected advertising but called for a fundamental rethink of the BBC's long-term funding and raised the possibility of the privatisation of Radios 1 and 2 and of replacing the licence fee with a subscription system. Peacock also proposed that a proportion of its programmes should be made by independents and that the licence fee should be pegged to the retail price index. This was a particularly important proposal as it would guarantee the BBC stability at a time when it might otherwise have been at its most vulnerable. Even though the United Kingdom was going through the most comprehensive privatisation of public assets in its history, the suggestion of selling off Radios 1 and 2 was quietly shelved. Subscription remains one possible means of dealing with the further proliferation of radio and television channels, but no government has subsequently sought to introduce it as a replacement for the licence fee.

Change was in the air, but it was change in the commercial sector, representing the first major relaxation of regulatory control since the launch of both ITV and ILR. The first legislation after the Peacock Report (1986) was the Broadcasting Act 1990, which split the functions of the Independent Broadcasting Authority and set up the Radio Authority and the Independent

Television Commission. The cynical rumour that the IBA had only turned its attention to radio on Friday afternoons was dispelled, since for the commercial sector the medium now had its own regulator. Crucially, the Radio Authority was empowered to advertise for and appoint contractors to run three national commercial radio stations: at last, Independent Radio was to be allowed to grow up. The Act also established the Broadcasting Complaints Commission (BCC) and the Broadcasting Standards Council (BSC), giving each of them the right to adjudicate on complaints received from listeners and viewers and to impose fines and/or order retractions and apologies. Prior to this, content in the private and public sectors had been regulated by the IBA and the BBC respectively. Henceforth, external bodies would have the power to take the BBC to task over what it broadcast.

The Broadcasting Act 1996 merged the BCC and the BSC, allowed for the development of digital radio services using a system known as Digital Audio Broadcasting (DAB), and enabled the licences of the commercial radio companies to be more easily extended. When the licence to provide an ILR service for a particular area was about to expire, the Radio Authority was no longer obliged to readvertise it, but could offer an extension to an existing licensee who agreed to simulcast on DAB. This, together with the commitment of the BBC to the new technology and a considerable investment in the first national multiplex by the GWR Group, enabled DAB to grow at a faster pace in the UK than in any other country. Over the following ten years the UK was to become one of only a handful of European states to adopt the Eureka 147 standard and develop a credible alternative to analogue radio. Meanwhile, the Act left the BBC unscathed: with Margaret Thatcher long gone, a government that was hugely unpopular with the electorate, and Conservative rule coming to an end amid accusations of sleaze, the licence fee seemed more secure. The mid-1990s ushered in a new era, though one which would be driven by technology rather than ideology – and technological change was happening fast.

Digital dawn: the Communications Act 2003 and the birth of Ofcom

The impact of the new technology on radio production is something we will consider in a later chapter, but the exponential rise in the use of digits to encode and distribute media content also had far-reaching implications for broadcasting policy. The first major legislation of the new millennium was the Communications Act 2003 (www.opsi.gov.uk/acts), whose main role was to acknowledge the fact of media convergence. The audience's interest in 'old' media was now being challenged by 'new' media, each of which was developing certain characteristics of the others. Radio could now be received through television sets and via the Internet, which in turn was distributed over telephone lines, and in order to carry out their functions the competing regulatory bodies could find themselves tripping over one another. Rather than refusing to acknowledge the popularity of the new services, as it had done in the 1960s and 1970s, the Labour government established the Office of Communications (Ofcom) not only as the successor to the Independent Television Commission and the Radio Authority, but as the regulator of all telecommunications.

Though primarily in charge of commercial broadcasting, Ofcom was given certain powers over the BBC too. The latter would be obliged to comply with its fairness code, its competition policy and its quotas on programme imports and independent production. Although the Broadcasting Standards Commission and its predecessor had been able to censure the BBC, this was the first time that the principal regulator of commercial radio and television had been given the power to discipline it. In June 2006 Ofcom upheld complaints about language on the Chris Moyles and Scott Mills shows on Radio 1 and warned the BBC that if the corporation failed to comply with its code on decency it would take action. In July 2007 it did so for the first time, albeit in respect of television: the BBC was fined £50,000 for deceiving the *Blue Peter* audience by manipulating a competition. This had an immediate effect on the BBC's demeanour: if their language exposed the network to regulatory action in future, the Radio 1 Controller Andy Parfitt warned his presenters that he would fine them himself. Far from being an angry government's revenge for the Gilligan Affair, as some have hastily suggested, Ofcom's power can be traced back to 2001 and the initial drafts of the Communications Bill.

The regulation of commercial radio: walking the dog on a very long lead

However, the Act broadly perpetuated the old dual system, with the public sector – the BBC, under the control of its Board of Governors – kept largely separate from the 'independent' sector. It seemed as though the future of the BBC was secure in the medium term: it had weathered the stormiest of seas and could now enjoy a period of calm. Ofcom was given responsibility for both the licensing of the independent stations and the broad character of their programming, but was intended to be a fairly relaxed regulator. It would facilitate the multiple ownership of radio and television stations, and foreign and cross-media takeovers would grow likelier. For programming it was required to set up a 'Content Board' (ss. 12, 13) which superseded the Broadcasting Complaints Commission, but not to be tightly prescriptive. Such news as was heard on the radio must be impartial and accurate (s. 319) and the stations must not editorialise (s. 320), but they would be free to reduce, if they wished, the seriousness of the news they covered and/or the frequency and length of their bulletins.

In this respect, the Act contains some illuminating references to local radio. Stations were obliged to include local material only to the extent that Ofcom considered appropriate for any particular area (s. 314). By 'local' was meant material that is of especial interest to persons living or working within the area for which the service is provided, but there is no requirement that this material be locally originated. Since 2003 there has been an emerging Ofcom policy of judging the performance of the local stations by 'output' rather than 'process' criteria. In other words, if what audiences hear on their radios reflects a due awareness of local issues and events, local preoccupations and local tastes, its actual source and the process by which it has been assembled become irrelevant. The effect of this policy has been to encourage out-of-area newsrooms or 'news hubs' that are able to provide customised bulletins to large numbers of different stations across whole regions of the country. By dramatically reducing journalistic presence within actual editorial areas, these will undoubtedly have a negative impact on employment.

Turmoil at the Beeb: the Gilligan Affair

With regard to the BBC, the Communications Act left unresolved a number of matters relating to regulation and future funding, but in the same year a serious dispute arose between the corporation and the government that would have serious policy consequences for the former. At 6.07 on 29 May, the BBC's defence correspondent, Andrew Gilligan, asserted during an interview with John Humphrys on Radio 4's *Today* programme that the government had 'sexed up' its report on Iraq's weapons of mass destruction by claiming that they could be mobilised within 45 minutes, even though it knew that this claim was probably untrue. Gilligan's source for his assertion, whom he refused to disclose at the time, was a respected scientist in the civil service named David Kelly. Dr Kelly had expressed disquiet to Gilligan and another BBC journalist about the way in which military intelligence was being used to bolster the case for a war on Iraq, believing that a hitherto neutral civil service was being pressed to act as an apologist for the government. Gilligan used Kelly's opinion as the basis for further reports on BBC radio and for a number of articles he wrote for the *Mail on Sunday*. An infuriated government, led by Alastair Campbell, its chief spin doctor and the main author of the weapons report, denied Gilligan's charge and demanded to know his source. Pressure mounted on Kelly, who a few days after having appeared before the parliamentary Foreign Affairs Committee was found dead, apparently from suicide (Born 2005: 455).

The government appointed a senior judge, Lord Hutton, to hold an inquiry into the matter, but in the meantime the BBC made two fatal errors. Its Director General, Greg Dyke, an enthusiastic champion of investigative journalism, moved to defend Gilligan before closely checking his report, and with similar impetuosity the Board of Governors then backed Dyke (Born 2005: 459–60). But within the corporation, alarm bells were already ringing: editorial guidelines were tightened, journalists were forbidden to write political material for outside publications, and the editor of *Today*, Kevin Marsh, conceded that he thought Gilligan's report had been flawed.

The Hutton Report and its aftermath

Hutton published the results of his inquiry in January 2004 and exonerated the government. He had discovered nothing to suggest that it had made a claim it knew to be false, but he found much fault with the journalistic practices of the BBC. He criticised Gilligan's reliance on a single and unconfirmed source and his failure to take a full set of notes of the information supplied by Kelly, for such notes as survived did not support all the allegations he had made on air. Hutton also averred that because of the gravity of the allegations, the 6.07 broadcast should have followed a script, and that in any event, the programme should have given the government an opportunity to rebut them.

Gavyn Davies, the Chairman of the Board of Governors, Dyke and Gilligan all resigned. At first Dyke had thought he could weather the storm, and indeed 30 pages of his autobiography consist of a chapter entitled 'Why Hutton Was Wrong' (Dyke 2004: 287–317). But in the event he lost the support of the governors. Those more academic critiques of the Hutton Report accept some of its findings about failings in journalistic practice, but criticise it for not taking a broader approach to the contexts within which the controversy over Dr Kelly arose (Barnett 2005: 328–410).

Meanwhile the government had already ordered a comprehensive review of the BBC's Charter, into which four smaller inquiries would feed: Ofcom's into public service broadcasting; Lord Burns's into the BBC and its dependence on the licence fee; an inquiry into the BBC's online services; and an inquiry into its new digital TV and radio networks (Born 2005: 461). Critics of the government were quick to perceive the danger to the BBC. They claimed that there were scores to settle and that the Charter review could damage or even destroy the corporation. As the review began, the then Secretary of State for Culture, Media and Sport, Tessa Jowell, declared it would concentrate on ensuring that the BBC was extending the range of its broadcasting appropriately and continuing to raise standards. The review would also examine the *size*, *scope* and *accountability* of the corporation, and in particular its provision of digital services ahead of the proposed termination of analogue television in about 2010.

For the incoming management of the BBC, these were anxious times. Bloodied but not entirely cowed, the BBC adopted a posture that was designed to protect its interests. Over the second half of 2004 it carried out four internal reviews – 'Content Supply', 'Out of London', 'Commercial Review' and 'Value for Money' – publishing their conclusions and inviting public reactions. The second review proposed, not altogether altruistically, that the public would be better served if more production were devolved out of London so that the BBC could play a part in the economic regeneration of certain regions. The grand plan was to move some radio and television production to 'the North'. This would entail the relocation of hundreds of staff to a then undetermined area, together with substantial local recruitment in order to fill the vacancies created by those employees who refused to leave London.

Back from the brink

In the event, the BBC emerged unscathed and, indeed, with a new lease of life. The review period was protracted and the old complaints were heard again – more loudly than ever from those in the commercial sector who felt that the licence fee gave their rival an unfair advantage. There were repeated demands that regulation should be conducted on a 'level playing field': one of the loudest was that the BBC should be made accountable to Ofcom. There was particular resentment that almost overnight Radio 2 had been able to shed its previous format as a middle-of-the-road station for an ageing audience and reconstitute itself as the natural home of those who had grown up listening to Radio 1. In contrast, the commercial sector was held by Ofcom to specific agreements about content and format, so stations were unable to change in response to perceived market demand.

Nevertheless, the commercial radio lobby carried none of the 'clout' of the Murdoch press in previous years, so this and calls for the partial privatisation of the BBC fell on deaf ears. Murdoch's domination of pay TV through the now successful BSkyB and his ability to outbid the BBC for television, film and sports rights meant his perspective had changed, and in order to succeed financially he no longer felt the need to attack the corporation. In one sense, the press became the guarantors of the BBC's survival: largely opposed to the ongoing war in Iraq, and happy to run with any negative stories about it that they could find, they may have made the government more grateful for its relatively even-handed treatment from the corporation. There was even a widespread feeling in the press that the BBC had had a raw deal from Hutton and now needed all the friends it could find.

Instead of taking the narrowest view of 'public service' and allowing it to do only those things that were beyond the resources of the private sector, the government resisted any temptation to curb the size and scope of the BBC. The easiest target would have been its internet operation; 'bbc.co.uk' was one of the world's most visited websites and exposed the BBC to the charge that it was involved in things which were far outside its brief and which denied the private sector some important sources of income. Yet to disaggregate the BBC's broadcast operations from its web presence would have been to paddle against the tide of technological convergence. Already, television and radio content were being distributed via the web both live and on a time-shift basis ('Listen Again'), for broadcasting now meant much more than the simple transmission of analogue signals that had characterised its infancy.

Judges or defenders? The problem of the BBC's governors

On accountability, however, the BBC fared less well, for the Gilligan Affair had exposed two weaknesses within it. The first was *structural* and related to the role of its Board of Governors, and the second was *professional*, relating to the way in which its journalists performed their duties. When the BBC became a public corporation in 1927, it was provided with a Board of Governors who would oversee its activities and act as 'trustees of the national interest'. But how is 'the national interest' to be defined? It was initially perceived as something that transcends the interests of both government on the one hand and the BBC on the other. The Board's independence of the government was reflected in the fact that those appointed to be its chair and vice-chair were usually of contrasting political persuasions, and its other members, though mostly distinguished professional or public figures, were not prominent in political life. But its independence of the BBC was also declared in the fact that the members were not media professionals such as journalists or programme producers, but embodied the old idea of the cultivated amateur. They were part-time, and in being drawn from public service, the arts, business and industry, broadly representative of the educated classes, bringing both intelligence and detachment to the role they performed.

However, from time to time problems arose when the government on the one hand and the BBC on the other regarded the national interest as being more closely allied to their own. The government then expected the Board of Governors to act on its behalf (it had, after all, appointed them) – to curb the corporation if it was becoming too independent or critical, and ensure that it was giving good value for the public money it received. But the BBC expected the Board of Governors to act as a bulwark against editorial pressures from the government. (The Board was, after all, housed within the corporation and had a close working relationship with the Director General.) Hence the governors somewhat resembled Janus, the ancient Roman god of gates and doors, who because he needed to watch in two directions had one face at the front of his head and another at the back. The Board was the agent of both sides – obliged to act as judge on behalf of the government and as protector of the BBC.

Nevertheless, history has a way of determining what theory has left ambiguous. After some initial difficulties with its more wayward members (Stuart 1975: 140), Reith largely succeeded in turning the Board of Governors into a creature of the BBC, and for the most part this is how it remained – a situation that was probably better than if it had been in thrall to the government. But a negative consequence of Reith's action was that the Board was recognised as the creature of *someone*: it was no longer acting for a transcendent 'national interest'. In the 1980s, Mrs Thatcher and her colleagues therefore resolved to wrest it from the BBC and bring it under the heel of the government. In swift succession they appointed two Conservatives to chair the Board, Stuart Young and Marmaduke Hussey, and broke with tradition by appointing another Conservative, William Rees Mogg, as vice-chair. In 1987, Hussey sacked the politically neutral Director General, Alastair Milne, and replaced him with John Birt, who, if not a Tory himself, was a devout managerialist and apostle of the market. Nevertheless, by the end of the 1990s, the Board had drifted back into the ambit of the BBC, and when the Gilligan Affair broke, it did not, as we have seen, behave in a measured, judicial manner but hastily lent its support to Greg Dyke.

The proposals of the government White Paper

Hence, in its White Paper of 2006, one of the main tasks that the government set itself was to address the issue of the governance of the BBC. In her foreword to the paper, the Secretary of State for Culture, Media and Sport put the matter lucidly:

> Since 1927, the Board of Governors, appointed by Government, have been the cheer-leaders of the BBC's management, as well as guardians of the Corporation's independence and the court of appeal for complaints against it. In an age where transparency and separation of powers have transformed the structures of almost every public institution, it is anomalous that the BBC should continue with a system whereby the Governors are both judge and jury. ... So we will go ahead with our plans to replace the Governors with a new BBC Trust and an Executive Board. The Board will be responsible for delivering the BBC's services, and the Trust for holding it to account and consulting widely and regularly with licence fee payers and industry.

(DCMS 2006: 2–3)

The White Paper itself explains what the job of the trust will be:

> The new BBC Trust will represent the interests of the licence fee payer more clearly than the existing Board of Governors and the new system will be more transparent, independent of Government and more outward facing. It will clearly separate the current Board of Governors' dual and sometimes conflicting roles of representing both the public interest and the BBC management.
>
> (DCMS 2006: 46)

The Trust would be the sovereign body of the corporation, with 12 salaried, and probably part-time, members who would be appointed by the government (DCMS 2006: 50). Like those of the old Board of Governors, they would be of an eclectic background and, other than of the constituent nations of the United Kingdom, not representative of particular sections of the community (DCMS 2006: 49). The Executive Board would also be salaried and its role would be to support the BBC's management. Its chair would be appointed by the Trust and at least a third of its members would be outsiders (DCMS 2006: 50). The White Paper makes clear that the new BBC Trust would not be a creature of the BBC, but what is less clear, since its members will be appointed and in effect salaried by the government, is how far it will be allowed to serve the broader national interest and how far it will be reduced to serving that of the government.

The second issue which the White Paper addressed was that of the BBC's funding, and it concluded that the licence fee remained the best method and would be retained until 2016 (DCMS 2006: 61), but it would be kept under constant review. Moreover, for the time being the BBC would continue to be the sole beneficiary of licence revenue. But probably towards the end of the period of conversion to digital technology, in about 2012, the government would revisit the possibility of allocating some of the licence revenue to other providers of public service content, notably Channel 4 (DCMS 2006: 63).

A further subject for review was to be the possibility of funding the BBC, either in whole or in part, from subscription. 'Subscription' means different things in different broadcasting contexts. In the United States, it has long meant voluntary donations to support National Public Radio (NPR) and, in television, the Public Broadcasting System (PBS). But conditional access technology has now made subscription more of a 'non-voluntary' matter, for premium television and radio channels are receivable only by those who will pay a published price for them. If the BBC were to adopt this form of subscription, it would reach only those listeners and viewers who were prepared to pay for it, and thus signify the end of a cardinal principle that Reith held dear. The principle is that after payment of the relatively modest licence fee, whose income the BBC can redistribute according to the cost of making good programmes rather than the size of the audience they will attract, nobody is debarred by poverty from enjoying any kind of programme that it is possible for broadcasting to provide. But whether the licence fee were replaced by this or by the more traditional form of subscription, it is clear that many who now help to support the BBC would cease to do so. Maintaining the corporation's current operations would therefore cost each subscriber proportionately more and there is a real danger that a vicious circle of increasing subscription charges would reduce the range and quality of its output.

Ofcom was also required to consider the impact of BBC policies and activities on the wider commercial sector. At the time the White Paper was published there was a preoccupation with the idea of introducing competition into public service provision, which served only to reflect how little the principle of public service broadcasting was understood; for its original purpose was, of course, to *transcend* the limitations of competition by providing what the free market could not. However, if news provision continues to be at the heart of the BBC's public service endeavour, it may offset some of the loss of jobs in journalism that looks likely to occur in the commercial sector.

The Neil Report of 2004

The second weakness within the BBC that the Gilligan Affair exposed was professional, relating to the editorial and journalistic practices that were criticised by Lord Hutton. The BBC immediately ordered a review of its practices, which was conducted by a working group under Ronald Neil, its former Director of News and Current Affairs. In his report, which appeared in June 2004, Neil listed five traditional principles of journalism: truth and accuracy; serving the public interest; impartiality and diversity of opinion; independence; and accountability (Neil *et al.* 2004: 6). He also recommended that extreme care should be taken in using anonymous sources. Journalists must fully explain why the source needs to be anonymous but also why it is regarded as trustworthy and well informed. However, the importance and credibility of the source should not be exaggerated, and the notes and/or recordings obtained from it should be accurate, reliable and retained (Neil *et al.* 2004: 11). Neil also recommended that no journalist who is employed by the BBC should be permitted to write a regular newspaper or magazine column that would express an opinion on some aspect of current affairs (Neil *et al.* 2004: 17).

However, the major recommendation related to journalism training. Neil observed that hitherto, the BBC's in-service journalism training had been fragmented and merely voluntary, and that training records had been insufficiently monitored. Henceforth, journalists should undergo training not simply in 'journalism', but in *BBC* journalism. The training should not only be continuous but yield competencies that would be a prerequisite for career advancement. He therefore proposed the founding of a 'college of journalism' that would be residential, industry-wide and under the leadership of an academic principal (Neil et al. 2004: 19–20). The corporation readily agreed, and the college, not made of bricks and mortar but providing distance learning and short residential courses, was launched in 2005.

The launch meant that by 2008 the BBC's annual spend on journalism training would double to £10 million. While building journalists' awareness of key themes and issues, such as Europe and the Middle East, the training concentrates on Neil's five core principles, which are essentially matters of ethics and values. The requirement that seasoned BBC journalists should undergo continual in-service training is highly significant, not least because it is so obviously traceable back to a judgment – Lord Hutton's – that was hotly contested within the corporation (Dyke 2004: 316). It is a reflection of the contrition felt by the successors to Davies and Dyke that they are so committed to the project; all journalistic staff must receive a minimum amount of annual training and further engagement with the college is a prerequisite of promotion.

However, as Hutton recedes into history, that commitment could be diluted. Since its launch, the BBC has been rather coy about the college: successive directors have declined invitations to discuss its organisation, structures or pedagogy. Yet the BBC's journalism continues to come under scrutiny and incurred further bad publicity in 2007. There were revelations first of a series of deceptions relating to the use of premium rate telephone lines on BBC and commercial television programmes, and then of tendentious editing in 'reality' shows. The press denounced the editorial distortions of a programme that featured the Queen, and the issue of ethics and accuracy in representation returned to the top of the corporation's agenda (Starkey 2007). Good policy in broadcasting regulation recognizes the fallibility of journalism and seeks to reinforce, not undermine, standards.

Radio's third sector: community broadcasting

Before closing this chapter, we should explain a development that over the last few years has culminated in the creation of a third sector of radio in the United Kingdom. This is the phenomenon of 'community radio', and means that those who are concerned with broadcasting policy and the future of the radio industry can no longer think only in terms of the duopoly of the BBC and the 'independent' sector that we have used to structure our analysis. The development of 'community' radio deserves much more than a footnote, although due to its niche status its real impact has yet to be determined. First, though, a little more history. Non-broadcast hospital radio, carried via rudimentary cabling systems to patients in need of light and optimistic programming, has existed since 1926. Volunteer enthusiasts collect requests from patients and visitors, tour wards and present programmes. In a similar way, student radio began in 1967, initially using low-powered 'induction loop' systems to transmit programmes to campus halls, and also making use of volunteers, a minority of whom, as in hospital radio, have become professionals and pursued successful careers in 'mainstream' broadcasting.

Since the late 1980s 'special event' and, from 1991, 'restricted service' licences have been granted to virtually anyone prepared to pay for them in order to conduct a temporary broadcast of up to 28 days at a time (Gordon 2001). Latterly 400 to 500 licences have been awarded each year, and 20,000 to 30,000 people have been involved in the broadcasts. However in audience terms, their impact on the BBC and the commercial sector has been negligible. In 1983 the Community Radio Association (later the Community Media Association) began campaigning for the legalisation of a new sector, community radio. Staffed mainly by volunteers, such stations would be authorised on a permanent basis, transmitting on the public spectrum, freely broadcasting over the editorial areas of their choice, and thus available to all who might wish to tune in.

Not surprisingly, the established radio industry was reluctant to cede part of the limited frequency spectrum to a potential competitor, and various governments have been equally reluctant to give air space to groups who might broadcast propaganda against them. In the mid-1980s the Home Office, as the government department which was then responsible for broadcasting, invited applications to run community radio stations but then took fright at the nature of many of the applicants – groups who were overtly left-wing and fiercely opposed to the Thatcher government. The scheme was quietly dropped (Lewis and Booth 1989). Nevertheless the Radio Authority revived the idea, and out of the success of a pilot project in 2001 that involved 15 stations (Everitt 2003) came the 2004 Community Radio Order, a statutory instrument empowering Ofcom to license for periods of five years stations which would provide some tangible benefit to identified communities. The first licences have been awarded to services for various ethnic and religious groups, children and older people, and speakers of languages other than English.

The hurdles facing an aspiring community radio station are high, and some of them have been put in place in response to pressures from the commercial sector. It must be a non-profit organisation, and no more than 50 per cent of its funding may come from any one source – including advertising. The benefit to the community must be defined as some 'social gain'. This might be the profits that the station ploughs back into it or simply a reinforcement of the community's identity and sense of its own worth. Furthermore, the licence requires each station to provide training in radio skills to the members of its community, who might then reasonably expect to participate in programme making. In theory, the stronger the links with the community and the greater the potential for social gain, the bigger the chance of winning a licence. In practice, stations that are reliant on donations either in cash or in kind, on subscriptions, and on deals with charitable bodies and other community groups will rarely support more than a couple of salaried posts. Many analysts describe community radio as 'more community than radio', and it is largely unable to provide paid employment for journalists. Depending on what importance a station assigns to the news, community radio could, however, offer a good training ground for journalists, and particularly one that encourages entry into the industry from demographic groups who are presently under-represented.

For better or for worse? The impact of policy on radio journalism

How, then, can we sum up the impact of all these recent policy developments? For journalists, radio presents a mixed picture, created partly by new technology and partly by the increasing polarisation of the public and independent sectors. To a greater extent even than their television counterparts, the commercial radio stations have been relieved of their public service duty to provide a comprehensive news service at local, national and international levels. On the other hand, news is perhaps more integral to the BBC's public service endeavour than ever before, and as we suggested in Chapter 2, radio plays at least as big a part in this as television. Here, then, the prospects are brighter, though with the caveat that new technologies – the Internet, laptop recording, editing and transmission, and a universal digital code that facilitates the transfer of material from one medium to another – will have a reductive effect on employment. To understand these factors more clearly, we now need to take a look at contemporary journalistic practices.

4

DIGITAL DEXTERITY AND THE NOSE FOR A STORY: CONTEMPORARY PRACTICES

The peculiar nature of radio journalism

We have looked at how radio journalism has developed and at the institutional and legislative contexts within which it has thrived. But what is the contemporary practice of radio journalism and what distinguishes it from other forms of journalism in an age when convergence is increasingly blurring such distinctions? It is clear that bi- and tri-media working is becoming more common: radio journalists are increasingly expected to integrate practices from television and online journalism, just as some print journalists now produce audio and video content to accompany their own output. Certainly, our opening analogy of the travelling stranger telling of people and places beyond the horizon is far removed from the modern-day realities of communicating electronically via a popular and ubiquitous mass medium – one that is highly dependent on technology and sharply defined by notions of professionalism.

We have also seen how disastrous it can be when radio journalism goes wrong. Fortunately, the Gilligan Affair, the controversy which surrounded it and its aftermath are atypical of news production. Just as most politicians are neither corrupt nor incompetent, so most journalists are undeserving of the low esteem in which they are held in some opinion polls (Pew Research Center 1999). Most newsgathering adheres to well-established conventions that produce few such controversies and which casual observers might mistakenly perceive to be boring because of their heavy dependence on repetitive routines. Far removed from secret meetings with anonymous sources, life and death decisions and high-profile public inquiries, most radio journalism is highly dependent on such practices as rewriting agency copy, making regular check calls to the emergency services and meeting the immovable deadlines imposed by the discipline of the hourly news bulletin – read on the hour, every hour, to audiences who, by the very nature of the services they choose to tune into, seem to be more focused on ephemeral music and chat than on the more significant events in the world around them that the journalist is able to describe and explain.

In fact, it is in the medium of radio that journalism can be at its most challenging and stimulating for those who practise it. Unconstrained by the relative infrequency of a daily or a weekly edition, radio offers greater immediacy than print. That immediacy has been greatly enhanced by the development of a technology that allows live and recorded material to be sourced over long distances and processed for transmission quickly and with high production values. Yet radio has none of television's dependency on images, a considerable advantage that allows it to remain authoritative and relevant even when reacting to events that are neither telegenic nor easily accessed by a camera.

Moreover, most radio stations have sizeable, identifiable audiences, often clearly demarcated by geographical and even demographic characteristics that enable the journalist to know not only that someone is probably listening, but the type of listener s/he is likely to be. In this, radio differs from the interactive media, where the sheer number of websites and web pages, blogs, podcasts and RSS (Really Simple Syndication) feeds means that each is likely to reach only a tiny fraction of those for whom it was intended (Starkey 2007: 46–7). Such media generate a virtual cacophony that is vulnerable to non-discovery, their existence reaching little further than hyperspace.

Neither is radio journalism confined to the hourly bulletins by which it is often characterised. Breaking news of importance to the target audience can be readily accommodated within the often live programming that surrounds the bulletins, without seeming so incongruous as to repel that audience. The newsflash between songs on a music station, or between callers to a phone-in, together with a promise of more details to come, requires very few of the logistical feats necessary to interrupt a pre-recorded television programme or a feature film. In this way, listeners to BBC Radio Five Live on 7 July 2005 were among the very first to hear eye-witness accounts of devastating bomb explosions disrupting London's transport infrastructure, even if the accounts were accompanied by presenter Matthew Bannister's warnings that no official confirmation of a terrorist attack had yet been received. Moreover, radio programming can be quickly rescheduled to react to a breaking news agenda. Once it began reporting the attacks on the World Trade Center in New York on 11 September 2001, five days elapsed before Five Live resumed its sports coverage as a 'rolling news and sport' network (Starkey 2004a: 35).

The range of radio journalism: opportunities in the public sector

Thankfully, such a story is atypical, too. We will return to it later, but let us first consider how more routine radio journalism is accommodated within the dichotomy of the public/private divide that we have already identified as fundamental to broadcasting in the United Kingdom. It is important to recognize that radio journalism includes a broader range of activities than those that originate from the newsdesk. Examples include documentaries and features, magazine programming and even the drama-documentary. While many journalists thrive on the often stressful demands of the news-desk, others enjoy the latitude afforded by longer deadlines – perhaps work-ing on a single story over weeks rather than hours, and sometimes engaging in the kind of 'investigative' journalism that demands painstaking efforts to expose wrongdoing by officialdom or big business, teasing out information that some would prefer to be kept hidden.

The ability to work at an unhurried pace, to hone whole programmes to the point of perfection, and to be name-checked in the listings magazine *Radio Times* – as well as receiving glowing critical reviews in newspaper columns – is almost entirely the privilege of those who are employed in the public sector. Radio 4's *Analysis* and its 'flagship' investigative programme *File on Four* ably demonstrate the point. Neither programme would have been initiated or sustained by the independent sector, requiring as they do the relatively large production budgets demanded by weekly 40- and 45-minute slots in the programme schedules. It is worth noting that in partial fulfilment of their early commitment to provide a 'full service', many of the very first ILR stations carried a weekly programme entitled *Decision Makers*, produced by LBC/IRN and distributed, on demand, across the network. However, this commitment was short-lived and the programme was soon sacrificed on the altar of the profit motive (Crook 1998: 50), while the will-ingness of individual stations to re-broadcast the programme would almost certainly not have outlived the IBA and its long-dead regulatory require-ment for 'meaningful speech'.

News and talk in the commercial sector: a tale of mixed fortunes

Paradoxically, a small number of news and talk stations remain in the private sector, notably LBC's two AM and FM services in London, the national analogue service talkSPORT, and Talk 107 in Edinburgh, but commercial radio in the United Kingdom is overwhelmingly dedicated to music. A number of attempts to sustain digital-only stations on DAB have been unsuccessful, with the successive closure of ITN News Radio, Bloomberg Business News and then, in 2006, just as Channel 4 Television was proposing investing in speech radio, Digital News Network (DNN). DNN was replaced in the regions by a relay of London's LBC 97.3, with some customization to insert local news and travel at predetermined points in peak hours. Against this background, Channel 4 – as 4Radio – ran a long campaign to woo potential audiences and actual decision-makers in Ofcom alike, in support of its eventual bid in 2007 for the second national digital multiplex. Commissioning a range of different speech programmes both for online listening and as podcasts, it went on to beat its one competitor, National Grid Wireless, with a proposal for ten new national stations. Some of them included bespoke speech programming (although to be viable this would have had to be on a much larger scale than the initial collection of podcasts), and one was to be a rolling service of Sky News Radio. We will consider in Chapter 7 how Channel 4's early approach to radio journalism bears comparison to the BBC's and what this portends for the future of both broadcasters.

Even on Merseyside, though, where arguably some of the most garrulous of Britons reside, the country's first all-talk commercial station outside London, City Talk, folded within two years of its launch, to be replaced in 1991 by a service of golden oldies. Established in 1989 as Radio City's answer to the call for an AM/FM split, City Talk mixed all-speech breakfast and drive-time news and current affairs with 'softer' interview and phone-in programming interspersed with occasional music. It drew upon the relatively generous resources of one of the most successful ILR services outside London, including a full-time political editor and a three-strong sports team, as well as a 24-hour newsdesk at which one of the authors (then senior producer at the station) once counted no fewer than 13 journalists on duty. Perhaps because its first audience figures were disappointing, or perhaps because the tide of fashion was already running against the AM waveband, the relatively ambitious venture simply failed to outlive the economic recession of 1991. The original aim at City Talk of denting the Radio 4 audience on Merseyside was wildly over-optimistic, given the national network's much larger budget, its far greater range of programming and its long-standing reputation for excellence among the ABC1 demographic.

Surprisingly, in the 2006 bidding round for an additional FM licence for Liverpool, City Talk's creator, Terry Smith, proposed a revived speech service with the same name. This time, as one of ten licence bids submitted to Ofcom for the same frequency, the EMAP group were promising a 24-hour service, to be run in parallel with their Radio City 96.7 and Magic 1548 brands. These were already broadcasting on FM and AM respectively from studios atop the St John's Beacon towering high above Liverpool. Despite any concerns Ofcom may have had that history might repeat itself, the 'Son of City Talk' beat off stiff competition from the other proposals for music services of various kinds, promising to avoid overdependence on phone-ins, and to exploit synergies with the news services of EMAP's two existing music brands in the area.

It is hoped that City Talk 105.9 will be a big success, and perhaps Sky News Radio too, but success may not come overnight. In Edinburgh, Talk 107's first audience figures were disappointing – even lower than for Radio 3 – prompting schedule changes and a management reshuffle. A reach of only 2 per cent conspired with very low average listening hours of 3.8 per listener per week to produce a share of just 0.4 per cent of all listening in the area. TalkSPORT's share of listening nationally was 1.8 per cent in 2006, and LBC's FM and AM services in London achieved 3.4 and 0.9 per cent respectively in the capital (RAJAR 2006). In Liverpool, Smith promised his new service would be 'closer to the edge' and less dependent on phone-ins than other talk services elsewhere in the UK. However, he intended to hire no more than 'between twenty-five and thirty' new staff (*Radio Magazine* 2006), and it is precisely because of cost that such commercial all-talk services as exist have overwhelmingly adopted not the shorter 'built' programmes that constitute the bulk of Radio 4's output, but interview and chat formats. It seems reasonable to conclude, then, that except where local interest coincides with an uncharacteristic willingness to invest in speech, documentary production will remain the almost exclusive preserve of the BBC. Likewise, drama-documentary (sometimes described as feature production), with its requirement for extensive scriptwriting, casting and the use of actors, is both an intensive and expensive enterprise, and therefore unlikely to be found in the commercial sector.

News and magazine journalism in the BBC

However, in the BBC, extended journalism of this kind thrives under the protective wing of the licence fee, and it is also highly valued by producers and audiences alike. Many of the corporation's senior personnel served earlier in their careers as reporters on *Analysis* and *File on Four*, including such high-flyers as Helen Boaden, in 2006 the Director of BBC News. Because they have themselves experienced the demands and rewards of sustained journalistic activity on a single story, the prospects for this kind of radio journalism inside the BBC remain good, as long as the level of the licence fee is generous enough to support it. Radio 4's budgets allow allocations of £6,000 or more per half hour, which although meagre in televisual terms, comfortably support sustained journalistic enterprise in radio and are the envy of the commercial sector, as its repeated pleas for a 'level playing field' in funding and other regulatory areas attest (CRCA 2006). Furthermore, as current affairs has become increasingly marginalised on BBC *television* – with

Panorama recently being shunted out of its traditional 8pm slot in peak time and into the late evening, for example – there is no corresponding pressure to move downmarket on Radios 4 or Five Live, with their impressive audience shares of 11.7 and 4.6 per cent respectively (RAJAR 2006).

Nonetheless, and even in the BBC, a much larger corpus of radio journalists is engaged in programme making within the magazine genre (Starkey 2004b: 119-42). First, consider the resource demands of the daily three-hour-long news and current affairs sequence *Today*, arguably setting the nation's political agenda six times per week, as it has done for much of its 50-year history (Donovan 1997). Despite its scheduling at breakfast-time, work on each edition begins the day before, so that when the editorial and presentation team arrive in the small hours of the morning, much of the output has already been determined. Then consider Radio 4's corresponding *World at One*, *PM* and *The World Tonight*, the near round-the-clock live programming of Five Live, the heavy speech content of the BBC's 40 English local radio stations and the national regional services of Scotland, Wales and Northern Ireland, and a picture emerges of a small army of BBC journalists producing hundreds of weekly hours of content in addition to the regular news bulletins. Some of that content is more specialised, or contextualised within paradigms other than news and current affairs: Radio 4's daily hour-long *You and Yours* concentrates on family and consumer issues and the network's *Veg Talk* is, perhaps like its listeners, fascinated by vegetables.

Then – to return to our point of departure – there is 'the news', capable of responding *in extremis* to breaking stories of sprawling dimensions, but on most ordinary newsdays focused almost entirely on regular bulletins of different lengths and in different styles. Bulletin length depends on a number of variables: from the assumed attention spans of the target listeners – the younger the demographic, of course, the shorter popular wisdom considers it must be – to the style of the output which surrounds it. Listeners to a speech station, it may be safely assumed, are inherently less resistant to speech, whereas on a station whose lifeblood is music, speech of whatever nature may be considered an unwelcome interruption to the flow of carefully programmed music. The interruption can be mitigated by playing an instrumental bed underneath it or by punctuating it at appropriate points with short electronic or musical stabs of the kind pioneered in the UK by the offshore pirates in the 1960s and subsequently adopted by the BBC on Radio 1's *Newsbeat*. At the other extreme are the half-hour news bulletins of Radio 4, read dry (without musical accompaniment) at a steady pace, conveying at once gravitas and authority, and those of the BBC World Service. The latter are, like their audience, international in outlook, serious in tone, and mindful of the need to avoid colloquialisms that might seem cryptic to those whose mother tongues are not English.

Some common features of radio journalism

What contemporary practices in radio journalism are common to the variety of forms in which it exists? At its best, radio journalism follows principles that are intended to ensure accuracy and avoid misleading its audiences. Professional and regulatory codes of practice, such as the National Union of Journalists' *Code of Conduct* (2004) and the BBC *Editorial Guidelines* (2005), set standards and norms of professional practice which those bodies expect journalists to observe. While in theory NUJ members are bound by its code, partisanship and proprietorial influence in the press render the prescriptions of fairness and impartiality patently unrealistic. However, in broadcasting, where in the commercial sector journalists are bound by Ofcom's *Broadcasting Code* (2005), such issues are taken more seriously and a concern for impartiality is inextricably linked to widely-shared notions of professionalism. We shall return to issues around fairness, distortion and misrepresentation in Chapter 6, but for now it is worth noting that most journalistic practice in BBC radio – and also, of course, in the commercial sector – remains unchanged by the Neil Report (Neil et al. 2004).

The three stages of accessing, producing and distributing news and other journalistic content in radio differ little across the public/private divide, except in terms of the available resources, where it is usually the BBC that is the better endowed. In terms of sheer numbers of staff, typically the journalists in BBC local radio stations outnumber their colleagues in commercial stations with similar editorial areas by a factor of three to one. This figure may be deceptive, however, as the speech content of sequence programmes on those BBC stations will almost always be greater, and with the blurring of boundaries between news and programming that this entails, some of that journalistic activity will be focused on programming rather than on bulletins. Despite their separation by such syntactical devices as station and programme idents, the playing of programme trails up to the hour, and the use on some stations of the Greenwich Time Signal to herald the beginning of another hour, the news programmes and news bulletins enjoy the benefits of considerable synergies achieved by the pooling of resources. The BBC's national and regional networks are resourced beyond the dreams of most stations in the commercial sector. Yet the programme teams behind *File on Four, Analysis, You and Yours* and so on, work as discrete units rather than adjuncts of a central newsgathering operation which is, by contrast, often the model in local radio. Similarly, the BBC's local stations may look on with envy at the far greater budgets of its national channels: there exists the institutional *apartheid* of a monetary pecking order not only of networks over local stations but also of television – the breadwinner – over radio.

Some radio journalists in the BBC are, though, no strangers to tight budgets and their implications for newsgathering. Successive experimentation with local radio formats has led to some very small and often short-lived stations being set up and then dismantled when the money has run out or the experiment has run its course. Seeking to devolve some budgets and production to the north of the principality, BBC Wales set up small subsidiary operations such as Radio Clwyd in the market town of Mold. Using skeleton staffing and local opt-outs on dedicated frequencies, they were intended to redress the fact that the main network was centred on Cardiff. However, despite protests to the House of Commons, and irrespective of the impact they might have had on their communities, they were soon closed down. Radio Clwyd had broadcast for little more than two hours per day (Hansard 2003).

Filtration at the station: how news values influence the choice of stories

Whether the newsdesk is close to the community it serves or remote from large parts of it, it necessarily acts as a conduit – or more accurately a filter – through which news travels from the discovery of the original event to an awaiting radio audience. That filtering is necessary because clearly not everything that happens in the world may be included in a single bulletin – or even a series of bulletins. Neither would broadcasters wish to report everything that happens nor audiences wish to be told of it. Only in the context of the relatively new phenomenon misleadingly dubbed 'reality TV' (Bignell 2005: 61), and on the Internet with its virtually infinite capacity for the sort of narrowcasting achieved through blogs, podcasts and web pages, is the truly banal routinely elevated to the level of public interest. Filtering, the various levels of selection between an original event and its representation in the media, or 'gatekeeping' as Galtung and Ruge (1965) term it, is essential in reducing the sum of human and natural activity to portions small enough and few enough not to overwhelm the easily-sated appetites of most listeners. This filtering requires the application of fixed or negotiable news values, which attempt to reconcile audience interest and stamina with the mass of reportable material in existence: it is the process by which every editor chooses what to put into a bulletin and what to leave out. News values are not absolutes. They are *subjective* because different editors will have different perceptions of what is important, *transitory* because relative importance changes over time, and *controvertible* because not everyone will agree with an editor's decision. Consequently, a range of academic literature has developed which considers news values, a subject to which we will return in Chapter 6. Much of the literature has been neatly summarized by Allan (2004: 57–8).

In essence, news values differ in the manner described above and according to the target audience, but they also relate very closely to the personal values of the journalist who exercises them and the institutional values of the organisation on whose behalf they are being deployed. For instance, to expect every radio news bulletin to lead on the same story, and for it to be reported in the same way, would be unrealistic, given the range of audiences they will be attempting to serve, and the interpretations placed on them by the various news editors in the light of the different institutional values they are required to implement. In countries that do not impose the impartiality that is required of broadcasters in the UK, the audiences are much more likely to regard the broadcasters as biased. In the USA, for example, many right-wing commentators denounce National Public Radio (NPR) as 'liberal' (Sutter 2001: 439–41), while shock jocks such as Rush Limbaugh are the *bêtes noires* of the political left. There is more than anecdotal evidence for such views: they are shared widely enough to be confirmed by the biennial national poll of 3,000 respondents conducted by the Pew Research Center for the People and the Press (2004). Wherever an ideological divide exists, such a lack of impartiality may be inherent. This is what has been termed *institutional* bias. For instance, it may be the case that the BBC's reliance on the hypothecated tax that is in essence the licence fee means that the corporation is more likely to support – or at least tolerate – state intervention than the commercial sector would be, founded as commercial operations are by entrepreneurs using private capital (Starkey 2007: 44–5).

A silent presence: the crucial role of the listener

Pragmatically, though, determining what a station's news values should be depends on the nature of those who are listening – or at least those whom a station would like to listen. When stations wish to change the nature of their audiences, perhaps moving the demographic upmarket or increasing the numbers of younger listeners, it is usually in order to increase the overall size of the audience or, in the case of the commercial sector, to increase the attractiveness of the audience to potential advertisers. In the 1990s, BBC Radio 1 socially-engineered its audience, targeting contemporary youth and shedding millions of older listeners who had grown up with the station since their teens (Garfield 1998: 67–93). The station made net losses of over 6 million listeners in the process, but by widening its radio provision to reach what had by then become an underserved audience, it did achieve one of the corporation's key objectives at the time, and by 2005 the station had started to reverse its decline (RAJAR 2005). This social engineering was mainly achieved by dramatic changes in music policy and presenter line-up, but re-targeting a station also involves ensuring that the aspiration is supported by corresponding changes in news values and news presentation.

For example, while the ageing Radio 1 audience may have had a direct interest in a change by the Bank of England to its base lending rate because of the effect on mortgage payments, such a story would be of little interest to younger people, who mostly live in their parents' homes or in rented accommodation. That is not to say that a single news event may be of interest to only one demographic group. Everything depends on how it is contextualised and presented. If the rise in interest rate is expressed as 'the cost of borrowing' going up, a younger audience might readily see the direct relevance to themselves, especially if the story is further contextualised with a reference to credit card repayments.

Other factors than age can determine an audience's priorities. Consider how news values differ within the BBC, between, for example, the World Service, one of the national networks and a local radio station. The World Service's unique funding arrangement, a direct grant from the Foreign and Commonwealth Office, is necessary to sustain an essentially ambassadorial service which clearly lies outside the public service remit of the licence fee, and which, ever since the establishment of the Empire Service in 1932, successive governments have perceived to be important to the UK. Because the transmissions are relayed worldwide and targeted at foreign English-speakers and UK expatriates, its audience is international. Many of them live in conflict zones or states where freedom of expression and the supply of information are restricted. To most of those listeners, interest rates in the UK would be of little or no concern, so in its regular bulletin of 'world' news the particular news values of the World Service would probably mean that it would offer minimal or no coverage of the story. But the story would almost certainly feature on the national network, contextualised, as we have seen, to relate to the target demographic, and it would also be heard on the local station because such national phenomena directly affect local communities.

News values determine not only the choice but the prioritisation of stories. The rate rise may be the biggest national story, and so lead the network bulletin, but it may be eclipsed on the local station if some other story, of interest only in the locality, is valued more highly. Consequently, the rate rise would be placed second or even later in the local bulletin. But a national or international story will often feature in a local bulletin if it has been recontextualised in some way to increase its local appeal. On BBC Southern Counties Radio, it may only be 'a Sussex man' among the dozens of fatalities caused by an air crash in China that secures it a place in the news bulletin, yet in an editorial area with a large Chinese community, the story would be given a higher priority. Similarly, the award or cancellation of a government contract to build a new warship may be of interest only in a region with shipyards because of its impact on jobs there. Content analysis of a station's news output can tell us a lot about the assumptions that have been made about its audience, and making such assumptions is an important part of the news editor's job.

News trafficking in BBC radio

The ability of local stations to cover those national and international stories which satisfy their news agendas depends on the resources at their disposal. Similarly, if it was unable to call on local reporters, a national newsroom based in London might struggle to cover important stories which break outside the capital. When it is needed, global news coverage depends entirely on the ability to exchange material through formal and informal arrangements, and these ideally need to be in place long before a story breaks. These arrangements have long been established in both the BBC and the commercial sector, even though they are quite different in nature. The BBC's newsgathering operation has been developed over a long period of time, and with its comparatively generous funding, it is able to sustain a team of foreign correspondents based in 42 overseas bureaux located in major news centres around the world.

In the UK, a domestic news agenda that is widely shared by all but the most cosmopolitan of broadsheet newspapers places little importance on international news, unless it is sensational or directly connected to an ongoing theme, such as the 'war on terror' or the conflict over the disputed lands of Israel and Palestine. Consequently, most of the BBC's foreign correspondents find that the World Service has the greatest appetite for their reporting. However, many of them are regular contributors to the long-running Radio 4 series *From Our Own Correspondent*, which consists of a number of detailed observational monologues each lasting about six or even seven minutes, and which draw on the contributors' wider experiences of life and the noteworthy if not always newsworthy events on their patch. Each correspondent covers a region, and in response to a breaking story and a request from London may be expected to move quickly to a hot spot within it. Some of these correspondents have been critical of the BBC's tendency to fly in 'star' reporters once the importance of a big international story has become apparent, and to compound their frustration, such reporters often depend on the regional correspondent to provide a background briefing and access to contacts and interpreters, and to assist them with transport, accommodation and making contact with London. Because of their supposed significance at home, some foreign news stories can be covered at extraordinary length and cost. In 1997, the handover to China of the former British colony of Hong Kong, for example, was covered by legions of BBC reporters, nearly all of whom were dispatched there on assignment, to file reports and make documentaries for the corporation's various radio and television services. Yet the cost was quite disproportionate to the level of interest in the story in the UK.

Similar arrangements are in place to cover domestic news. The local and regional news teams in the stations which constitute 'BBC Nations and

Regions' will provide London with coverage on demand, since because of their proximity to the story they are able to respond at speed. But they will also be eclipsed by 'stars' if the story's importance and longevity seem, in the opinion of London, to deserve it. Plans to devolve to Manchester by 2012 much of the newsgathering and programme making which forms the basis of Radio Five Live are intended to tackle, at least in part, this London-centricity. Some of the 'star' reporters are actually subject-specialists, concentrating on economic affairs, entertainment, politics, royalty, sport or legal issues, so often their involvement with a big national story is necessitated by its relevance to wider contexts. The appearance of a front bench politician in a distant constituency, for example, may be of greater interest to the national networks if that politician is involved in some current controversy of national, rather than just local, significance.

News trafficking in commercial radio

We will return shortly to the BBC, and how such a large and complicated operation works. First, though, let us note that the commercial sector lacks the funding to operate such an elaborate system of foreign correspondents. Although IRN has at times maintained a small number of correspondents overseas (Crook 1998: 277–9), and despite the fact that the commercial stations are far more numerous than was foreseen in 1973, it was caught between the rock of competition from Sky and the hard place of the sector's unwillingness to invest large sums in international news. Because IRN was not the only news provider available to the commercial stations, it was unable to charge the kind of fees for its service that would enable it to rival the BBC. In fact, in order to take greater control of its own destiny, it became self-financing in 1988 through the introduction of *Newslink*. This is a rare quasi-national advertising sales opportunity which is loosely incorporated on a 'must-carry' basis within the hourly bulletin and allows advertisers to reach listeners to all stations which either take IRN live or use its news copy and audio as source material (Crook 1998: 272).

At the time of writing, Sky, however, was in a position to invest more heavily in its news provision, but lacking the BBC's origins in radio it was understandably more focused on its television operation. The comparatively small radio team at Sky's Osterley headquarters in West London often re-packages live television reports from Sky News for re-broadcast on subscribing radio stations, and initially, when they included unrelated ambient sound that pictures would have made intelligible, they could seem very obviously like the television soundtracks they were. In a report on the state of the economy, the relevance of industrial machinery as a backdrop might be immediately

apparent to television viewers, but without some brief explanation of the
context for the report, radio listeners could not even guess what was making the noise in the background, and it would seem more like interference.
However, the increasing sophistication of Sky's production software has latterly allowed the disaggregation of the constituent parts of a soundtrack, so
that unwanted ambient sound can be largely stripped out of the radio version. In 2008 IRN ended its supply agreement with ITN, switching to Sky.
The launch of Sky News Radio as a rolling news channel would represent a
significant raising of Sky's profile in the provision of radio news.

Paradoxically, and despite its sizeable presence at Osterley, Sky did not
benefit like IRN from a large network of subscribing stations around the
country, which can be relied upon to file reports from their own editorial
areas. Compared with IRN's 290 subscribing stations, in July 2006 Sky had
supply agreements in place with only 30, although its customers did include
the high-profile nationals, Virgin Radio and talkSPORT. The pooling of
material from around the country is one of IRN's considerable strengths,
and has benefited it since its inception. It does not need to send reporters to
the provinces, as local reporters with background knowledge and contacts
in place are already there. Despite the growing number of niche stations targeting particular demographics, stations taking IRN already produce their
local material to a common style in order to complement the national material they re-broadcast. Hence it is a straightforward matter for them to relay
the IRN bulletin overnight and at weekends. Producing an IRN-style report
for the network, perhaps with added context for those who are new to what
is locally a long-running story, is not only well within the capabilities of
most of the local stations that take IRN, but offers an opportunity for local
journalists to reach a larger audience than usual. Thus, an explosion at a
nearby gas terminal might give a local journalist some all too rare access to
the national limelight, and provide a brief but effective boost to an otherwise parochial career.

Where news stories come from

It is worth reminding ourselves that journalists are neither omniscient nor
clairvoyant. The presence of a BBC foreign correspondent in a region does
not guarantee that he or she will know about a news event before an editor
in London hears of it and requests some coverage of it. Neither will a local
journalist hear about all that is newsworthy on his or her own patch. Radio
journalism relies, like any other kind, on a wide range of triggers to the
act of newsgathering that follows. Most of them, while forming part of contemporary practice, are hardly new. The simplest of these is the tip-off:
someone tells the journalist about something that might be of interest.

Many of these lead nowhere, being mistaken or misleading in nature, but occasionally they can provide a scoop worth paying for, as the case study at the end of this chapter shows. More commonly of use is the agency report. Often focused on the press, a news agency may operate on a local, national or international scale, depending on its size and remit. News agencies commonly maintain a presence in the criminal or civil courts which stations would be unable to resource themselves yet which might produce some unexpected stories that need a minimum of rewriting for radio, or even prompt a follow-up of some kind. A brief word of caution, though: court reporting is, of course, subject to the range of legal restrictions on the press and broadcasting that are detailed in the latest edition of *McNae's Essential Law for Journalists* (Welsh et al., 2007). These are far too extensive to be reproduced here, but every journalist must be familiar with them.

A big criminal trial resulting from a murder or some other widely reported incident would not be unexpected, and local – perhaps even national – newsrooms would have noted its expected date in the news diary and planned in advance to cover it. The timing of many news events is entirely predictable, and morning and other editorial meetings of any news team are usually focused on the predetermined prospects for that day's or the next day's coverage that such careful planning can provide. For instance, unless particularly difficult economic circumstances or a change of government policy were to force a departure from its practice of the past decade or so, the Bank of England would alter its lending rate only after a monthly meeting of its Monetary Committee. This allows radio journalists operating at whatever level to plan and prepare coverage of newsworthy events in the near future. By entering in the news diary sufficient information for a new or continuing story to be taken up on the appropriate day, they can minimise the risks of being taken by surprise or having to struggle to fill bulletins.

The biggest news agencies are international in scope and deserve their high reputations. Those with the greatest brand recognition among the public include Reuters, a US$2.4 billion business with 2,300 correspondents in 196 bureaux spanning the globe. Others include Associated Press (AP) and United Press International (UPI), while many countries have news agencies of their own, such as Agence France-Press (AFP) and Agencia Efe (EFE) in Spain. These may be less well known but they play a bigger role than we might imagine in providing the news to their domestic audiences. On a much smaller scale, but often unexpectedly useful, is the freelance stringer, working alone, but aware of stations' news values and sometimes able to supply coverage that would otherwise have passed them by. Stringers are as close as radio gets to having *paparazzi*: they earn an income by selling stories rather than pictures.

Watching the detectives: how stations steal stories from each other

The final news source is the competition. In case they run a story it has missed, the newsroom of every radio station monitors its rivals, just as foreign correspondents keep a close watch on CNN and the domestic news output of the media of those countries they cover. Though this may seem incestuous, news agencies also keep an eye on each other, sometimes having supply agreements in place so that a domestic wire service might alert Reuters to a breaking story while, in order to keep abreast of events, it also monitors Reuters' output. Many national and international news agencies monitor Al-Jazeera because of the Arabic channel's record of breaking stories about Islamic groups that are generally regarded in the West as terrorist (El-Nawawy and Iskandar Farag 2002).

Although a long-established practice, this has become easier because of the diversification of news output and the development of easily accessible electronic platforms across different media. Radio newsrooms can monitor a range of radio, television and web sources through the various digital platforms now available, including satellite transmissions and the Internet. Depending on what stories are breaking, interest in particular news outlets will rise and fall, with CNN's coverage suddenly becoming useful to a local radio station, perhaps, because someone from the area has become caught up in a news event far away from home. If CNN's newsdesk agrees to put the station in contact, the CNN correspondent may even be persuaded to report for it on the phone or via the Internet, and such *ad hoc* or even more formal agreements are often arrived at in return for an on-air credit. Some commercial stations came to such agreements with Sky News, a service which, despite the quality of its output, lacks the heritage and brand awareness of the BBC and can benefit from such wider exposure as a radio credit can bring.

Before one newsroom can use the output of another, there does not need to be a formal agreement in place, although the way in which it may be used is dependent on copyright law. The Copyright, Designs and Patents Act 1988 protects the originators of artistic, literary and musical works, including written news copy and live or recorded audio. For this reason, commercial stations may not use the BBC's audio wholesale or vice versa. In principle, this is logical since without having to contribute to their funding one broadcaster would otherwise be able to exploit the resources of another at will. Commentary rights for sporting events are similarly protected. Hence talkSPORT was ordered by the High Court to stop pretending on air that its 'live' Euro 2000 football commentaries originated from the stadia. Covering the Championship without the broadcasting rights, talkSPORT's commentators had been watching whole matches on television, and describing for their own listeners what the cameras showed. However, there is a defence under the Act known as 'fair dealing', under which small amounts of copyright material may be used for the purposes of review or to allow the free dissemination of news and information. How much of a work may be used through fair dealing is undefined in the legislation, but a court would almost certainly not consider a whole news report to be allowed, any more than it would the whole of a commentary. For this reason, in 2006 a reformed talkSPORT, now owned by UTV (formerly Ulster Television), entered and won a 'proper' bidding war to secure exclusive commentary rights to 32 Saturday afternoon Premier League matches each week over three seasons.

How stealing isn't always theft and runners-up can still be winners

This was a considerable blow to the losers, but good journalistic practice goes a long way to circumvent the problem of lacking commentary rights. To use verbatim reports of an event, lifted without permission off a rival radio station or a television channel or from some other secondary source, is to invite legal action over breach of copyright. However, one of the fundamental principles of copyright law is that facts cannot themselves be copyright, so dissemination of the fact that an event has occurred is perfectly legal but it must be done in an original way. The ability to rewrite someone else's copy, quickly, without omitting important information or introducing inaccuracies, is a valuable one. Ethically, claiming someone else's 'exclusive' as one's own is problematic – however much it may be a common practice in the press – and there is always the risk that such false claims will attract wider attention and lead to embarrassment. Being able to report an event in one's own way means that a rival station will not have an exclusive for long. Nevertheless, since a big breaking story can sometimes achieve considerable 'talk about' status, it is important that a station should not allow its rival to gain the reputation of *always* being first with the news.

Over 40 years after the assassination of President John Fitzgerald Kennedy on 22 November 1963, in Dallas, Texas, it is still common for many of those who were alive then to recall where they were 'at the time'. In fact, they probably mean where they were when they heard the *news* of the event and with the broadcast media much less developed than it is today, it was much more likely to have been by word of mouth. When news broke of the attacks on the World Trade Center many millions of people around the world turned to the television to see the unprecedented images for themselves. When news of the next big story breaks, it will be of little consequence for a particular media outlet if others broke it first. As long as its listeners hear about it from them soon afterwards, this is all they will remember. It is harder for a radio station to borrow audio than adapt written copy, but a quick call to a rival's newsdesk might secure an agreement to lend its audio in return for an on-air credit, in the manner described above. At the beginning of the Gulf War of 1991, radio and television stations around the world lacked correspondents in the Iraqi capital and therefore relayed CNN's Peter Arnett commentating from his Baghdad hotel room on the first shots to be fired (MacGregor 1997: 12). Given the distances involved, and the dangerous nature of the news event, there was no alternative to relaying CNN or including highlights in recorded packages.

Sometimes a radio station might use audio that was recorded and transmitted by a rival and obtained in the presence of other news organisations. The most obvious example is at a press conference. In response to a question from the authors, the editor of one network news service, run on a budget that did not allow him to send staff to every event he wanted to cover, explained off the record that the presence of a number of microphones made it impossible for a rival service to prove he had stolen their audio – it could have come from one of the other journalists present, with whom he might have had an agreement. The BBC and other more reputable broadcasters may appear to be above such chicanery, but only because they are so well resourced that they rarely need to resort to it.

Sound grabbing: how audio is captured and edited

Legitimate audio can be originated in a number of ways. Until recent advances in digital technology, a reporter's options were limited to getting low-grade audio from distant interviewees or filing reports on location over ordinary telephones, or travelling to and from the location with a microphone, lead and portable tape recorder, most commonly a Uher. Despite the great weight of the Uher, whose strap gave so many reporters shoulder strain, it is fondly remembered for the acceptable compromise it represented between ease of use, broadcast quality and portability. But many have welcomed the later generations of hardware, including Digital Audio Tape (DAT), MiniDisc and hard disk recorders. For ease of use, portability and concealability (in situations where, for reasons of personal safety, reporters might prefer to blend into their surroundings), the recently developed microphones that record on to a chip housed within their own stem, and an associated USB port for downloading the audio as data into any computer, are attractive alternatives. A Flashmic, for example, obviates the need for a microphone lead which, even in the most ideal of acoustics and with a correctly selected and positioned microphone, could still ruin or disrupt a recording through faulty connectors or microphone rattle (Starkey 2004b:

10–11). For every radio journalist who was sent out to collect audio, 'Mike Rattle' was at one time a phantom to be dreaded.

Digital technology has also facilitated the establishment of live connections between the newsdesk and remote locations. Expensive, fixed, broadcast-quality analogue landlines and often hard-to-set-up VHF radio links from outside broadcast vehicles have, for the moment, been eclipsed by ISDN lines, which deploy digital/analogue converters (codecs), satellite uplinking and the Internet. However, this technology brings its own problems. For ISDN, the codec needed at the remote end is expensive and it needs to be *in situ* before the interview can begin, so unless their homes happen to be suitably equipped it is unlikely to be very useful in getting immediate reactions from individuals early in the morning and at short notice. Satellite uplinking requires generous resourcing because even the more modestly-priced reporter kits are expensive and require pre-arranged access to a communications satellite, a power source and somewhere to site the portable dish. Given its great potential for other applications, it is perhaps inevitable that the Internet is at present one of the simplest means of getting original, quality audio to the modern radio newsdesk. Using production software such as Adobe Audition or Audacity, audio downloaded into a laptop can be edited on the site, saved as an MP3 file, and, perhaps using other developments in mobile phone technology, sent over the Internet in a fraction of the time it once took radio journalists to return to base and then edit it using traditional techniques (with a chinagraph pencil to mark edit points, a razor blade to cut the audio tape and splicing tape to stick the usable sections back together).

Even though experienced reporters once developed great speed and dexterity at the fiddly practice of editing tape, expertise with modern PC or MAC-based audio software has enabled exponential improvements in their work rate. On occasions, important sections of audio tape would get lost or damaged in the cutting and sticking process, but the non-destructive nature of much audio editing – especially using the undo facility – now enables such errors to be swiftly repaired. The better software allows more elaborate production values to be easily applied to recordings: atmosphere and effects may be added, and music or wild track that was recorded at the scene may be mixed, where appropriate, with interview material and voice reports. Now simple packages and wraps are achievable within a time-scale that was unimaginable in the days when production was characterized by cut-and-paste operations. A package might include two or three interview clips from different people, some actuality and a linking script from the reporter to pull it all together, to give it a clear sense of direction and purpose and to ensure the piece clearly 'tells' the story. When handling sensitive stories, where the identity of a victim, a witness or a minor needs concealing, the audio processing functions of the new software can easily disguise a voice by raising or lowering its pitch, changing its tone through equalisation, or even by making minor alterations to its speed.

Assembling and presenting radio news

Information technology has also revolutionised the news-handling process. Most of the effort in busy radio newsrooms is now focused on computers used for research, communication, production, editing and playout – and in many of them bespoke software draws all these functions seamlessly together. Such applications as Burli, NewsBoss, ENPS (Electronic News Production System) and Scoop each present radio journalists with an easily navigable interface between ordinary internet sources, the news agencies, network hubs and their outposts and material generated by the station's own team of staff and freelancers. The BBC's news operation uses ENPS, which integrates all its newsrooms, allowing different editors to access copy from other newsrooms in the corporation, whether national or regional, and either unedited or subbed. Typically, and with great speed, newsroom software enables news copy and any accompanying audio to be edited, sorted, filed and sequenced in the desired order of an upcoming bulletin. Different versions for different services can be prepared with ease and, if required, extended versions of copy and audio cuts can be saved for use in a longer evening bulletin at the end of the day – a frequent practice on local stations. Such planning and preparation as takes place in the newsroom culminates in bulletin presentation from a dedicated booth or even at the spare microphone in a studio being used for the programming that surrounds it.

The bulletin may consist solely of copy read live, or it may be punctuated by pre-recorded audio, including packages and voicers. Presentation of a news bulletin requires appropriate attention to voice production – enunciation should be clear but not over deliberate, correct but not seeming to less formal audiences to be too pedantic, and pace should be measured, neither rushed nor ponderous. Voice training focuses on *understanding* the copy and its meaning, because that is what the newsreader has to convey. Copy that is garbled, rushed and mispronounced in ways that make the listeners doubt its authoritativeness may be copy that is wasted: however heroic or well-resourced the journalistic endeavour behind it, however ethical, newsworthy, exclusive or suited to the interests of the target audience it might be, its impact will be blunted. To convey meaning requires the variation of tone which brings both light and shade to a monologue that would otherwise not command attention. It is only the human voice that can bring surprise, happiness, sadness and many other emotions to words that would otherwise lie dead on the page. Of course, it is all too possible for a newsreader to over-emphasise this light and shade, to become a self-parody and lose credibility by straying too far away from a professional balance. Presentation style comes naturally to few but may be taught and improved through practice. Of course, styles will vary across genres – documentary presentation differing even in subtle ways from bulletins, and magazine formats lending their presenters more scope for informality.

Wraps, billboards and packages: the versatility of radio journalism

The realia that can bring immediacy, first-hand experience and a strong sense of authenticity to a bulletin – or to radio journalism in all its other forms – are to radio as pictures are to television, print and internet journalism. As we have seen, they may simply be clips of pre-recorded interview, a live interview with a specialist contributor, a reporter or a correspondent, or they may take the form of a report: the straight voicepiece (or 'voicer') or a short package (often called a 'wrap' or a 'billboard'). According to culture, heritage and institutional practice, such nomenclature varies from newsroom to newsroom. The word *billboard* is firmly rooted in IRN culture and hence that of its subscribing stations, but rarely heard at the BBC, except perhaps among those journalists who have crossed the rubicon between the two. The audibility and radiogeneity of such material has to be a consideration. While technical quality must be of broadcast standard, radio journalists obviously need a speaking voice that will, in aesthetic terms, withstand repeated exposure to its audience. Yet interviewees who sound odd or discordant may be far more acceptable to listeners because their inevitably shorter contributions have been included for their expertise, their eyewitness account or perhaps some other characteristic that renders them interesting or credible, while the onus on a journalist is, understandably, to 'sound like' one.

The copy written for voicers, packages and the spoken cues which precede them, as well as any other audio generated, can often be repackaged for different purposes. Increasingly, and as a consequence of both the proliferation of different news media and the pervasiveness of information technology, radio journalists are being encouraged to exploit this material in ways that might have been inconceivable just a decade or so ago. Material prepared for the radio can be quite quickly reworked for the Internet (where the radio station may have its own web presence or service other websites) and even for distribution through other media, such as mobile phones. Television normally requires pictures, but often a good radio interview on *Today*, for example, can give so pivotal a twist in an unfolding course of political events that television producers will use it, perhaps accompanied by a caption or loosely-related images known as 'library footage'. Conversely, television sound can often be used on radio – perhaps with some extra contextualisation – and, increasingly, print journalists are being asked to provide audio for use on newspaper websites, such as *Guardian Unlimited*.

The growth of 'tri-media' – and the continuing vitality of radio

If in the 1990s a buzzword in the BBC was 'bi-media', tri-media working is now increasingly common in the industry. Particularly in regional and local newsrooms, where a local radio station and a television news opt-out from BBC1 are serviced in parallel, journalists need considerable levels of multi-skilling to move material between media, often adapting, recontextualising and reframing it for different target demographics. The Broadcast Journalism Training Council (BJTC) looks favourably on courses which integrate radio, television and online practice, and practical textbooks such as Hudson and Rowlands (2007) show how it can be done. Despite the early restrictions on newspaper ownership of the first ILR stations, lighter-touch regulation and the proliferation of services since then have enabled governments to ratio-nalise the relaxation of such constraints. As early as the 1980s, some ILR sta-tions launched their own free newspapers as extensions of their commercial activities, but like the *Preston Red Rose Advertiser* (1987–90), many were light on editorial content. Broadcasting in the Basingstoke area, 107.6 Kestrel FM claims to be the first radio station to have introduced a newspaper *per se*. Although a free title supported by advertising, much of the *Basingstoke Observer*, which was launched in 1998, was produced by a bi-media (radio and print) newsroom. The 2005 purchase of the Wireless Group, including talkSPORT, by Ulster Television, together with the concurrent formation of the KM–FM Group of five stations by the *Kent Messenger*, suggest that further synergies in news production between radio, television and print are to be expected in the commercial sector. These are not inevitable, though, as the editorial distance between the content of most EMAP radio stations and that group's specialist consumer magazines was usually too great to be bridged by local newsrooms in the large metropolitan 'heritage' stations, such as Metro Radio, Radio City and Radio Aire. Bi- and tri-media journalism is, however, here to stay, and in Chapter 7 we will consider its implications for the future.

Finally, while recognising the importance of such developments for con-temporary practice in radio journalism, let us note, briefly for now, that some attempts to straddle more than one medium are less successful than others. Just as we have considered how the television soundtrack is not always an appropriate substitute for a radio report, the differences between copy written for print and the spoken word can be considerable. Writing intended for broadcast must allow for the transient nature of both radio and television output, whereas readers generally have the output of print journalism in their hands for some time. They can refer elsewhere in an article for clarification, or, while remaining generally interested in it, they may prefer to skip detail that appears too specialised for their tastes. As we shall discover in the next chapter, radio listeners engage in other ways with their medium, often regarding those whom they hear on it as their friends. The more conversational style this permits must, however, be constrained by the need for immediate intelligibility, for a logical and economical narrative, for the maintenance of an authoritative tone and for constant relevance. Yet the audience's attention may be held by using a more colloquial – if not necessarily informal – style that can make researching, writing and presenting journalistic output on radio so very rewarding. When planning or presenting any content for radio, every broadcaster must remember, though, that a listener who switches off or tunes away may be a listener lost forever. This means that in the way it is produced and presented, radio journalism must at all times be as accessible, engaging and compelling as possible.

Case study: handling breaking news – Kate Arkless Gray

Before we proceed to a discussion of international radio journalism, we offer an example of contemporary practice in reacting to breaking news which demonstrates the importance of professionalism, proper procedures and a 'nose' for a story. Arguably the biggest domestic news event of summer 2006 was a major security alert at all international airports in the United Kingdom. Early on the morning of Thursday 10 August, anti-terrorist police moved to disrupt a suspected plot to bring down a number of aircraft flying that day to the United States. Twenty-four people were arrested in east London and the Home Counties on suspicion of involvement in the plot. It was thought to centre on the in-flight mixing of liquids that, although separately harmless, would, when combined, result in mid-air explosions and many hundreds of fatalities. At 0200 the Joint Terrorism Assessment Centre formally raised the UK security threat level to 'critical', indicating fears of an imminent attack. At all major airports swingeing new security arrangements were put in place in order to prevent terrorists from using their hand luggage to smuggle such liquids into aircraft passenger compartments. All but the most basic of items would have to be loaded into the hold, and taking liquids into departure lounges was banned. In one of the busiest weeks of the year for holiday flights into and out of the country, airlines, airport managers and travellers faced one of their most challenging days ever. Even outside the holiday season, most stations would have led with a story such as this, but the huge numbers of Britons personally affected by the ensuing disruption to their travel made this story yet more compelling.

(Continued)

At 0400 the freelance journalist Kate Arkless Gray arrived at Gatwick Airport on her way to a one-week break in Cuba to witness the 80th birthday celebrations of its president, Fidel Castro. When she attempted to check in she was told that only passports, tickets and money could be taken on to the plane. Airport staff were saying only that this was due to 'heightened security', and no other information was available. However, Kate was quick to realise the implications for all airports and travellers as more passengers arrived, and that for such a measure to be put in place something must be seriously wrong. As a freelancer who had worked in programming as well as recently completing a postgraduate diploma in broadcast journalism, Kate had already been planning to exploit any opportunities that might present themselves while she was on vacation. While President Castro was lying in hospital recovering from emergency abdominal surgery, his impending 80th birthday celebrations could yet turn into a national wake. However, even having one's contacts book handy – or at least a selection of key numbers stored in one's mobile – can be unhelpful at an hour when many newsrooms are just waking up, and some are unprepared to deal adequately with a tip-off that could turn into a scoop.

Mindful of her need to proceed through the lengthening queues to the departure lounge, Kate began making calls. Some numbers were unanswered because mobiles were turned off, and switchboards blinked in vain where a lone journalist was otherwise preoccupied. She called the last remaining number she had for her current workplace: the on-air number. It was answered by a broadcast assistant in Birmingham who explained that she had no links to the network's newsroom and no contact numbers for it. Despite this Kate persisted, repeating that she freelanced on the network, so she was finally given a number for the BBC's travel centre. But the number turned out to be incorrect.

Journalists and other programme makers must always be wary of being hoaxed, and without knowing the caller it is reasonable – in fact essential – to seek independent verification: without prior knowledge of the security alert Kate's story could well have turned out to be false. However, in an industry where breaking reliable news is a core activity, to miss a story such as this by not following it through would be unfortunate. It is also important to react quickly to sudden and dramatic changes in the day's news agenda by always being able to allocate resources where they are needed most.

Working through her contacts, Kate managed to call a friend working on the breakfast show at Heart 106.2. He was able to go into the Chrysalis Group's London newsroom and ask someone to take the call. So it was LBC that broke the story minutes later, using clips it had recorded with her before she had to check in her mobile with the rest of her luggage. Some more quick thinking then led to LBC News 1152 doing a two-way with Kate at 0615, via a pay-phone, in the final minutes before she caught her plane. Live on air as the only reporter on the scene, she was able to describe at first hand the security restrictions and reactions from staff and travellers. She gave the station's listeners an eye-witness account of the first signs of the travel chaos which, coupled with the terrorist threat and the further news of the police arrests, made the story so compelling that it led radio and television bulletins for several days. In Kate Arkless Gray's words:

> The check-in staff knew nothing – no one knew anything! The guys carrying the big guns just smiled and said nothing was happening. ... I just knew there was. LBC had no idea at first, but by the time I did the two-way they had called the relevant people and worked out what was going on. They told me it was affecting all airports and that people had been arrested.

Conclusions

This episode illustrates not only the skills that any good journalist should possess, but some that are special to the radio journalist. First, there is the 'nose' for a story – in this case, the ability to go behind the official and reassuringly opaque explanation of 'heightened security' and quickly grasp the actual and chaotic consequences such security would have. Second, there is the fact that this journalist's preoccupation with one story, the possible demise of President Castro, did not blind her to the possibility that another and more immediate one was developing – one which would turn out to be far bigger than anything that would happen to Castro. Third, there was her pertinacity in continuing to make calls to newsdesks and contacts. Finally, there was her ability to provide instant 'radio' on her mobile phone, to answer questions, improvise a description of the scene and give the reactions of staff and travellers – all under the pressure of continuously unfolding events and to unseen interviewers and listeners.

5

THE WORLD AT ONE — OR AT SIXES AND SEVENS? INTERNATIONAL PERSPECTIVES

Radio journalism: a BBC export

So far we have concentrated on institutions and practices within the United Kingdom, but to consider radio journalism within a single country would be misleading, and there is much to learn from a comparative approach that recognises the importance of journalistic activity in the rest of the world. Just as we have used the divide between the public and private sectors in this country to organise much of our analysis, a second duality exists in that the flow of influence and practice between radio journalists here and abroad is certainly not unidirectional. On a superficial level, though, it might easily appear to be so, for both practical and cultural reasons. At their heart lies the BBC, with its long history, its international reputation and its unparalleled scale of operation, reaching way beyond these shores.

Let us begin with the more overt aspects of the corporation's activities. Not entirely without coincidence, one of the United Kingdom's most influential exports has been the values and approaches to journalism embodied in the BBC Radio Training Unit. Now inevitably subsumed within a cross-media department called BBC Training and Development, the Radio Training Unit played host to hundreds of broadcasters from other countries, many of them in the Third World, and provided basic and advanced courses in journalism and programme making. Among the courses on offer at the Unit were not just the brief introductions to radio production devised initially for new recruits to the corporation, but also more advanced ones for experienced broadcasters requiring professional updating and seeking career progression. The corridor walls of the former Langham Hotel in London's Oxford Street, where the unit was based, bore group photographs of small cohorts of journalists and producers from overseas who had come to learn the ways of the BBC. Even though the building has now reverted to its original use as a hotel, its luxurious appointment contrasting starkly with its more frugal décor when it was a centre of excellence in training, that tradition continues unabated, with the BBC as well equipped to teach modern journalists as it was to guide their predecessors.

Many of the trainees receiving such instruction are non-indigenous staff and freelancers working in the UK for the BBC World Service. Their knowledge and even fluency in foreign languages has made them potentially useful journalists and programme makers in one or more of its different departments based in Bush House in London. The practice of providing BBC training for complete novices and experienced journalists alike may have resulted in a certain standardisation of approach among those who have later returned overseas with their accumulated experience and skills. Working as a studio manager at Bush House, with a variety of journalists from the different foreign language sections, led Brian Lister, for many years afterwards a respected manager in commercial radio, to recall that in the 1970s his colleagues, whatever their origin or cultural background, readily adapted to standard BBC practices, each team producing essentially similar versions of a standard bulletin followed by feature material to suit a targeted audience.[1]

Another successful arm of the BBC, but with a much greater profile overseas than its training operation, is the BBC World Service Trust, a charitable organisation running media training projects that have taken it in recent years to India, Nigeria, Iraq and several other countries. Its collective experience and ability have been welcomed everywhere, by enthusiastic but ill-equipped journalists keen to raise their own professional standards to those they perceive in the BBC. Among the Trust's more recent achievements: the BBC School of Broadcast Journalism opened in war-torn Bosnia in 1996; in Afghanistan a series of five-day workshops in 2002 was attended by women who had previously been prevented from working by the Taliban regime; and a partnership with other bodies led to the creation of Support to Independent Media in Ukraine in 2003. In 2006 the BBC World Service Trust's Somali Journalism Training Project reported considerable success in helping such stations as Radio Horn Afrik and Radio Shabelle to develop their journalistic output. This was achieved through both group tuition and the development of online materials for continuing professional development. Sustained periods of training for up to six months may well, as the Trust claims, have shown 'determined, enthusiastic and eager to learn' Somalis used to 'reporting rumour, innuendo and opinion, and presenting it all as fact' that 'news reporting in an unbiased manner can be just as interesting and captivating to the audience as gossip and unverified features' (EU 2006).

The influence of the BBC World Service

Aside from such specific and highly practical initiatives, the BBC World Service has over the decades become so greatly respected that it may also have influenced international journalistic practice. This is in addition to any individual links that have been forged with what has inevitably been a minority of overseas practitioners. Today the BBC's output is available through many other means than the original short-wave broadcasts. These were, and are, often poor in quality, difficult to find and subject to atmospheric conditions that cause them to fade in and fade out around the clock (Starkey 2007: 116), yet listeners in many countries have depended on them since the BBC began its overseas broadcasting in 1927. Those early trial broadcasts to the British Empire were the precursor to a regular service that became a vital source of news and information to a wide range of different audiences – some of them deprived of freedom of expression at home, others simply wanting to access different perspectives from those more readily available through their domestic media. During the Cold War years many listeners were obliged to listen clandestinely, often through the discordant jamming signals with which Soviet and East European governments tried to block them. In many different territories, accessing the BBC's output has in more recent years become easier than ever before.

Now, in addition to new and still developing platforms such as satellite, digital terrestrial and cable, the core English versions of the World Service (and in some cases foreign language variants of it) are relayed by many traditional broadcasters as enhancements of their own services. By agreement, even such giants as the Australian Broadcasting Corporation (ABC) include relays of the BBC between locally produced programming. Less prominent internationally, but highly significant in their own areas nonetheless, are the dozens of local and national stations in the USA and Canada, Africa, Europe and Asia which do the same. Radio New Zealand's National Radio re-broadcasts BBC World Service feature programming during evenings and at weekends. Then there are permanent relays on FM in such diverse locations as Singapore and Mongolia, and on AM in Hong Kong, Moscow and St Petersburg, all of which add to the BBC's ubiquity in the broadcasting landscapes of many overseas countries.

Two-way traffic: how the BBC learns from the rest of the world

Its audible international presence has enabled the BBC to lead by example, establishing itself as the 'beacon for impartiality, journalistic freedom and quality', described by World Service Director Nigel Chapman (BBC 2007). His assessment of the service is widely shared: it is for demonstrating values such as these that it has long enjoyed great respect internationally. To a large extent, the BBC's high reputation is deserved, but such assessments should be treated with a measure of caution.

In broadcasting as in any other human endeavour, it would be far too imperialistic of the British to imagine they have nothing to learn either culturally or practically from the rest of the world, and over the decades the BBC has absorbed, if only through osmosis, as well as given. The regular secondment of staff from various national, regional and local newsrooms to teaching posts within the Radio Training Unit has doubtless resulted in the adoption of some good overseas practices within the BBC when they return to their regular duties. Given the impressive ability of career journalists to rise within the organisation's ranks, often at a faster pace than staff working within other genres, unorthodox attitudes and values may even have penetrated its corporate mind. Some of those attitudes and values may have been less welcome or less necessary. Certainly, the Somalis could have shown their BBC World Service Trust trainers how to stretch meagre budgets further than their comparatively generous resourcing might require.

Neither can BBC journalism have developed in complete ignorance of professional practice in better-developed countries overseas – particularly in the Anglophone continents of North America and Australasia. After all, and as we noted in Chapter 4, journalists monitor the output of other journalists, and especially so when they are on assignment overseas. Along with Britain's armed forces, democratic institutions and police force, 'BBC journalism' is often proclaimed loudly as being the best in the world – by Britons. But such confidence may be misplaced, founded as it is on little, if any, systematic analysis of practice elsewhere. In truth, journalism abroad may be at least as good, and sometimes better, for even the BBC, pre-Hutton and post-Neil, has been forced to accept that its practice may at times be flawed (Neil et al. 2004).

Mistakes aside, and notwithstanding the BBC's relatively generous funding compared to what is received by others at home and abroad, the corporation would probably argue that its resources produce enormous amounts of content which can be exploited across its various platforms and which thus provide the licence payer with good value for money: given the range of activities they are expected to support, these resources are even somewhat stretched. Now, having responded to the Hutton Report by opening its College of Journalism in 2005, the corporation has more than its *Editorial Guidelines* (BBC 2005) to cite as exemplifying its pursuit of high journalistic standards.

Overseas contexts: North America

What, then, are the wider contexts within which radio journalism takes place? Although in the United States radio first developed along commercial lines just as the BBC was beginning its near half-century of monopoly provision, the public/private divide we have already identified as significant in the development of journalistic practice has been mirrored elsewhere, and widely so. In fact, the privately-owned commercial stations that the United States initially licensed were regulated by a number of public bodies whose roles were later merged in 1934 into the Federal Communications Commission (FCC). Albeit belatedly and on a rather flimsy basis, the USA also sanctioned the creation of a public broadcasting sector with National Public Radio (NPR) in 1970.

As a loose confederation of stations, NPR is, thanks to its often precarious financial situation, stilted in style and lacking in impact. Without the security of universal licence revenue, it is obliged to resort to fundraising activities in order to supplement its regular income from sponsorship and voluntary subscriptions (McCauley 2005). A mere 13 per cent of its income comes from the Corporation for Public Broadcasting, a non-profit body set up by Congress in 1967 with the purpose of distributing federal funds to those radio and television stations which pursue public service objectives. NPR developed out of the National Association of Educational Broadcasters, itself funded largely by philanthropic grants rather than a licence fee or state funding, and its failure to challenge the commercial sector in the audience ratings is telling. Yet despite its meagre funding, NPR remains highly regarded in the USA, and NPR news, like its programming, offers an alternative to the right-wing slant found elsewhere in the US media. It is not only public service broadcasters who can deliver reliable and reputable news services, though, and within the strong commercial sector, such stations as CNN Radio News have won credibility for the reach and depth of their coverage. CNN itself provides news feeds, copy and live bulletins to affiliated stations across the United States.

Canada began licensing its first private stations in 1922, but because of fears of Americanisation a 1932 parliamentary committee recommended the creation of a public sector, and the Canadian Radio Broadcasting Commission (CRBC) brought competition to the market. In 1936 the CRBC became the Canadian Broadcasting Corporation (CBC) of today. In Australia, the ABC was formed in 1932, but the private sector dates back even further and takes the lion's share of this highly regionalised market whose constituent parts are separated within the continent by vast distances. An unequal relationship pertains in New Zealand where a sweeping privatisation of the broadcast frequency spectrum has marginalised the state broadcaster, and two non-Kiwi groups have rapidly come to dominate the national radio market (Shanahan and Neill 2005).

Overseas contexts: Europe

Some countries outside the Anglophone world have also developed systems of sound broadcasting that have been characterised by a public/private divide. In France, for example, a number of private stations which competed with the early state-owned stations were 'tolerated' by the government (Kuhn 1995: 84) and today Radio France and the commercial sector continue to coexist. However, the emerging pluralism of the 1920s was by no means universal. With the formation of the Unione Radiofonica Italiana in 1924, the Italian government merely reserved two hours per day for itself, as well as the right to interrupt other programming with 'important' announcements (Monteleone 2003: 23). By contrast, some western democracies adopted a public service monopoly model rather like that of the United Kingdom: Danmarks Radio launched in 1925 and in Norway NRK began in 1934. In the Netherlands, a rolling time-share arrangement allocated frequencies to different religious and political groups, broadcasting from state-owned transmitters at Hilversum. For Dutch governments this was a relatively innocuous way of regulating access to the airways and controlling the means of transmission.

Since its creation in 1950 the European Broadcasting Union (EBU) has supported public radio, initially in Europe but later in North Africa and the Middle East as well. Based in Geneva, it currently has 74 members in 54 countries. In addition to regular programme exchanges, the EBU typically coordinates members' coverage of over 100 major news events per year. The Eurovision News Exchange for television and the parallel operation Euroradio together promote cooperation in the dissemination of news copy and actuality between member organisations, facilitating coverage of European stories in different territories (Harrison 2006: 93).

However, some of the state broadcasters of today are remnants of the authoritarian regimes of the past, underfunded, struggling and demoralised vestiges of a once cherished monopoly. They are now foundering on the rocks of competition that is commercially-supported yet unconstrained by public-service values and commitments, and rather than merely playing songs interspersed with presenter chat, are struggling to produce expensive speech programming. On visiting Moldavian state radio in 2006, the EBU's Director of Radio, Raina Konstantinova, found a rump of committed but very poorly resourced journalists struggling with outdated and failing equipment that hampered their work routines and produced none of the digital dividends in time-saving practices we have already identified in modern newsrooms and production studios.[2] A rampant private sector in a broadcasting market freed from the constraints of communist dogma has also drawn away much of the radio audience in a country of only 4 million people which is culturally and linguistically divided and politically and geographically isolated from potential allies abroad.

Inevitably, though, given the various privatising and nationalising forces at work around the world over the last 80 years, and between the extremes exemplified by the UK and Moldavia, the division of the radio audience

Table 5.1   Public sector share of listening in different European radio markets, 2003 (source: EBU 2004)

Country	2003
Austria	82.0%
Belgium (Flemish)	80.7%
Germany (Nordrhein-Westfalen)	66.3%
Switzerland	66.1%
Sweden	66.0%
Denmark	65.0%
Germany (Baden-Wurttemberg)	59.6%
Norway	59.0%
Finland	49.5%
Germany (Bayern)	48.1%
Bulgaria	43.9%
Ireland	43.0%
Germany (Berlin)	42.2%
United Kingdom	42.0%
Belgium (French)	36.1%
Netherlands	33.0%
Hungary	27.8%
Lithuania	25.3%
Slovenia	25.1%
Spain	23.4%
Poland	22.3%
France	22.2%
Italy	18.7%
Czech Republic	18.4%

It is worth noting that the public sector is strongest in the Nordic countries, while some of the lowest shares are to be found in the southern European states – Spain, Italy and France. (Greece was not included in the survey.)

between public and private sectors varies dramatically, as shown in Table 5.1. While the BBC's market-leadership in domestic radio is often characterised by its competitors as unhealthy, it is arguable that a healthy PSB provision, well-resourced and widely consumed by its audiences, may help to raise and maintain journalistic standards. The EBU, the BBC and other pillars of public service broadcasting provide an important bulwark against the forces that threaten such standards. One of them is globalisation – a modern phenomenon rarely identified with the BBC's overseas broadcasting, perhaps because its original name – the Empire Service – was so quickly and unceremoniously consigned to the dustbin of history. Today the BBC World Service is sustained by a direct grant from the Foreign and Commonwealth Office, and with finance provided by a government paymaster rather than licence revenue, it is all too easily perceived as beholden to the instruments of state.

The impact of globalisation on domestic journalism

Yet other broadcasters than the BBC are more routinely accused of globalising ambitions and it may be useful to consider how resistant domestic journalistic practice is to globalising forces when they manifest themselves in the related fields of television and film. The considerable irony of the United States having fought its war of independence from Britain and now appearing to seek world domination through various forms of popular culture is not lost on many commentators. In what they fear to be a rising tide of globalisation, some of them identify considerable dangers to economic independence, national identity, cultural heritage and development, and political autonomy. Despite McLuhan's insistence in 1964 that the shrinking 'global village' is not a homogenising influence on societies (2001: 334), recent theorising about the mass media has been characterised by cultural predictions that are increasingly apocalyptic. It is argued that the world has changed significantly since 1964, and as the pace of change quickens, an important battle is being lost – in Europe, as elsewhere in the world.

The media might indeed seem to be important agents of globalisation, and of course there is plenty of evidence to support such a proposition. Gutenberg's printing press predated the first 'wireless' radio transmissions by 450 years, but since then, and at an exponentially quickening pace, newspapers and magazines have exploited such technological developments as the electronic transmission of pages over wires in order to overcome the logistical difficulties of publishing across frontiers (Starkey 2007: 115). The subsequent consolidation of cross-frontier newspaper ownership has enabled Rupert Murdoch to control not only a large share of Australia's newspaper industry (Jackson 2003) in addition to an impressive portfolio of newspaper holdings in Britain and elsewhere in Europe, but important holdings in television and film, such as Star in Australasia, Sky in Europe and Fox in the United States. It is easy to conclude today that the world's media, with radio among them, are about to be overwhelmed by a predominantly American 'axis of evil', with all the cultural consequences that could have. Furthermore, where American *ownership* fails to penetrate, the adoption of American *practices* seems to threaten national, regional and local identities, particularly where, in response to frequent demands for 'modernisation', consultants have been used to promote change.

Globalisation – ravenous beast or paper tiger?

However, McLuhan may yet have the last laugh – and it is not hard to find scholars who remain sceptical about the threat posed by globalisation. Terry Flew observes that, of the four biggest media conglomerates, only Murdoch's News Corporation has genuine global *presence* as opposed to mere global reach, and that, ironically, media companies tend to be less globalised than companies in other sectors of the economy (Flew 2007: 86–7). David Hendy argues that fears of globalisation often centre on ownership, where evidence aplenty may be found to support them. He suggests, though, that too simplistic an assessment of such trends and their impact may conceal counter-movements rooted in a greater diversification of outlets and easier access by listeners (Hendy 2000b: 9–10). Put simply, the prognosis for radio journalism in an increasingly globalised world may not be as dire as the pessimists suggest because social and technological factors can disrupt its more harmful effects. In this book, we have only just begun to describe the relentless growth of different radio and television services. It is merely the tip of an enormous and apparently endlessly growing iceberg of mediatisation, but it is in part a *reaction* to the forces of globalisation.

Let us consider the press again, and the effect of technological development on existing structures. Just as Murdoch takes control of what some perceive as an unhealthily large share of the newspaper industry, a whole new medium invents itself and print is confronted with competition from other, faster and less cumbersome methods of distributing text and pictures. The democratising nature of the Internet lies in the simplicity and relative cheapness of constructing and maintaining even a fairly elaborate website. Consequently, except where states repress their peoples' ability to access material from the web, as has recently been the case in China, the normal issues of access and gatekeeping that are associated with ownership of the press and regulation of broadcasting simply do not apply. The development of blogging has created thousands of amateur reporter-editor-publishers, and while the production values of the broadcast industries are more difficult to emulate on low budgets, all the traditional forms of journalism face challenges from the amateur podcast, the digital camcorder and the bedroom webcam. Moreover, far from winning the mass audiences outside America that satellite and cable television now enables it to reach, the American model of television rolling news programming, as exemplified by CNN, Fox News and MSNBC, has instead spawned dozens of home-grown imitators across the developed world, from BBC News 24 (rebranded as BBC News in 2008) and Al-Jazeera to Deutsche Welle TV (Starkey 2007: 123). France alone boasts three such television channels: La Chaîne Info, BFM and i>télé.

Faced with a vigorous and acquisitive American commercial media sector, the nation-state's final defence lies in regulation. However willing some may be to reciprocate in the lowering of trade barriers, national governments do not need to concede all control of their domestic media to acquisitive multinational conglomerates, any more than they would have considered yielding power to foreign governments in times of war. The long-established restrictions on foreign ownership may be under pressure, but they do not have to be abandoned completely. In the United Kingdom, the originally federal structure of the main terrestrial independent television network, ITV, was recently consolidated, and this, together with the merger of the two largest radio groups to form GCap Media, provoked immediate fears that both commercial television and commercial radio would soon succumb to foreign control. Yet, whoever owns these companies is still subject to the single regulator, Ofcom, and the provisions of broadcasting legislation. Likewise Global, in its acquisition of GCap in 2008. Even Rupert Murdoch's Sky TV enjoys few of the freedoms of expression that are wielded so often – and, against his political rivals, sometimes savagely – by his newspaper titles.

Some jokers in the pack: public service and community radio

Within this controlled broadcasting environment, there is also the 'public service' factor. Notwithstanding the example of Moldavia, where 'public service' is still tainted with the old Soviet notion of 'public control', and in contrast to the relatively small audiences achieved by NPR and Public Broadcasting Service (PBS) television in the United States, public service broadcasting remains important in most European countries. Since its first networks and stations were launched, all that has really changed is the potential size of the commercial competition, yet as that competition has grown, the public's appetite for PSB remains largely buoyant. We noted that in the United Kingdom the huge growth in the number of commercial stations since the launch of LBC has not fulfilled the early predictions that the BBC would be annihilated in the ratings. Despite the enlargement of choice that it provided, the audience's enthusiasm for commercial radio appears to have peaked between 1996 and 1998, when the BBC's share briefly fell behind. Since 1999, the BBC has unexpectedly regained lost ground, winning back a clear lead over the commercial sector (Starkey 2003: 304) and consolidating it in the most recent surveys (RAJAR 2006).

Regulation, and the public service broadcasting it often accommodates, has had to be adjusted to changing circumstances. By the 1970s the original concept of the nation-state as the locus of monopolistic – or at least duopolistic – broadcasters was unequal to the rise of 'free' radio and television services that were transmitted either across national borders or in defiance of national law. Just as in the 1930s the BBC's monopoly in the United Kingdom was routinely broken by commercial rivals broadcasting from Luxembourg, Normandy, Toulouse and other continental European locations, so in 1966 Radio Monte Carlo began regular broadcasting in Italian to Italy and Tele Monte Carlo joined it in 1974. In the same year, the Italian constitutional court ruled that cable television was outside state regulation (Anania 1995) and soon Italy had hundreds of private radio and television stations, leading Europe in the liberalisation of the broadcast media.

Since then, consolidation of *radio libres* has taken place in a number of European countries, sometimes at the expense of what is often characterised as community radio. Likewise, in 1978, the creation in Italy of *de facto* television networks by the entrepreneur and politician Silvio Berlusconi resulted in the mopping up of small independent stations. But given the political will, regulation can be used both to resist globalisation at national level and protect the autonomy of radio and television stations at community level. However, the United Kingdom has been among the most sluggish states in Europe to concede official status to broadcast community radio. Ofcom was almost overwhelmed by the interest demonstrated in the first wave of applications: of 192, 107 were successful while the others were rejected, many for lack of frequencies, particularly in London.

It is, of course, true that resistance to the globalisation of (American) culture is of varying effectiveness. Community radio may be a new and growing phenomenon in the United Kingdom, but if it addresses only niche audiences and operates on only a semi-professional basis, its impact on the plurality of news provision is likely to be small. A strong BBC and a commercial sector whose content is tightly regulated may offer rather better prospects for resistance to globalisation, if not without cost. The *status quo*, which has now been maintained for over 30 years, was partly conceived with such resistance in mind. Yet in at least two respects UK radio provision is the poorer for it. While the importation of the 'shock jock' concept from American all-talk stations resulted in the spectacular flop that characterised the launch of the original Talk Radio UK (subsequently relaunched as talkSPORT), the absence from the country's radio landscape of a permanent, *analogue*, national service of rolling news reveals a serious failing in regulatory leadership.

Two global influences that passed us by: news-talk and radio rolling news

'News-talk' is often cited as being the most popular radio format in the United States, but it is a glib classification, lumping together news, phone-ins and other kinds of content that in music would be classified quite separately. In other words, music stations far outnumber those majoring in speech, but because music formats are more narrowly defined as 'adult contemporary', 'soft adult contemporary', 'urban' and so on, they do not appear to do so. A more accurate description of talk radio in the USA would distinguish news-talk from the minority of stations that major in sports, business, politics or agriculture rather than merely in 'current affairs'. However, news-talk remains an important forum for the public expression of opinion on news and current affairs in the USA, yet is largely absent from the British broadcasting landscape. For a population one-fifth of the size of that of the United States, LBC 97.3, available in London on FM and some regions on DAB, talkSPORT in certain off-peak periods, and a handful of local services including Talk 107 in Edinburgh amount to a surprising paucity of provision within a format that can not only be popular but commercially successful.

Rolling news, as a service of continuously updated news bulletins, is also lamentably absent from the British radio dial. LBC News 1152 in London is the only such service on radio, despite the willingness of the BBC and Sky to maintain it on television – at far greater expense. BBC Radio Five Live was conceived after a long debate which took place both inside and outside the BBC on the desirability of a permanent service of rolling radio news; but contrary to initial expectations, it provides a much more general diet of news-related talk that is easily diverted by the sporting agenda into running commentaries on football, tennis, cricket and even athletics. Such is the network's split personality that it might give live coverage to an important press conference, but only if it has not already begun to cover a sporting event it deems more important. Some of these events, such as one-day international cricket matches and the Wimbledon fortnight, take instant preference over all but the most dramatic crises elsewhere. So despite radio's great portability and its potential for informing people on the move, rolling news has all but disappeared from sound broadcasting (Starkey 2004a). It remains to be seen whether further exploitation of DAB through the second national UK multiplex and the promised launch of Sky Radio News will prompt its revival.

By contrast, there is a strong commitment to rolling news among our near neighbours, the French. Radio France maintains a network of FM transmitters providing nationwide coverage for France Info, a 24-hour operation that runs a regular 'clock' of news, business, sport, entertainment, traffic and weather, all at fixed points around the hour. Overnight this is sustained by re-broadcasts of, among others, French Canadian, Swiss and Senegalese bulletins. A typical daytime hour is shown overleaf:

Figure 5.1   The 'clock' for a typical daytime hour on France Info

11H00'	Bulletin	30'	Bulletin
07'	Weather	37'	Weather
08'	France Info Sport	38'	France Info Sport
10'	TV highlights	40'	Reportage
12'	Racing	42'	Traffic
15'	Editorial	45'	Headlines
17'	Package	47'	Economy
19'	Book of the Day	51'	Music news
21'	Consumer news	53'	Headlines
23'	Headlines	55'	Package
25'	Package	57'	Personal money
27'	Financial markets		

The more it rolls, the more it stands still

At the heart of most forms of continuous news coverage lies a dichotomy. However vital it may be, and however compellingly presented, news usually happens more slowly than the time that is needed to report it, and this is not only because most events are best summed up rather than described in great detail. Rarely is a whole press conference of interest to a general audience, and the coverage of most court proceedings, however extensive it might be, would fail to make congenial news copy out of dry legal arguments. This obvious point presents producers of rolling news with a problem: by the time the bulletin 'rolls round' to the beginning, the lead story is unlikely to have developed very much since the last time it was reported. It can of course be rewritten, in the manner described in the previous chapter, but unless it has been replaced by another breaking story it will in most details be unchanged.

Wherever the format is used, the editorial dilemma is the same: how long to make the sequence of rolling news, before repeating it. This dilemma gives a clue to the reason why, after years of equivocation, the BBC shied away from the format when it launched Five Live. When ITN introduced News Direct into the London market in 1996 on what had originally been LBC's FM frequency, it opted for a 30-minute sequence, with quarter-hourly headline reads and 'travel on the ones' – that is, a traffic and travel update for the capital's busy road and public transport infrastructure every ten minutes, at 1, 11, 21, 31, 41 and 51 minutes past the hour (Crook 1998: 10–11). However, the format attracted poor ratings: the repetition of material three times an hour instead of twice meant that, inevitably, less material was used to fill a fixed amount of airtime, so the format was altered to accommodate three 20-minute sequences. Though more convenient for listeners wanting a quick digest of the latest news, a shorter sequence inevitably means greater repetition and a disincentive to listen for very long, and that impacts on two of the most important measures of the audience: hours listened and thus share of listening.

Unless audiences can be tempted to listen repeatedly, re-tuning from whatever other station they may be enjoying, a format which relies so heavily on repetition will inevitably struggle in terms of audience ratings. In the event of a real national crisis, the tendency of music radio stations to switch if they can to emergency schedules of news coverage and related comment means the rolling news station cannot even depend on occasional public panics, natural disasters, large-scale accidents or terrorist outrages to win expanded audiences in occasional bursts. Yet within the rolling news schedule, some flexibility is possible: although on France Info the bulletins are half hourly, some items are hourly, to reduce repetition. Many of them are 'soft' items, though, more typical of magazine programming, and it is arguable whether they constitute news at all.

Tailoring the news to different audiences

A form of rolling news does, however, lend itself to the less ratings-conscious context of international broadcasting, particularly on a radio station that broadcasts in several languages. Each section of the news is targeted at a different audience, often separated from its other audiences by thousands of miles and also by language, if not by culture and ideology. Even today, such international broadcasters as Radio Prague, Radio Sweden and Radio Beijing organise their schedules according to the possibly misguided assumption that despite all the other sources of mediatised news and entertainment now at their disposal, sufficient numbers of people will tune in to their broadcasts at a particular moment in order to hear the news in their own language. A major problem with serving such diverse audiences, and one which also affects the BBC World Service, is the lack of a common news agenda other than that of the nation which provides the service.

British listeners tuning in to the BBC while abroad are often struck, for example, by the lack of *British* news on the World Service. This is because the highly domestic news agenda of the British media, which rarely report world events unless they relate to Britons caught up in some tragedy overseas, British foreign policy in such places as Iraq and Afghanistan or the visits of British politicians to other countries, is of no great interest to listeners elsewhere. The World Service does feature news from Britain, but the main bulletins of world news which figure most prominently in the schedules are much less introspective than those of the domestic networks, and rightly so. Were this not the case, the BBC's reach overseas would be much smaller than it is: stories such as a murder in Merseyside, a price hike at the petrol pumps or a change in the political leadership of an opposition party, compelling as they are to Britons, are of neither relevance nor interest abroad. Similarly, the overseas territories that the BBC may wish to reach will be too numerous to address individually, so while their audiences may be preoccupied with domestic stories that overshadow the events that are relevant to whole continents, it will be the importance of the latter that the BBC will seek to emphasise.

An international news agenda: real possibility or castle in the air?

So, to return to a central theme of this chapter: Can there ever be an internationally shared news agenda? And if so, can it attract substantial audiences other than at times of great international tension, such as the outbreak of a war or a cataclysmic disaster, whether natural or the result of human intervention? In addressing these questions it is worth noting Hendy's observation that among the broadcast media the impact of radio may have been underestimated because in many less developed parts of the world access to television and even the power to run a television set is restricted (Hendy 2000b: 62). The equipment required to receive television broadcasts from abroad makes the average short-wave radio set seem a humble object: but such sets are far more common in the Third World, where domestic news coverage is either limited in quality or constrained by anti-democratic influences. If we acknowledge this greater accessibility of radio and also accept the contention that a globalising effect of television news is to shape the attitudes of audiences worldwide (Gurevitch 1996), the production of 'world' news may not, after all, be a futile enterprise. Perhaps audiences for it develop in the same way as those of a soap opera, which creates a desire to follow the development of its different narratives and the characters who populate them.

However, the modest audiences captured by the external radio services of a number of countries do suggest that such an effect is limited. In comparison to the ready availability of domestic services, not only can it be hard to access short-wave and even Internet broadcasts, but language differences can pose a further problem. It may simply be that the appetite for international stories is small. This is suggested by the fact that throughout the Cold War the BBC, the Voice of America and Radios Liberty and Free Europe were widely valued as sources of 'free' news and information by audiences behind the Iron Curtain. But with the end of the war and the establishment of democracy, the audiences fell dramatically (Nelson 1997). In the 1970s Radio Sweden's international service broadcast an anarchic late-night comedy programme in English, which achieved a certain cult status among 'DX-ing' (long-distance listening) enthusiasts in the UK, but the station never dented the audience figures of the domestic stations and was too small to register on any survey.

On any but those vast questions that relate to the entire human race, is it realistic to expect a world audience to share a single perspective? Despite McLuhan's increasingly apposite predictions (2001) that our planet would shrink and become ever more efficiently intra-connected, the issues that divide humanity seem as intractable as ever. The deep ideological divide between governments of the west and those of the USSR and its satellite states has all but gone. It has been replaced, though, on three different levels. First, there are the divisions rooted in religious belief and in the lengths certain individuals, and governments, will go to defend and promote them. Second, there are growing inequalities in income, capital and infrastructure between the developed and 'third' worlds. Allan (2004: 190) notes that most of the world's population has never even made a telephone call. Third, there are conflicting assessments of the impact on the global and local environments of sustained economic development, and a widespread reluctance to reduce carbon emissions through the greater exploitation of renewable energy sources.

Your terrorist is my freedom fighter: some unbridgeable chasms

Far from a robust global news agenda which may be used in the prioritisation of stories and the sourcing of material to cover them, there may only be a collection of conflicting and perhaps ultimately irreconcilable perspectives on the world. Among these we may discern western liberalism, the attitudes of the economically emergent third world and religious fundamentalism. They amount to a 'cultural chaos' described by McNair as rooted variously in politics, technology, economics and ideology (2005: 156–60). For an international news editor to find commonalities of interest within such a miscellaneous public is all but impossible. How, for instance, can one present to everybody's satisfaction a story that would be perceived by some as an instance of global terrorism and by others as an act of heroic resistance to western hegemony?

An environmental story that from one perspective is about pollution may from another be about a welcome economic development. For instance, the destruction of the Brazilian rainforest threatens the ozone layer and countless species of wildlife but also creates employment for communities who have no other means of survival. In some respects, war, famine and natural or man-made disasters are a gift to journalists because no matter how far away they occur, their uniqueness and potential consequences enable them to be described in ways that are compelling to wide audiences. The difficulty lies in how to present military victory and defeat, the opposing combatants in a war, causal factors and strategic implications, for it is in describing allegiances and underlying ideological differences that curiosity and shock value give way to partisan interpretation by the journalists and a rejection of it by sections of the audience.

The ubiquity of propaganda among state broadcasters

In the face of this challenge, international news services inevitably have to settle for a compromise that is compatible with the objectives of their paymasters. Where these are state broadcasters, the funding and organisational structures that underpin them may require journalists to sacrifice impartiality and promote that state's foreign policy in an uncritical way. The Voice of America is just such a broadcaster, and proven links between the CIA and Radio Free Europe (Cone 1998: 148–46) suggest that it is simply not possible for its journalists and broadcasters to dissent from official US policy – or even to decline to reinforce it. Despite its direct funding from the Foreign and Commonwealth Office, the BBC World Service manages fairly adroitly to balance the interests of its sponsor and its reputation for impartiality, rarely courting the kind of controversy that it attracted during the Falklands War, when it was accused of revealing too much information about British military tactics. However, it would be naïve to deny that the BBC is still perceived in some parts of the world as a tool of old-fashioned western imperialism.

Those broadcasting services that are run by the armed forces are expected to boost morale among service personnel serving overseas, and where civilian populations can tune in to the American Forces Network, for example, they are likely to hear a diet of news and programming which is more partial than not. In the Middle East, Galei Zahal is recognised as the voice of the Israeli Army, and its news and comment are regarded as important indicators of the military's understanding of a situation but unlikely to inspire much empathy among non-Israelis. Similarly, western travellers in many parts of the world may be surprised to hear news bulletins infused with anti-western rhetoric. Yet in their way these are no more biased than the refusal of our own bulletins to impugn a range of ideological assumptions relating to capitalism, free trade, industrial and scientific progress, and western models of democratic governance. We shall return to such notions in the next chapter.

In those developing countries where democracy is less robustly established than here, we should not be surprised to find that journalism is sometimes indistinguishable from propaganda. Where the state controls the radio station, and the state is answerable to nobody, it is likely that journalists will be required to produce propaganda on the state's behalf. Yet if the likes of the BBC World Service, the Voice of America and the Dutch Radio Nederland are, if somewhat subtler in their approach, essentially the tools of western cultural imperialism, are they really so different? Across the range of international contexts there will inevitably be differences about what constitutes 'journalism' in its radio forms. Attitudes will differ over how domestic and international news agendas should be conceived, the standards of proof that should be applied, and the rigour with which the checking of sources should be done in order to guarantee minimum standards of accuracy – as well as the degree to which news and comment should be kept separate. At one extreme, government statements are in certain countries given unquestioning currency, even when a cursory investigation of the alleged facts would prove them wrong. Some stories are given undue prominence and others are ignored because in compiling the bulletin the journalist is obliged to present an authorised view of the world. At the other, even under great pressure, journalists may routinely put up fierce resistance to attempts to coerce them into bending their reports to fit someone else's political agenda; Tim Crook lists a number of heroic attempts by journalists to overcome obstacles and defy threats in order to tell the truth (Crook 1998: 281–6).

Another threat to truth: low journalistic standards

Between these extremes are circumstances where – often simply due to a lack of resources or training – journalistic practice fails to meet the standards that trainers from the BBC World Service Trust would wish to leave behind them. Equally, and even in democratic societies, issues over resources mean that such relatively minor compromises as an over-reliance on international news agencies are common (Harrison 2006: 92–3). Also widespread is 'hobby' journalism, where private, 'free' or community radio stations – and latterly podcasters – rely on input which, however well-meaning, lacks the professional standards that are required in the UK for BJTC or NCTJ certification. There are similarities here with the way that the relatively recent phenomenon of blogging allows some untrained and often misguided enthusiasts to place in the public domain material that no respectable print journalist would countenance.

At sixes and sevens till the cows come home

In the light of radio's great potential for cross-frontier broadcasting, we have discussed the possibility of an international news agenda for radio journalists and, beyond the coverage of such visceral matters as disaster and war, have found little evidence of a sufficient unity of perspective to sustain one. Given differences in motivation, the number of constraints faced by journalists working in different contexts, and the variability of available resources and training, we also suggest that the worldwide inconsistency in journalistic standards is inevitable. Yet it would be wrong to suppose that wherever in the world it is practised, journalism is influenced only by pragmatic concerns – and it is to a number of theoretical considerations that we now turn.

Notes

1 Interview with the authors, 27 September 2006.
2 Interview with the authors, 8 June 2006.

6

SOUND IDEAS: WAYS OF THEORISING THE FIELD

Radio journalism: smart theorists wanted

Radio journalism is as much a product of the world it seeks to represent to its audiences as it is a reflection of that world. So our understanding of it would be woefully incomplete if we failed to embrace a number of theoretical perspectives on journalistic practice and output. Despite its age, radio is, through no apparent fault of its own, a relatively under-theorised medium. On 24 December 1906, the first broadcast of the Canadian Reginald Fessenden heralded the beginning, albeit faltering, of a durable and illustrious form of mass communication. This was a mere 11 years after the Lumière brothers opened the first cinema in Paris, and all of 30 years before the BBC began the world's first regular television service.

Academics, though, were slow to perceive radio as worthy of study. In 1933, F.R. Leavis and Denys Thompson became the pioneers of the emerging field that has become known in the United Kingdom as media studies. Leavis and Thompson sought to protect children from what they perceived to be the pernicious influences of the cinema, by teaching them to discriminate between 'good' and 'bad' elements in their viewing (Starkey 2004c: 25). Radio, though, was not considered to be such a threat, and while film appreciation, even if somewhat maverick in nature, soon became accepted as a discipline in schools, radio studies did not. Perhaps this omission was simply because the BBC, still imbued with Reithian values, was perceived as a trusted source.

Developing over decades, the media studies curriculum concentrated on film, television and the press – and similarly the academic study of journalism has tended to focus on print and television. It is worth noting that journalism education may be either vocationally oriented or more conceptual in nature, or even a mixture of both. The different ingredients of this mixture may broadly be categorised as skill training, a critical engagement with ethical issues in journalism and an academic exploration of issues and controversies around professional practice (Franklin et al. 2005: 127–8). We feel that none of these may be successfully taught in isolation because practice without a theoretical underpinning is likely to be shallow, uninformed and more preoccupied with routines than an intelligent profession requires, whereas theorising practice does itself require an element of pragmatism that might prevent the drawing of unrealistic conclusions. Those who theorise journalism often draw on academic traditions in broadly liberal subjects in the arts – English, sociology, and communication studies among them – and like those whose work inclines towards 'media' studies, they are often drawn to the analysis of 'given' images, usually in print or on screen.

This is not to say that radio journalism has been totally neglected, nor is it a claim that a more generalised theorising of the field is irrelevant to the specific context of radio. In Chapter 8 we discuss a number of very useful contributions to the literature on the subject, and indeed a number of works refer to 'broadcast' journalism where there are similarities between radio and television. Many important books were written in the 1980s and 1990s, well before the dawn of the digital age. The increasing convergence of the media, and the development since the mid-1990s of the bi- and even tri-media working that we discussed earlier, makes an integrated approach more appropriate now than ever. However, there remain clear differences between many aspects of *radio* journalism and other journalistic activity, just as there are many respects in which the more generalised theories of journalism are eminently relevant to radio, despite its distinctiveness.

The radio medium: limitations and strengths

Just as pictures illustrate a story in other journalistic media, be they still (as in print or on the web) or moving (as in television and the more elaborate web productions), it is the way radio articulates its own messages that accounts for much of that distinctiveness. This is not to be mistaken for a sense of inferiority, similar to that which McNair (2003: 141) perceives as a siege mentality that radio has adopted against the sustained onslaught of television. For radio works in different ways that are neither inferior nor bound to bring about its demise, and it is worth reminding ourselves of the distinctive character of the medium. This is, in essence, a *blindness* – the fact that it provides no visual images of the things that it refers to. In one sense this is an obvious limitation. In former times, radio felt uneasy even in competition with cinema, despite the fact that cinema could not match its 'liveness'. This explains why the BBC decided to give a visual connotation to one of its earliest current affairs programmes by naming it *Radio Newsreel* (Donovan 1992: 221). Then, during the 1950s, radio audiences were decimated by the rise of television and have never looked like returning to their pristine size. But its blindness also places it at a disadvantage to the print medium because although, with the limited exception of still photographs, newspapers also lack visual images of the things they refer to, they do at least provide visible *text*. Unlike those of radio, the words of a newspaper are fixed and stable, and since they exist in space rather than time they can also cover stories in greater length and detail. In a nutshell, radio provides neither images of the real world of news and current affairs, as television does, nor even images of the words that describe these things, as newspapers do.

Yet what is true of many things is also true of radio: turned inside out, a disadvantage becomes an advantage. What cannot be seen must be imagined, and imagining is more strenuous than seeing and normally achieves a less vivid result. But imagining is a pleasurably private and idiosyncratic activity and the lack of vividness allows the radio listener to do other things while listening. Radio is, in other words, a *secondary* medium, and thus much more pervasive than television or newspapers: we can absorb its messages while driving or cooking, or even with our eyes shut (Crisell 1994: 3–14). These factors seem to create a uniquely personal relationship between the medium and its listeners and, however reduced their number, evoke a fierce loyalty in the latter.

As we noted in Chapter 1, the blindness of radio confers a further advantage, especially in respect of news and current affairs. While the medium cannot *show* the people and events that make the news, its primary code of words is wholly capable of *describing* them and – in the same breath, so to speak – of going on to deal with the underlying causes of the news and the issues surrounding it in a way that the literal and overwhelming images of television would inhibit. Watching the latter, we may be so horrified by the pictures of carnage and suffering caused by a car bomb in Baghdad that we half ignore the accompanying commentary that assigns the cause to the presence of American troops or the feud between Shi'ite and Sunni Muslims. Even a 'talking head' – the image of a war correspondent standing before a background of palm trees and city streets – adds an element of distraction to a report. But with its disembodied words, the elderly and blind medium of radio is, like print, entirely comfortable with ideas and abstractions (Crisell 2004b: 7–10). It reminds us that *talk* – reports, interviews, announcements, debates – is the very essence of news and current affairs, even on television, but that a pure sound medium handles it better.

Encoding and decoding the message: a semiotic approach to radio

Yet as well as stimulating the imagination, literal blindness has the positive effect of sharpening the other senses because it is only by focusing on these that someone truly without sight may survive. It is in that more strenuous experience of choosing to *listen* to the radio that the voluntary blindness of the medium lies (Starkey 2004b: 25–6), so that whatever their primary activity, the willingness of radio listeners to depend on their hearing in order to get the most from a sound broadcast, means that they get better at it. They learn to decode what they hear on the radio so as to extract the maximum amount of information from it, just as truly blind people rely on the tone and expression in a human voice to determine the mood or demeanour of the person they hear. Knowing this, a radio producer encodes extra layers of meaning into a broadcast in order to help the listeners in their own subsequent act of decoding the broadcast. In drama this often takes the form of signifying a change of scene by fading dialogue to silence, waiting a second or two, then fading up dialogue or sound effects from another time or place. Listeners quickly learn that this is a convention of drama – it is often used in drama-documentary, as well as in fiction – and once they understand the code they readily interpret the technique in the way the producer intended. In other words, they understand that what they are hearing is a change of scene, even though it is quite unlike the normal human experience of moving from one location to another or living through the passage of time.

The relationship between signifiers and the signified was explored by Ferdinand de Saussure (1983 [1916]). Semiotics is the study of signs and how they construct meaning in order for it to be decoded by those who perceive them. Both linguistics and culture influence the ways in which the recipient 'reads' a message, because that act of reading will inevitably be shaped by the interpretative framework within which the recipient's understanding has developed. Although most of the academic literature on the subject contextualises these processes within visual media, many of the conclusions drawn are nonetheless transferable to radio (Starkey 2004b: 29–30; Crisell 1994: 42–62). Depending on how literally they represented the meanings they were intended to convey, C.S. Peirce (1960: vol. I, 196; vol. II, 143, 161, 165, 168–9) organised signs into three groups: the icon, the index and the symbol. In essence, the icon most closely resembles the subject, and the symbol tends more towards the abstract. Some signifiers can be *polysemic* – capable of having more than one meaning, in the way that the sound of an alarm may be iconic of a burglar alarm going off, indexical of a break-in or even symbolic of crime in general. Hence, a package for a radio news report on crime might begin with the sound of a siren, even though no actual burglary has just taken place: the reporter merely wishes to evoke a comprehensive sense of criminal activity.

The radio text: words, ambiguity and a potential for deception

Where sound has the potential for such ambiguity, it is often through words that the radio broadcast seeks to limit that ambiguity, directing the listener to a particular interpretation by eliminating other possibilities. If the script begins by referring to a burglary as having just taken place, the listener is led towards the iconic meaning of the sound of the alarm and is more likely to imagine the actual alarm making the sound, perhaps above a door or a window. If in a more general piece about the impact of crime on its victims, the reporter refers only obliquely to burglary, the same listener may be more inclined to picture other aspects of crime because the alarm symbolises a range of instances of lawbreaking and the efforts to deal with its consequences.

Directing a listener towards a 'preferred' reading of a text is called *anchorage*, and is similar in function to a newspaper caption which seeks to specify the meaning of the photograph under which it is placed. In television, a voiceover may anchor video footage to a particular meaning by eliminating a whole range of potential ambiguities about what is being shown. Frustratingly for producers, the aim to give preferred readings to media texts can be thwarted by the tendency of individuals within the audience to read a single media text in different ways (Hall 1981: 67). Depending on their perspectives on what is being described, a particular radio news report, for example, may produce an emotional response from one listener, but complete indifference in another. Their readings may often be polarised. One listener may feel sympathy for a deer slaughtered by an illegal hunt, while another may be pleased that a countryside tradition has not yet disappeared. When this became more clearly understood, many scholars investigating media artefacts turned their attention to 'reception studies', the Glasgow University Media Group among them.

Yet the potential for ambiguity in radio production can also work to the journalist's advantage: it is not necessary, for example, to capture the exact sound of a particular burglar alarm to illustrate a report about a specific burglary. In such a purely illustrative role, any number of archive recordings of such alarms may well be quite acceptable and easier to access from a database. The journalist who, in order to save time and effort, passes off an archive recording as a piece of actuality is clearly raising an ethical issue, especially if such recordings are used so often that the listeners begin to recognise them. This is not so confusing, though, as using filmed images of the wrong building on television, nor as significant – and potentially libellous – as attributing to one person a statement that has been made by another. There are clear expectations that journalists should be truthful and avoid misrepresenting the stories they cover, but in practice some do cut corners which they consider unimportant.

Usually they rationalise this compromise by reminding themselves that the essence of the story and any facts around it are unchanged. In ethical terms, there is little difference, though, between this and the accepted practice of television reporters who voice commentaries over newsreel footage they have received from an agency and thus connive at the viewer's assumption that they were the eye-witness of the event it depicts. By relying on archive actuality of fire engines and firefighters to illustrate reports that were filed from the relative comfort of the studio, but were *otherwise* accurate in material detail, one former radio reporter, who is named elsewhere in this book but who must presently remain anonymous, gained a reputation for beating rival news organisations with his coverage of major building fires.

Perspectives from journalism studies: the gatekeeping concept

We have explored, although not exhaustively, some of the characteristics of radio as a medium, and in so doing identified some of its potential and some of the issues that are raised by working in this lively medium. What, then, do the widely accepted perspectives on *journalistic* practice tell us about radio journalism? Behind every journalistic representation lies an act of selection that separates what is newsworthy from what is not. This is essential because no bulletin, documentary, magazine programme or round-table discussion can convey the sum of human and natural activity taking place in the world. The only representation a radio journalist can make within the time constraints imposed by programme schedules and formats must, by definition, be a partial – or incomplete – version of what is happening in the world (Starkey 2006: xvii–xviii, 1–20). Deciding what to cover and what to leave out has long been rationalised as the application of news values, and this is sometimes characterised as 'gatekeeping' (White 1950: 63–71; Carter 1958: 133–44). In this once popular analysis, the gatekeeper wields considerable power in deciding what is communicated to the audience and what is not, how much coverage each story receives, how much importance it is accorded by its relative positioning in the bulletin and which perspectives on any controversy are given exposure.

Galtung and Ruge (1965: 64–91) further rationalised this concept by producing a model of how gatekeeping works in practice. This was observed in the news coverage of four Norwegian newspapers, but Galtung and Ruge's analysis also used a number of interesting metaphors derived from the act of tuning in and listening to radio news broadcasts which might suggest that their work was at least partly influenced by their own consumption of radio journalism. They came to a number of conclusions about 'gatekeeping' which appear as relevant to radio today as they did in 1965. For this reason, their work has been a standard text in journalism education and training, even though issues around the appropriateness of their methodology remain. These arose because they concentrated on the coverage of three major international crises, rather than on days that yielded more mundane stories (Tunstall 1971: 21). They found that, in order to stand a better chance of getting coverage, news events must (1) be extraordinary, (2) be close to home or in a 'high ranking' nation, (3) be negative rather than positive, (4) relate to important people or celebrities, or (5) have a strong element of human interest – and if the latter, it should preferably be about someone who resembles the target audience. A story which scores well according to all of these criteria is most likely to receive coverage, and one which scores highly against many of them will fare better than one which scores well in only a few.

Some modifications of the gatekeeping concept

Because of the great complexity of their tasks and the increasing tendency of journalists to construct news from sometimes only loosely-related elements that together suggest a new direction in which to 'take' a story, the concept of the omnipotent gatekeeper has proved too simplistic to account for this process in an enduring way. The era of 24-hour news is well established, and has brought with it a constant need to refresh material that can quickly grow stale. Journalists can do this by finding a local angle on a national story and looking for material to substantiate it or by initiating surveys and opinion polls to give new topicality to a story that might otherwise be exhausted. More recent critical reassessments of Galtung and Ruge's study suggest that their neglect of the more routine stories led them to overlook much journalism that does not actually consist of reports of events, but instead describes 'pseudo events' and carries free advertising or public relations spin in order to attract publicity (Curran and Seaton 1997: 277–78). Other stories may even be media fabrications, for in a more recent study of the press, Harcup and O'Neill (2001: 277) noted 'the prominence of many apparently manufactured stories that have little relation to actual events'.

However, the systematic analysis of news bulletins on the radio does tend to confirm some of Galtung and Ruge's key findings: natural disasters, tragedies, unexpectedly violent acts, the perceived failings of government or large organisations, and the extraordinary experiences of ordinary people, often in the face of adversity, all tend to dominate the news agenda. The more 'tabloid' the station's approach, the truer this is, and the shorter the duration of bulletins, particularly on music radio stations, the fewer in number the 'pseudo stories' and 'manufactured stories' seem to be. Radio journalists often have less space to fill than their colleagues in the press. Consequently, in order to be included on the radio, foreign news needs to be especially striking, and an industrial stoppage in another country will only be newsworthy if it impacts on Britons travelling to or from it for business or on holiday. Remoteness is a clear disadvantage, although clear cultural, historical or ideological links may prove advantageous. For example, the British media more readily report events in Australia than those in many of our near neighbours. However, because of the human suffering they create and the images they generate, earthquakes, famine, war, terrorism and the like transcend normal criteria.

Who are the radio gatekeepers?

But in the radio context, who performs these acts of selection? And without the given images that drive print and television, are their decisions different? At the newsdesk it is the duty editor who makes the routine decisions. In determining which stories are covered, how much coverage they get and where in the bulletin they are positioned, the editor works to the station's broader editorial policy, interpreting and reinterpreting it as circumstances require in the light of the perceived interests of the target audience. But in *programmes* as opposed to news *bulletins*, the decisions will be taken by the series producer, whose selection will be guided by a different editorial process and a different context. Sometimes there will be an element of specialisation, a tendency towards softer items, or a greater emphasis on human interest.

However, the individual journalist, researcher, interviewer or presenter also plays a role in agenda setting, reinterpreting the source material, bringing a perspective to the selection of material and choosing which illustrative audio (if any) to use. In order to secure its inclusion in a bulletin or programme, a reporter has to 'sell' a story to the editor, and so needs to make it compelling. In the light of this, the reporter will make choices over whom to interview, and the line to take in the course of the questioning. At each stage in the process there exists a layer of hermeneutic transfer between the original event or issue being covered and the listener who will hear the eventual representation of it. Inevitably, this raises issues around bias and, where regulatory or legal constraints require it, the 'impartiality' that is so often cited by journalists as a mark of their professionalism (Sheridan Burns 2002: 11–12).

Balance and bias in radio journalism

Notions of balance and fairness in reporting, particularly where party politics, social conflict or industrial disputes are concerned, are often controversial. Not only might the individual protagonists of particular stories complain that they have been disadvantaged by the coverage (or lack of it) that they receive, but the relationship between balance and bias in journalism often provides the focus of academic analysis. This is rarely welcomed by practitioners, and is sometimes met with open hostility. The early work of the Glasgow University Media Group in analysing television news (1976) was a prime example of this, but such hostility may simply have resulted from practitioners being unused to the kind of scrutiny to which they routinely subject others. Now such academic analyses, if not actually routine, are increasingly common, particularly in election periods. They sometimes relate specifically to radio, and some of their findings can be striking (Starkey 2007: 139–52).

Other ethical issues

Theorising the field can embrace the discussion of a range of issues beyond fairness in representation, and courses in journalism usually dwell at some length on what is labelled 'ethics'. For wholly pragmatic reasons, this often revolves around the professional handling of sources – sometimes these are informants who, if they are not to face repercussions for helping the media with a story, providing some background information, or even leaking sensitive information which proves valuable to the journalist, must be allowed to remain anonymous. When Andrew Gilligan met David Kelly in 2003 to discuss weapons of mass destruction in Iraq, neither could have known how great would be the consequences of their meeting. Once Gilligan's now infamous 29 May two-way for the *Today* programme had been broadcast, one of his initial concerns in the media storm which blew up was to protect his source (Barnett 2005: 333). The subsequent identification of Dr Kelly by the media and by his employers, and the grim aftermath, serve as a reminder of how such a transaction can go terribly wrong. If it is to continue, the relationship with a source is one that in most cases needs protection. Ethical considerations are rarely straightforward, though; reluctant though they may be to break a confidence, most journalists set a higher value on uncovering stories than protecting vested interests.

There are also ethical debates about privacy and intrusion, particularly when legislation to protect individuals or groups is either proposed or already in place (Harrison 2006: 192). The boundary between revealing something in the public interest and satisfying public prurience will always be controvertible, and the more tabloid the house style, the more likely it is that journalists will want to push at that boundary (Franklin 1997: 17). Because radio and television broadcasters do not enjoy the relatively unchallenging luxury of self-regulation by the British press, but are regulated by Ofcom, their news bulletins will normally avoid the excesses of the tabloid newspapers. Programming, though, particularly in phone-ins and on music stations, provides an easier environment for celebrity gossip to thrive, some of it potentially defamatory even if lacking the permanency and relative formality of newspaper copy. Furthermore, those who produce this kind of programming often lack the rigorous training of the NCTJ-qualified news journalist, a fact which can have disastrous consequences.

When the aim is to expose wrongdoing by collecting clandestine material of useable quality or unmistakable authenticity, this is a much easier task for radio than for television or print. An audio recording of a discussion is simpler to make than one with pictures for television, because secretly positioning a microphone in such a way as to secure a broadcastable recording is much easier than having to position a hidden camera as well. Television does not like poorly framed shots, their essential lack of photogeneity seeming incongruous in a medium enjoyed by audiences for its aesthetic appeal. Because it sounds so authentic, an audio recording broadcast on radio has far greater impact than a simple printed transcript in a newspaper, which audiences might readily suspect to be inaccurate, exaggerated or even invented. However, in practice, decisions over the use of clandestine recordings are not wholly left to the judgement of the individual journalist. Again, it is the tighter regulatory environment within which radio journalism operates that reduces some of the autonomy that newspaper journalists, editors and proprietors enjoy under a relatively *laissez-faire* Press Complaints Commission (PCC) (Roberts 2003: 21). Both the BBC *Editorial Guidelines* and the Ofcom *Broadcasting Code* are quite specific about the use of clandestine or surreptitious recordings, requiring considerable justification on public interest grounds and, in the case of the BBC, the express permission of senior personnel (BBC 2005; Ofcom 2005).

Journalism theory and issues of media ownership

As well as ethical issues, journalistic theory also addresses matters of political economy. On the commercial side of the institutional divide there has been little of the controversy in radio that, from the time Rupert Murdoch entered the British market in the 1980s, has raged over ownership of the press and satellite television. With the commercial sector's share of the radio audience only briefly surpassing that of the BBC (RAJAR 1997, 1998, 1999), and tight controls on ownership imposed by successive regulators since the days of the Independent Broadcasting Authority (IBA), no single owner has achieved the kind of market domination that has made Murdoch the *bête noire* of many a media theorist. Even in the wake of the Communications Act 2003, ownership restrictions on commercial radio still ensure a plurality of voice in local or regional markets that prevents any single operator from exercising undue influence. Coupled with the regulatory requirement of impartiality that prevents the broadcast media from indulging themselves in the political partisanship that is so prevalent in the press (Starkey 2007: 49–67), it is easy to see why radio gives at least the appearance of occupying a neutral position in the political economy of the United Kingdom.

This neutrality, though, is a sham. The 'independent' radio stations, and for national and international news the big groups that control most of them, depend largely on a single provider, IRN. The limited inroads that Sky and other news organisations had made into the sector meant that in 2006 between them IRN and the BBC supplied news to stations which accounted for 88 per cent of radio listening (RAJAR 2006). By contrast, the national daily sales of the two largest newspaper groups *combined* (News International and Associated Newspapers) amounted to just 5,934,565 out of 10,505,768 copies, merely 56.5 per cent of that market (ABC 2006). Yet rarely do analysts, media academics among them, complain about lack of diversity in the supply of radio news. It is a continuation, then, of the BBC's public service status and ownership regulation in the commercial sector that masks a lack of pluralism in radio news provision that would seem intolerable in the newspaper industry. Significantly, in 2008 Sky began supplying news to IRN.

Given the stricter content regulation to which radio journalism is subject, it is reasonable to ask whether this matters. In the medium of radio, it is perhaps acceptable that the public should be protected through content regulation rather than seeking to ensure that a range of opinions are disseminated by relying, as in the press, on pluralism of ownership. There is a rich irony in the fact that in different sectors of the media the freedom of speech argument is used to rationalise both regulation and the absence of regulation (Street 2001: 118). However, the argument for regulation draws strength from the tendency of the press barons, despite their individual characteristics and interests, to support similar positions: until the mid-1990s they were broadly pro-Conservative, and in the period preceding the 1997 general election broadly pro-Labour (McNair 2003: 156–61). But the argument for less regulation can point to IRN's dominance of the commercial sector, a dominance which is all the greater for being invisible, or rather inaudible: the 'out' cues within and at the end of the bulletins and voice reports which ITN supplies to subscribing stations ceased to credit the organisation as long ago as the 1990s. In practice, however, it may only be when one of them gets it wrong that we should worry that most national and international radio news in the UK comes from just two providers. If Radio 4 were not the most listened-to station in London, perhaps the Gilligan controversy of 2003 would not have been so acute.

Does media proliferation make ownership less important?

In 2006 an Ofcom review of radio provision suggested that both the convergence and proliferation of media outlets made ownership a less crucial issue than ever before. In essence, because there are now so many different news sources to be accessed through a variety of different media platforms, including those sources which are 'alternative' and amateur, audiences are freer than ever to exercise real choice over what they consume. For that choice to be meaningful, though, audiences may need more information over the provenance of their news than they are currently offered. A more reliable alternative to the free market might be the setting of radio audience share quotas, above which neither the BBC nor IRN may go. In the same way as the BBC is obliged to source certain percentages of its television and national radio output from independent producers, perhaps it should be required to commission and re-broadcast some of its news output from minority providers who pass appropriate quality thresholds.

There would certainly be a great deal of resistance to such a suggestion, from both within and outside the BBC. Despite the various setbacks the corporation may have suffered, including those shortcomings identified by the Neil Report (Neil et al. 2004), as a body corporate and as a collection of individuals it retains a strong sense of self-worth. This sense of its worth is also to be found among its audiences and even pressure groups, such as The Voice of the Listener and Viewer, whose campaigning often focuses on protecting what it perceives as the irreplaceable qualities in the BBC, which, without its vocal support, may be lost to the nation. Even the BBC, though, has recognised that it needs to change. Successive Director Generals have acknowledged that the Reithian ideals which held sway early in the last century were distancing the organisation from its public. The puritanical nature of its pre-war Sunday output was eventually superseded by the introduction of the Forces Service (1940) and the Light Programme (1946). The launch of Radio 1 in 1967 reflected a further sensitivity to popular taste, and more recently there has been recognition that some demographic groups have been super-served with output of the highest quality while others have been overlooked.

The populist trend in radio news ...

So the corporation has moved steadily away from elitism towards populism, and radio news has been part of that trend. The presentation styles epitomised during and after the Second World War by the veteran newsreader Alvar Lidell would seem stuffy today but were long ago modified to suit the programming around the news, even on networks such as the World Service and Radio 4, which are intended for relatively informed and motivated audiences. In order to cater for what are assumed to be the short attention spans of very young listeners, the two youth-oriented services, Radio 1 and 1Xtra, introduced in 1967 and 2002 respectively, brought with them an increasing use of stings, beds and deliberately short sentences and audio clips. 'Newszac', as typified by Franklin (1997), even pervades the bulletins and programming on Radio 4 and occasionally evokes protests from disgruntled correspondents to *Feedback*, the network's listener reaction programme.

Yet are such developments necessarily for the worse? The debate initiated in 2006 by the announcement of Channel 4's 4Radio that it intended to apply for the second national digital multiplex revived the argument that Radio 4 was southern, white and middle-class in its outlook and ignored listeners in other demographic groups who were looking for something different. From this perspective, an increasing populism is by no means negative. Promising an alternative to *Today* that would sound less elitist, less pompous and more directly relevant to a national audience than its diet of largely 'Westminster Village' material, 4Radio might just have a point – if what was proposed would have added more choice rather than encouraging Radio 4 to follow suit. After all, even the southern, white middle-classes are entitled to their own service, and since 1994 – albeit on the relatively unfashionable and technically inferior AM band that instantly characterises it as having second-class status – the BBC has offered a more populist alternative in Radio Five Live.

...and the conservative rearguard

Ironically, all that stands between Five Live and its own national network of FM transmitters is Radio 3 – educated, cultural, often eclectic in its musical content, and cherished by a tiny audience that rarely raises the network's share of all listening above 1.5 per cent (RAJAR 2006). That audience is an influential one, though, including many opinion formers, lobbyists and power brokers. Sheer listener numbers may seem to be on the side of Five Live, but it seems unlikely that the BBC would displace Radio 3 in order to offer the Five Live audience a better signal. The conclusion we draw in this debate is that although there may be a range of pressures on the corporation to take some of its output further downmarket, it should resist those who want it to abandon the intelligentsia altogether, for to do so would be to create a newly disenfranchised minority, and one with the political muscle to exact revenge.

Just as news presentation elsewhere reflects the programming around it, Radio 3's is restrained, considered and occasionally reminiscent of the Third Programme, in which lie its pre-1967 roots. Delivering the copy are newsreaders employed for their voice and delivery rather than for being journalists: some move as freelancers from one network to another, adjusting their style to suit the requirements of each. The smooth, classless professionalism of the freelancer Vaughan Savage, for example, is to be heard at various times on Radio 3, Radio 4, and even the World Service. Moving between services which each reflect some of their tastes, experiences and aspirations, listeners may be equally mobile – perhaps more so than the broadcasters, in their attempts to rationalise the audiences' interests and thereby determine what should be their own news values, may imagine. Modern radio receivers, using RDS on FM and menus on DAB, actively encourage this, whereas early research often found listeners reluctant to tune an analogue dial away from a favourite station lest it be difficult to find again.

Audience studies: the traditional empirical approach

What, though, do listeners make of what they hear? Audience theory is no exact science – it is just theory, or more precisely a collection of often-conflicting theories that may be difficult to prove or disprove. This is an area of academic study for which practitioners tend to have little regard – they live by the empirical data produced by Radio Joint Audience Research (RAJAR) which, as we noted in Chapter 4, suggests how many people or what percentage of the population tune in ('reach'), how many hours they listen for ('listening hours') and how large a piece of the listening 'cake' a station manages to attract ('share'). Within this empirical data, especially where it is broken down by demographics, practitioners can observe partic ular phenomena such as the way in which the introduction of new features, presenters or schedules has impacted on listening figures.

External phenomena can also be observed in this raw data, such as the damage that the 2006 World Cup did to radio in the UK by tempting listeners to watch live matches on television. As the basis for its playlisting decisions, a radio station will often use separate research into listeners' musical preferences: it will play extracts of new songs and golden oldies to them either in groups or over the telephone in order to ascertain which ones they like and which they dislike. Because of the apparent tangibility of the methodologies involved, the programmers who rely on such findings consider them to be robust: they think the findings must be correct because the listeners' opinions have been collected systematically and they must be telling the truth. Ironically, it is uncommon for news editors to commission such systematic research among 'typical' listeners in order to ask what kind of news they would prefer. Just as music programmers are sometimes surprised by the research they do commission, it is highly possible that news editors are ignorant of the kind of news their audiences would prefer and mistaken in their routine assumptions.

However, the practitioners' confidence in industry data produced for programming purposes or through audience research may well be misplaced, and they should be cautious of the significance they attach to such phenomena as the 'World Cup effect'. Unfortunately, these phenomena often seem to generate new assumptions that have no firmer basis in fact than the old ones, for the data will reveal only an *effect*: because no questions are asked of those respondents providing the data, the *cause* can only be surmised. We see listening figures going down and we know of an event that took place at the time, so we might assume a connection between these two things. The relationship we ascribe to them seems convincing to us, but it remains no more than a possibility that one thing caused the other, and we have no way of testing that theory in retrospect. Sometimes academic research can provide answers to fill in the gaps in such 'knowledge'. For example, by placing small cameras behind television sets in a small number of homes and recording what 'viewers' were actually doing while the sets were switched on, Collett and Lamb (1986) showed television producers that their programmes do not always command the full attention of their audiences. There is no knowing, though, how typical Collett and Lamb's viewers were of the rest of the television-viewing population.

A critique of the traditional approach – and an alternative

However, following a recent debate about the validity of the traditional methodology used to collect data on listening activity – one that is based on human recall – audience research has become much more controversial. Specially-prepared diaries are given to samples of each population to be surveyed, and each respondent is asked to keep a written record of all radio listening over a specified week. Most diary completion is retrospective, though, and some demographic groups may be better than others at recalling detail in a meticulous way. Others may seriously misrepresent listening behaviour through mistaken or clumsy entries, or because they may wish their tastes to seem more 'highbrow' than they actually are. Between 2000 and 2004 controversy raged between the then Chief Executive of The Wireless Group, Kelvin MacKenzie, and a number of other major players in the industry over the desirability of replacing diaries with electronic metering (Starkey 2003). RAJAR, an industry body that is jointly owned by the BBC and the commercial sector, is charged with producing credible figures that are acceptable to both of its paymasters. So the organisation began a protracted period of comparative testing – comparing the results derived from different electronic devices that the listeners wore or carried around with them, and those derived from the traditional diary method.

MacKenzie had become suspicious of diary measurement after commissioning private research he dubbed the 'cricket test'. Independently of RAJAR, National Opinion Polls questioned listeners who had heard ball-by-ball commentary from the 2000–01 England v. Pakistan Test series. Since his station, talkSPORT, had recently wrested the rights to this event from the BBC by offering more money, he was surprised to find that most of the listeners thought they had heard the live commentary on Radio 4 or Five Live. Only a third identified the station correctly (MacKenzie 2002). Of course, various factors might account for this, but MacKenzie (2000) rationalised it as evidence that listener recall was demonstrably flawed, and that the very principle of using it as a source of audience data was misconceived. Whereas the BBC may have benefited in the cricket test from a false recognition derived from its greater heritage factor (the BBC had previously monopolised such coverage), electronic metering 'couldn't lie'. The tendency of the early trials of radio audience metering to boost figures for speech stations and depress those for music stations added to its appeal – at least for MacKenzie – and if metering had then been adopted by RAJAR, it would certainly have benefited talk formats in particular and radio journalism in general. However, RAJAR was not persuaded by its research findings from a number of different metering systems, and so in the UK it is likely that audience research data will continue to be derived – at least in part – from diaries.

Academic approaches to audience studies: the 'hypodermic' theories

Practitioners are often even less eager to espouse academic perspectives on radio audiences than the more conventional forms of research by which the industry lives. But what exactly are these perspectives? Again, we have to turn to more generic understandings of the media, and theories that have developed through scholarly activity that is not as focused on radio as it might be. Somewhat inconveniently, there is less of a consensus about the nature of audience behaviour than we would probably like. Over some 80 years, a number of competing theories have been developed, and *McQuail's Mass Communication Theory* (2005: 456–78) provides a detailed but easily digestible review of the wealth of literature on the subject. In summary, we could say that the first academics, professionals and lay commentators who considered audience behaviour assumed a fairly simple and direct relationship between content and effect. It was widely believed that the media were so powerful that audiences could be easily persuaded by propaganda into behaving as the propagandists wanted them to (e.g. Lasswell 1927). During the Second World War, Nazi Germany tested this theory almost to destruction by commandeering the powerful transmitters of Radio Luxembourg and using them to spread disinformation and unease among the British population. From a studio in Hamburg, an announcer who was nicknamed Lord Haw Haw by the *Daily Express* because of his hallmark opening drawl of 'Germany calling, Germany calling' read bogus news bulletins proclaiming allied defeats and German victories. This was widely perceived as a product of the German propaganda ministry of Joseph Goebbels, largely derided by the British public, and no matter how 'journalistic' the reporting may have seemed within the generic conventions of the day, ultimately unsuccessful as an attempt to undermine morale.

There are many other instances of radio 'news' being used to support imperialism or more bellicose activities around the world (Starkey 2007: 115–30). However, in times of war, and where journalism is produced by a perceived enemy, audiences may be naturally, even unthinkingly, more sceptical than when news is produced at home and by a trusted source. In theorising bias in the press, Edward Herman and Noam Chomsky (1994: 297) argued through their 'propaganda model' that journalism often protects elements of the *status quo* by filtering news, marginalising dissent and encouraging conditions in which both governments and commercial interests can communicate. It is thus able to impose 'preferred' information and attitudes on the public or to reinforce them. They contended that because inequality of wealth is inherent in capitalism, mass communication must preserve stability by regulating social and economic change. Journalists, the thesis continued, often accept without question the 'presuppositions' of the state (Chomsky 1989: 5). This means that in Britain, for example, the legitimacy of capitalistic values, parliamentary democracy, taxation, and the constitutional monarchy are rarely if ever impugned in the reporting of news and current affairs. In current controversies, alternative ideologies which might be represented as republican, anarchist or communist are not reflected in bulletins, and certain other issues, such as Britain's possible adoption of the euro, are rarely given exposure. It is appropriate to ask whether the communication of information can be a catalyst for social change or whether radio journalism's routine packaging of information as 'the news' and its transmission through outlets that are part of the institutional fabric of the nation merely reinforce a *status quo* that supports and tolerates a single view of the world.

What does the audience make of all this? Popular wisdom still suggests that the showing of violence on television makes people, particularly children, more violent and that the repeated showing of exciting toys and junk food causes children to demand that their parents buy the toys and feed them an unhealthy diet. Nevertheless, the theory that propaganda is uncritically consumed by its audiences has not found much favour among academics. Later models of passive audience behaviour include that of the 'hypodermic needle' (Livingstone 1990: 16–17), a once popular metaphor for the relationship between 'omnipotent' media and 'lumpen, unquestioning' audiences. It was so called because it compared the relationship between media products and media audiences to the injection of a drug into a muscle. Just as a drug provokes the same automatic reflex in everyone, so the 'injection' of information into the audiences' consciousness causes predictable and uniform reactions.

Academic theories of the autonomous audience

Such notions are readily attractive to people who complain about what they perceive to be either irresponsibility or malice on the part of the media, but from the late 1970s more persuasive academic perspectives have focused on *individuals within audiences*. These are much more diverse in terms of the 'readings' they make of received texts and their responses to them (Livingstone 1990: 62). We can observe this phenomenon ourselves: clearly, not everyone who hears of a killing in a radio news bulletin automatically sets out to kill somebody in the same way or, indeed, by using any other way. Even children display individuality in discriminating *between* advertised products. Katz, Blumler and Gurevitch (1974) are among those who rationalise diverse responses in terms of the 'uses and gratifications' model of audience behaviour. This suggests that as well as each being shaped by different circumstances and experiences (1974: 24), different people are individually discerning. According to their own beliefs and perspectives, individuals within an audience are each likely to make their own active readings of media texts. They also use the media to satisfy their own differing needs, 'using' any content which provides some form of gratification, and rejecting other content at will (McQuail et al. 1972). In news terms, individuals might seek out items on the radio which seem to have direct consequences for them, such as the cost of borrowing and the likelihood of getting caught in bad weather or in traffic congestion. Today, they are sophisticated enough to dismiss other stories they regard as irrelevant or fanciful, such as the sightings of UFOs and alien beings in the famous 1938 Orson Welles radio parody of news reporting. This terrorised much of the American radio audience but was in fact a dramatisation of the H.G. Wells novel, *War of the Worlds*.

Gerbner's cultivation theory

Despite its appeal to common sense, this explanation of audience behaviour remains controversial. At odds with the notion of audiences being made up of discerning individuals who cannot easily be duped into behaving like puppets is 'cultivation theory', as articulated by Gerbner over the last 40 years, and most recently in 2002 (Gerbner et al. 2002: 19–42). This posits the ability of the media to cultivate particular attitudes and values in audiences, which in turn affect their likely responses. The heavier an individual's use of the media, the greater the cultivation effect. Thus, the persistent coverage in 1990 of tragic but relatively rare incidents in which certain breeds of dog seemed more likely than others to bite children led to their being popularly labelled 'devil dogs'. By apparently inciting a public demand for something to be done, it also prepared the way for the introduction of the

Dangerous Dogs Act 1991. Similarly, an increasingly tabloid approach to radio news accommodates the coverage of celebrities and 'reality TV' personalities to the exclusion of serious items which may have more direct relevance to individual listeners. This approach may thus reinforce in audiences the idea that such personalities and their activities are in themselves newsworthy.

How context may contribute to media effects

Just as celebrities rise and fall in popularity, a range of contextual factors may cause media effects to rise and fall in intensity (Carey 1988). Certainly, when society is destabilised by a crisis – be it real, such as a natural disaster, war or economic depression, or merely perceived, such as a greater incidence of crime 'out there' or falling standards of discipline in the schools – people may collectively be more suggestible (McQuail 2005: 462–4). News editors often perceive among their audiences an appetite for stories which address topical concerns, but that topicality may itself have been created by earlier coverage of similar incidents. Many of these concerns develop in the same way as those which Cohen (1973) describes as 'moral panics'. These are themes which are developed either consciously or subconsciously across a range of media, drawing upon often isolated incidents to create a sense that something must be done urgently to resist an overwhelming social threat. An early example of this was the way Adolf Hitler was able to turn large sections of German opinion against the relatively prosperous Jewish community in the 1930s. Similar, though less extreme, reactions have been stirred up in Britain towards asylum seekers, who have been variously described as 'swamping' the country, 'flooding in' and overwhelming the social infrastructure. Another attempt to theorise the effects of journalism in various media focuses on 'agenda setting'. Audiences may not often be told *what* to think, but because editors' news values transfer into the public's sense of what constitutes social and political priorities, they are generally told what to think *about* (McCombs and Shaw 1972: 176–87).

Media effects: the responsibilities of the journalist

So, given the range of academic perspectives on the audience's responses to the media, what conclusions may we reasonably come to about the way that listeners react to radio news? If individuals within audiences were totally impervious to media content, there would be no advertising industry, nor would political parties put such effort and expense into 'spin', campaigning and party political broadcasts. News editors and other journalists routinely apply news values to their work which reflect not only their own professional training but a sense of the listeners' own interests and perspectives on the world around them, and this is born of the need to hold an audience's attention and make it keep coming back for more. There is undoubtedly, though, a sense that certain stories or themes will draw more effectively on current concerns than others, and selecting particular stories probably does stimulate interest for more of the same, particularly when they relate to an ongoing narrative that appears to be, for the moment, unresolved. It also seems likely that individuals within audiences will each react in different, if often not totally dissimilar, ways and that maverick responses will be restricted to small numbers of people. Yet while people may be resistant to blatant propagandising, could it be that they are less resistant when regularly confronted with compelling evidence that leads them to think in particular directions?

This imposes certain responsibilities on journalists. The pursuit of trends in reporting may bring high audience ratings, but feeding a moral panic with disproportionate coverage of a subject may also have a corrupting social effect. Here lies the perennial dilemma for an editor or producer: whether to cover a story because it is sure to yield high audience ratings, or whether to adopt the moral high ground by rejecting it because it is crass, misleading or unworthy of the coverage that competitors will give it. Because it is inextricably linked in many people's minds with 'dumbing down', the increasing tabloidisation of radio news makes it even harder for the journalist to take the moral high ground. This is particularly apparent on music stations, where news and speech programming are patently less significant than its primary content. Playing music beds under news may signify the bulletin is there more for its entertainment value than its potential to communicate information, while adopting more colloquial expressions and phrases – such as substituting 'uni' for 'university', 'devil dogs' for rottweilers and so on – can confirm this impression.

The tabloidisation of radio news: selling democracy or just dumbing down?

Such judgements can attract charges of elitism. Indeed, making the news more accessible benefits a democratic society because it makes 'ordinary' people more inclined to engage with current affairs. This may in turn mean that they are more likely to participate in the social and democratic processes which underpin the state in which they live, rather than remaining marginalised by a highly politicised discourse that they might otherwise consider rarefied and irrelevant to their own daily lives (Lewis et al. 2005: 6–7). Paradoxically, those who value the more substantial, better informed news coverage of Radio 4 and the BBC World Service would feel democratically impoverished if those services were to be similarly 'dumbed down'.

Tabloidisation is primarily, though, about the choice of stories, their prioritisation in the bulletin and the treatment they are given. So-called 'entertainment news' about the stars of cinema, music, 'reality TV' shows and the like has long been accommodated in the bulletins of radio news, but rather like its confinement to the gossip columns of the broadsheet newspapers, it was formerly placed at the end of the bulletin – the 'and finally … ' much parodied in light entertainment. It was included simply as a palliative to counter any distress or unease that might have been created by the more serious stories of misfortune, disaster and injustice at the top of the bulletin. Tabloid newspapers – relatively downmarket in character, narrow in their horizons and lacking any real ambition to educate or culturally stimulate their readerships – unashamedly feature such material even on their front pages, so focused are their news values on celebrity, scandal and a mawkish interest in the individual victims of calamity. The more radio journalism promotes this kind of material, the more it risks the charge that it is pandering to the ratings rather than maintaining high standards, and the more it will confirm Marxist suspicions that it is seeking to divert the 'masses' from a consciousness of their oppression by capitalism (Street 2001: 242–3).

Less Marx than McDonald's?

Radio journalism has great potential to inform and influence a democratic dialogue, forming part of the public sphere described by Jürgen Habermas (1989: 27) as a place where 'private people come together as a public'. The more it becomes preoccupied, though, with popular and relatively inconsequential 'newszac', the more it will justify the Marxist critique of the media. In practice, populist broadcasting may have more innocent intentions than to try to distract the 'masses' from their political predicament. Such activities may be a mere consequence of the McDonaldization that George Ritzer (1998) identified in the routinisation of production in a number of different industries, and which has been labelled McJournalism in respect of the media (Franklin 2005; Franklin *et al*. 2005: 142–3). A Marxist, however, might perceive McDonaldization to be a natural consequence of capitalism, even if Marx himself pre-dates the eras of fast-food and broadcasting. On the other hand, a conspiracy theorist, of whatever political persuasion, might simply perceive the tabloidisation of radio news as the corollary of progressive deregulation in broadcasting. This includes the increasingly lighter touch of the Radio Authority and now Ofcom, manifest in allowing an ever greater freedom to determine the nature, extent and content of news in the commercial radio sector, and the granting of permission to develop news hubs and the like. There is also the near certainty that wherever commercial competition goes, the BBC will soon follow.

So, if the tabloidisation of radio journalism is widespread, is it a conspiracy or an innocent consequence of working in a competitive market? Does it aim to promote social inclusion or merely create entertainment? Are the fears of those who opposed the introduction and development of commercial radio in the 1960s and 1970s now vindicated? There seems to be insufficient evident to prove either case: many practitioners of radio journalism will consider that they are merely doing their job rather than seeking to corrupt or repress their audiences. They will say they are responding to changes in listener demand but within regulatory and legislative constraints that are still quite considerable. They may be right. It is hoped that the proliferation of radio services that has been taking place over the past 30 years or so will continue to enrich provision and increase choice, to encourage innovation while preserving the best of established practice. The public sector, with its distinctive funding mechanism, may well provide an effective bulwark against the rising tide of newszac, and in sustaining the worthier end of the quality spectrum ensure that debates about elitism versus populism persist for years to come. Can we depend on it, though? Where is radio journalism heading in the future? Let us now consider that future, drawing conclusions where appropriate from both the present and the past.

7

NEWSRUNES: DIVINING THE FUTURE

Radio but not as we've known it: multi-platform delivery

When pondering the future of radio journalism, we can do no more than play an inspired guessing game. Everything depends on the changes that radio itself will undergo. Many of them will be substantial, but some perhaps will be more apparent than real. On the other hand, we shall see that within radio journalism certain changes that occur could be more real than apparent, in the sense that while news programmes might sound very much as they presently do, they could conceal a changed understanding of the news and new ways of gathering it. Moreover, since many of the technological and political issues that the medium faces are also faced by television, we shall often talk in this chapter about 'broadcasting' rather than just radio.

At the *transmission* end of radio, digital technology will deliver content from a range of platforms. Traditional over-air or 'wireless' radio will persist, but its stations and networks will proliferate. Sound broadcasting gradually became more abundant even in the old days of analogue technology. From 1922 until the mid-1950s, the reliance of radio signals on amplitude modulation (AM) meant that the spectrum could accommodate only a limited number of stations, but the development of frequency modulation (FM), which allowed clearer signals that seldom travel more than 80 miles, made many more stations possible. If they were a reasonable distance apart they could share the same frequency, and in Britain FM provided the impetus for local radio (Briggs 1995c: 647). Later, transistorisation and a general miniaturisation of components meant that transmitting equipment became less costly and more compact: it was this that prompted the growth of pirate stations during the 1980s (Crisell 1994: 36–7). Digital technology has reduced the cost yet further, and since several channels can occupy a single frequency, there could soon be hundreds of radio stations on the spectrum. This is not an easy transition for either the industry or the public, though.

While DAB has been a greater success in the UK than anywhere else, calls for the adoption of an improved system of transmission, DAB+, would, if answered, frustrate the early adopters of DAB, who would then find they were unable to receive any services that used the new standard. The trials of Digital Radio Mondiale (DRM) suggest that this alternative system might prove attractive for digital broadcasting over longer distances. It could perhaps bring a new lease of life to the AM band, where radio waves travel further.

Internet radio: webcasting and podcasting

However, broadcasting over the Internet will be – and already is – even cheaper, easier and more plentiful. We can usefully divide it into 'webcasting' and 'podcasting'. *Webcasting* is the transmission of linear, 'streaming' audio (or video) content over that international network of computers that we know as the 'Internet' or 'web' – often the very same content that a radio station is transmitting by traditional, atmospheric means. *Podcasting* is the internet transmission of content that is similar, but which can be accessed only by (sometimes paying) subscribers. Moreover, it is designed for playback on mobile devices as well as computers: it can be downloaded, using software that is capable of reading its formats, and it gets its name from its association with the iPod, the famous personal audio player created by Apple. The difference between webcasts and podcasts is that the linear content of the former is transient and not saved on to the receiving device, whereas podcasts are downloaded and saved. Because the content of a webcast is streamed, an internet connection is needed for its duration. On the other hand, once the content of a podcast has been downloaded from the net, the device that has received it does not need an internet connection to play it back.

In 2006, the podcasts created by the comedian Ricky Gervais were hugely popular and demonstrated that the British, who for generations have been accustomed to free-to-air radio, are nevertheless willing to pay for broadcast speech just as they have been willing to buy downloaded music. Even so, it is clear that many podcasters and web radio stations, especially those that do not run a parallel over-air service, will reach only minuscule audiences; unless listed in 'portal sites', they may be hard to access even by those who are seeking them. Yet there is no doubt that internet broadcasting has a democratising potential. Just as anyone, anywhere, can create a website, so anyone, anywhere, can webcast or podcast: only marginal start-up costs are involved and only a modest investment in material is needed. Moreover, webcasters and podcasters have a global reach and for the most part operate outside the regulatory regime that governs the traditional stations (Barnard 2000: 253–4).

Radio broadcasting: customisation, transfer and replication of content

Digital technology will have other impacts, whether on traditional or internet radio, and we will focus on just three of them here. First, it will produce a diversification of services because it allows an easy and rapid *customisation of content*, enabling a single newsroom to provide a variety of bulletins and news packages that are tailored to different presentation styles and the interests of different audiences. The newsroom of a local or regional station might, for instance, make supply agreements with new community stations that lack the resources to produce a credible news service of their own. Such agreements could hinge on the straightforward payment of a fee or on sponsorship, branding or advertising. The supplying station might provide news to a non-competing station in return for being identified on-air as the supplier, or it might require the non-competitor to carry particular advertising within the bulletins. The latter arrangement would somewhat resemble the 'Newslink' service by which IRN is partly funded. This enables advertisers to place a single commercial within the news bulletins that IRN supplies to its client stations.

Second, digital technology will facilitate the *transference of content* between one medium and another. It is this interchangeability that creates the need for proficiency in bi- and tri-media journalism. Its binary code is now the common currency of the mass media. The stories, interviews, features and music sessions that are used for a radio programme can be swiftly repackaged for a newspaper, website or CD (Hendy 2000a: 224). On the other hand, the first Finnish digital channel, YLE Radio Peili, made considerable use of the soundtracks of television news bulletins, re-versioning them slightly for sound-only consumption (Ala-Fossi 2004). It has, of course, always been possible to move content between media, but it is the ease and rapidity with which it can now be done that is significant. Media organisations cannot resist the economies of scale that it offers, but it may also involve some reduction of choice for audiences. In other words, despite the development of new media, and despite the growth of channels and outlets within each medium, whether old or new, there could be a considerable *replication of content*. Radio journalists may increasingly encounter print journalists who are capable of capturing, manipulating and packaging audio – for podcasting has already ceased to be the preserve of the traditional broadcasters. Individuals and corporate bodies have also begun using the techniques of broadcast journalism to communicate directly with potential audiences over the web, and as they become more proficient, the unmediated nature of their messages will acquire considerable potential for public relations.

The transference of content also has organisational implications that plainly militate against those democratising tendencies of internet broadcasting that we observed just now. It encourages a preoccupation among media companies with the content itself, which tends to be costly, rather than with the means of distribution, which is relatively cheap: the quality or saleability of the former becomes paramount and the latter almost irrelevant. Despite the best efforts of the media regulators, the consequence is likely to be a growth not only of conglomerates, companies with interests in a range of media, but *transnational* conglomerates, companies that produce and deliver content on a global scale. In Britain, foreign ownership of the media has been a sensitive issue since the rise of Sky TV in the late 1980s and its subsequent mutation into BSkyB. For obvious reasons, it is nowhere more sensitive than in the gathering and presentation of the news.

Is it still radio? The phenomenon of media convergence

The third impact of digital technology is already clear from our discussion of internet broadcasting: it will facilitate the *convergence of previously separate media*, enabling audiences to listen to the radio on their television sets, laptops, mobile phones and other portable devices. As long as they remain within reach of a wi-fi hub, the new internet radio sets retain the portability and ease of operation of a traditional transistor radio, yet are able to summon up hundreds of stations on the web. We have now progressed to the *reception* end of radio, but we should also observe that at one level some of these changes are more apparent than real. Radio which is received on a TV set, a mobile phone, a personal computer or an iPod is, for practical purposes, still radio. Yet if these devices can provide moving text and images, are the days of traditional, 'blind' radio numbered? Is there some sense in which the medium will lose its integrity and become merely ancillary to visual data?

It seems certain that radio will survive as a medium whose essence, whatever its visual accompaniments, is sound, because as we saw in the last chapter the fact that it has no *need* of vision gives it certain irreducible advantages, at least two of which are crucial to journalism and news. First, it is a secondary medium: because it does not engage the sight, it allows the listener to do other things while listening. Hence even in this era of round-the-clock television coverage, the news can still reach the radio listener before it reaches anyone else. Second, in its presentation of events and other physical phenomena radio enables – indeed requires – the exercise of the imagination, which though requiring more effort than seeing is a mostly pleasurable activity. And third, precisely because the imagination is less vivid than sight, radio is good at handling ideas and abstractions – not as good as the stable medium of print, perhaps, but much better than television – and ideas and abstractions are, of course, an essential element in the presentation and analysis of news.

Listeners are doing it for themselves: the growth of interactivity

However, at another level, the impact of the new technology is more complicated. Because some of the media that radio is converging with are two-way (phones, the Internet), radio itself will become much more *interactive*: by various means, listeners will be able to shape and even control its content. Here are just two of the implications. Xfm, the British commercial network that plays current and unsigned alternative music began, when owned by GCap Media, to enable its listeners to customise the radio station they receive under the brand. The next step will be to enable listeners to customise the *news* they consume. This may well prompt fears that audiences will 'dumb down' their own news by preferring entertainment stories to weightier ones, and that it will erode the 'shared national consciousness' that arises from the fact that on radio and television we have always been collectively exposed to what is a single agenda of serious and significant items.

Yet from a different perspective, these fears are surprising and stem from the peculiarly high expectations we have of broadcast as opposed to press news. Perhaps because we feel that our society will otherwise fragment, we continue to believe that there should be a shared national consciousness and that broadcasting should shape it. Our expectations have, of course, been built up over many decades: they originated in the notion of a universal public service to which the BBC was dedicated and which was later imposed, almost automatically, on its commercial rivals. Broadcasting of any kind was to offer comprehensive news that prioritised serious and responsible issues. Yet it has always been possible for the public to buy newspapers that do not prioritise these issues or not to read them even in the newspapers that do. Our higher expectations of broadcasting arise from its historical scarcity, and therefore from its overriding need to reflect concerns that were at the heart of the nation's life. Perhaps we have not yet adjusted to the extent that technology and deregulation have transformed it – that precisely because broadcasting is now plentiful and even more assimilated to everyday experience, there is a sense in which it has become *less* and not more important.

The second implication of interactivity is that there is likely to be a new emphasis on 'audience-originated content'. Listeners will be encouraged to gather their own news stories and perhaps even package their own audio. Eventually, the news agenda could be almost entirely audience-driven. Quite apart from the attendant risk of 'dumbing down' that we have already considered, what implications would this have for the notion of journalistic expertise? At the end of Chapter 2, we outlined the debate about whether journalism was merely a trade that required a postgraduate training in technical skills as a complementary experience to a first degree in some other subject, or whether it was a profession that demanded a sustained and specialised education in media and cultural studies. The notion of a whole army of 'lay' journalists challenges both these perspectives, for journalism would then become something that virtually anyone could do.

Audience-originated content: the implications for radio news

It is in respect of audience-originated content that the changes to radio might be more real than apparent. News bulletins could be broadcast to a reasonable technical standard and with all the trappings of authoritativeness that we have been used to, yet actually consist of little more than supposition, rumour and sheer invention. The 'softer' forms of news already thrive on an element of these things: Is such-and-such a pop singer pregnant? Are a Hollywood couple soon to divorce? Is a certain soccer star about to be transferred? But 'hard' news must be factually accurate, disinterestedly compiled and properly attributed. In the new digital era, there will therefore still be the need for a trustworthy 'gatekeeper', a body whose version of the news may be relied upon as truthful and authoritative – and this brings us to an interesting paradox.

In its early years, there was a need to regulate broadcasting because it was a *scarce* commodity. In Britain this need was met by the establishment of a publicly funded, publicly accountable broadcaster – the BBC – with an obligation to serve all sections of the public, not just those who were attractive to advertisers. But in future it seems that there will be a need to regulate broadcasting because it will be an *abundant* commodity. In so widely accessible and anarchic an environment, amid all the babble and cacophony of voices, which of the many broadcasters will we be able to believe? There must remain at least one whose output can be relied on as truthful, authoritative and editorially independent, and the obvious candidate is the BBC because it is the nation's public service broadcaster.

Yet public service broadcasting is not sustainable without the licence fee, and in an era of broadcasting abundance the imposition of that fee – on every householder who has a television set – becomes ever harder to justify. If I am a householder who, faced with a plethora of TV and radio channels, spends less and less of my time watching and listening to the BBC, why should I be expected to fund it? The question gains urgency from the fact that if I prefer to watch subscription channels, I will have to pay for these in addition to my TV licence. The solution is surely to apply the same principle to the BBC – to reinvent it as a public service provider which is funded not by the licence fee but by subscription. This could involve, for instance, turning Radio 4 into an all-news channel that can be accessed only by those who will pay for it.

However, Radio 4 would then be obliged, as newspapers are, to adjust its form and content to its subscribers' tastes, not to a disinterested pursuit of the truth. Moreover, the considerable cost of news-gathering would almost certainly make it a premium-rate service for the rich and not for anyone else. Hence two of the cardinal principles of public service broadcasting that we outlined in Chapter 1 would have been abandoned; Radio 4 would no longer be a cultural resource that was as widely accessible as possible, and it is likely that its news provision would no longer be 'comprehensive' and 'impartial', but primarily tailored to the sectional interests of those who were paying for it.

We need to appreciate a truth that the BBC, perhaps cowed by those fervid apostles of the market, seems strangely reluctant to stress: the licence fee is the *only* way to fund public service broadcasting. Neither subscriptions nor advertising can do so because they are market mechanisms and the whole purpose of public service is to *transcend* the market – to provide what the ordinary laws of supply and demand cannot, or will not, provide. If this were more widely understood, it is likely that audiences would continue to want a BBC that they pay for through the licence, because this would give them an adequately funded radio and television broadcaster whom they could always access and always trust.

Radio: still a sweet, old-fashioned thing?

There is another prediction that we might venture to make about radio and television. Despite the prospect of interactivity, media convergence and audience-originated content, a demand will persist for formal, old-fashioned, one-way and one-to-many broadcasting with decent production values. Why? Audiences do not always wish to be interactive, nor do they like programming that sounds or looks cheap. Sometimes they merely desire content that has been professionally created by someone else. If, among the other kinds of programming that it makes, a licence-funded BBC radio continues to produce serious, truthful and authoritative news, it is conceivable that at least one of its commercial rivals would eschew audience-originated content and offer news of a similar stature. When he was Chief Executive of Channel 4, Michael Grade famously remarked that 'It is the BBC which keeps us all honest' (Franklin 2005: 157). What he was suggesting was that if the corporation did not exist to make respectable programmes, the commercial broadcasters would have no incentive to do so. Not only is it democratically healthy but also economically feasible that in sound broadcasting, just as in the press, there should be a modicum of competition even within the sphere of quality news.

Threats and opportunities in the commercial sector

Nevertheless, we must begin by acknowledging that under the challenge of the new media, the commercial sector may be facing an irreversible decline in its advertising revenues, and when this happens expensive spoken-word programming is often the first casualty. In the past, the sector has cried wolf at every hiccup of the national economy, but some of the threats it now faces are unprecedented. The most obvious comes from the growth of commercial websites on the Internet, though by forcing the radio stations to find new ways of reaching advertisers for whom websites are a less desirable option, this could stimulate rather than depress the market. But the most palpable threat is internal, arising from the sheer proliferation of both on-air and internet radio stations. This will have a 'salami' effect on the overall listenership, slicing it into ever thinner portions. Commercial stations with tiny audiences will not attract lucrative advertising and will therefore make cheap programmes which, if anything, will mean audience losses, a further reduction of advertising revenue, even cheaper programmes, and so on, in a downward spiral that could end in extinction. The relatively few stations that can garner large audiences will therefore thrive, and it is likely that they will do so by espousing the old-fashioned broadcasting values we have outlined. The audience's demand for professionally-produced output of high quality will surely extend to news and current affairs, so that in one way or another, the professional radio journalist will still have an important role to play.

To have faith in the future of commercial radio as a purveyor of quality news, we must presently turn to Channel 4. Its consortium, the 4 Digital Group, was awarded the second national commercial multiplex, which was to rival the first, owned by the Digital One Network, and bring no fewer than ten new stations to the market via DAB and online means. Speaking at the 2007 Radio Festival in Cambridge, its chair, Nathalie Schwarz, was bullish about its ability to find new audiences for radio and attract new advertisers to the medium. Together with UBC Media, Carphone Warehouse, Emap Radio, Chrysalis (soon to become Global Radio) and UTV Radio, Channel 4 had identified a number of innovative services, such as E4 Radio based on the populist television spin-off, and Schwarz announced the group's intention to draw more listeners to DAB by investing in quality speech programming. Channel 4 also had a distinct advantage in its ability to cross-promote its radio services on television – an advantage that was crucially missing from traditional 'independent' radio. Hence if 4 Digital Group had not wobbled, a reinvigorated commercial sector would have emerged to challenge the BBC. The preliminary skirmishes were already taking place, when a change of management at GCap early in 2008 led to a sudden reigning-in of investment in DAB. At the time of writing, though, this is all we have, and our aim in the following case study is to explore how effective radio is as a medium of quality news and whether there is scope in the future for more than one version of such news.

Case study: a comparative analysis of BBC Radio 4's *Today* programme and Channel 4 Radio's *The Morning Report*

Introduction

Among other things this analysis will show how journalists exploit the strengths of radio and seek to minimise its limitations in order to create news programmes. It will become apparent that in a clamorous world of newspapers, television and the Internet, radio is still an effective news medium, and we have chosen the *Today* programme and *The Morning Report* because they are probably radio's closest equivalent to the 'quality' press and because each is the creation of a public service broadcaster and the latter is also in the commercial sector. *Today* can be heard six days a week on BBC Radio 4 and *The Morning Report* was produced by Channel 4 Radio until 13 July, 2008. Since those who listen to 'quality' news may be seen to comprise a single market, there is a considerable degree of similarity, even duplication, between these programmes. Yet for each of them to thrive, there must also be an element of difference, a targeting of some part of the market by one broadcaster which it feels the other has neglected. Consequently, our analysis of the programmes will not be merely consecutive and cumulative but comparative and contrastive, and the fact that the two broadcasters saw themselves as competitors is indicated by the war of words that accompanied the launch of Channel 4 Radio in June 2006.

Andy Duncan, the Chief Executive of Channel 4 Broadcasting, fired the opening shot. He declared his wish to end the BBC's dominance of radio, 'to contribute something new to the radio mix by offering a public service alternative to the BBC in news, current affairs, entertainment, lifestyle, music and comedy' (*The Times*, 5 June 2006). Then Channel 4's head of news, Dorothy Byrne, launched a direct attack on the *Today* programme, claiming that its values were those of 'a middle-aged man from Bournemouth, with a strong interest in bird-watching, whose wife wears cashmere twinsets and is active in the bowling club'. She told *Broadcast* magazine that when she listened, she felt that 'although [the presenters are] being incredibly rude in interviews ... actually they were all at a dinner party the night before and are in the same club'. She asserted that 'We don't want to be in that club' and added:

> I think that even people who work at the BBC agree that *Today* needs revitalising. It feels like a programme for white, middle-class people from the south. It's not diverse. I want to appeal to everybody, and it feels as if *Today* is primarily for one group.

(Sharp 2006)

(Continued)

One of the *Today* presenters, John Humphrys, hit back:

> It's a bit sad in a way that she feels the need to rubbish the most successful speech programme in Europe. It's a bit of an insult to people who don't fit that lazy caricature. ... It's perfectly true that when she enters *Today* she enters that world of university students who are interested in what's going on in the world, in arts, in politics. ... all these different challengers have come along, all saying that they are going to knock us off our perch – and our audience is higher than ever.

(Sharp 2006)

We can discount much of this as polemical overstatement: middle-aged birdwatchers from Bournemouth and even university students doubtless make up an infinitesimal part of the *Today* listenership. Yet it might also remind us that 'the news' does not exist in some idealised, platonic form. News is not simply new information, but only that new information that audiences wish to hear – and different audiences wish to hear different things. To a large extent, then, our analysis of the two programmes will be an analysis of their respective audiences, those who are implied in their structures and in their choice and treatment of stories.

We have matched the programmes as contemporaneously as we can, selecting their respective editions for the morning of 17 May 2007. We have analysed the *Today* programme between 7.00 and 7.30 (its most serious elements tend to be featured in the first half of the hour) and *The Morning Report*, which was transmitted on Oneword Radio (among other platforms) between 7.30 and 8.00 until Oneword was ominously closed down in January 2008 by its owners, UBC Media and Channel 4. It could, however, be objected that we are not comparing like with like – that while *The Morning Report* was a programme in itself, our sample from *Today* is only a fraction of what is actually a three-hour sequence, and that a truer comparison would include the latter in its entirety. Yet aside from the impracticality of analysing the amount of material this would generate, much of it repeated, we would argue that the very different structures of these programmes are themselves indicative of different understandings of quality news on the radio and of the audience that exists for it.

The *Today* Programme [TY] – BBC Radio 4: Thursday, 17 May 2007, 7.00–7.30 am

JOHN HUMPHRYS [JH]: It's seven o'clock on Thursday, the 17th of May. The government's going to confirm today plans to close two and a half thousand post offices to stem heavy losses. Gordon Brown is going to take over from Tony Blair without facing a vote by Labour Party members. And senior officers have been ordered to help salvage Prince Harry's army career after he was told he couldn't serve in Iraq. Today's newsreader is Harriet Cass. [0'.30"]

NEWSREADER:

1. 'Two and a half thousand more post offices are likely to close under plans being outlined today by the Trade and Industry Secretary, Alistair Darling. The government has been consulting on the future of the network which, with fourteen thousand branches, is losing four million pounds a week. Here's our business reporter, John Moylan.' Report from John Moylan.
2. Gordon Brown to succeed Tony Blair as Labour leader and Prime Minister without facing a vote by party members. Report by political correspondent, Mark Sanders, with recorded remarks by one of Brown's challengers, John McDonnell. Report concludes on the elections for the deputy party leader.
3. Portuguese police questioning a man in connection with the disappearance of four-year-old English girl, Madeleine McCann.
4. Army commanders considering Prince Harry's future role in the army. Report from royal correspondent, Peter Hunt.
5. A policy think-tank, Chatham House, warns that Iraq faces the prospect of collapse and fragmentation.
6. Before he quits as Prime Minister, Tony Blair is visiting George W. Bush for talks. Report from Washington correspondent, Justin Webb.
7. The President of the World Bank, Paul Wolfowitz, is discussing the terms of his departure.
8. A number of companies that offer to help people recover bank penalty charges are being investigated by the Ministry of Justice. Report from business correspondent, Greg Wood, including telephoned comments from the head of regulation with the Ministry of Justice.
9. The government to announce its position today on the creation of human/animal hybrid embryos for stem-cell research.
10. The Food Standards Agency expected to recommend the mandatory addition of folic acid to bread. 'The details from John Braine.' Report from John Braine.
11. US scientists make progress in the search for a cure for baldness. [8'.30"]

JH gives a time-check. Since Basra has always been known to be a dangerous place, he asks what has changed the army's intention to send Prince Harry to Iraq. He cues remarks from five military bloggers, which are read out out in different voices, then interviews Major General Patrick Cordingley, a veteran of the first Gulf War. [5'.00"]

CAROLYN QUINN [CQ] gives a time-check and then introduces an item on Gordon Brown's unchallenged claim to the posts of Prime Minister and leader

(Continued)

of the Labour Party. But there are six candidates for the post of deputy leader, who attended a meeting last night in central London. 'Ian Watson was there.'

- Report from Ian Watson on a sound-bed of actuality and containing remarks and sound-grabs from five of the candidates. [4'.00"]

JH back-announces, gives a time-check and introduces an item about British Telecom's plans to offer television to customers via their broadband internet connection. 'Greg?'

- Greg introduces the Chief Executive of BT Retail, Ian Livingston, and conducts an interview with him. [3'.00"]

CQ gives a time-check and announces that the Food Standards Agency is expected to recommend the addition of folic acid to bread. She then interviews health correspondent, Julia Hobson. [2'.00"]

JH gives a time-check and introduces an item about today's Algerian general election, which takes place against a background of terrorist attacks. He cues Middle East correspondent, Ian Pannell.

- On a sound-bed of actuality, Pannell reports from an election rally outside the central post office in Algiers. His report is punctuated by the recorded remarks of politicians, including a former Prime Minister, and the US ambassador to Algeria, Robert Ford. [4'.00"]

CQ back-announces, gives a time-check and introduces sports correspondent, Steve May, who is reporting from Lord's cricket ground on the opening day of the first test against the West Indies.

- May gives the latest pre-match news and then conducts an interview with England captain, Andy Strauss. He follows with other items of sports news, until the news headlines are repeated at 7.30 am. [3'.00"]

TOTAL DURATION: 30'.00"

The Morning Report [MR] – Channel 4 Radio: Thursday, 17 May 2007, 7.30–8.00 am

MELISSA PREEN [MP]: Hello and welcome to The Morning Report. It's Thursday, the 17th of May, and I'm Melissa Preen. [MUSIC PLAYED IN] Coming up: No contest – Gordon Brown will be the next British Prime Minister. [SOUND-GRAB FROM GORDON BROWN] Backlash against the decision not to send Prince Harry to Iraq. [SOUND-GRAB FROM PRINCE HARRY] Two and a half thousand post offices hear today if they will close. In the battle of the internet music titans, retail giant Amazon weighs in. [SOUND-GRAB FROM CNN REPORTER] Also, rising levels of water complaints and the first npower test against the Windies. Plus Donnie Darko on Cannes. [SOUND-GRAB FROM ACTOR, JAKE GYLLENHAAL] The weather: much of England and Wales will see cloudy and patchy rain giving way to sunny spells. This is *The Morning Report* from Channel 4 News. [MUSIC FADES UP AND ENDS] [1'.15"]

MP announces that Gordon Brown will become the next Prime Minister without having to face a leadership contest. She then cues:

- Sound-bite of recent speech by Gordon Brown to the CBI outlining the challenges of climate change, terrorism and security, global economic competition, and the re-building of communities.

'I'm now joined by our reporter in Westminster, Peter Murphy.'
An informal interview with Murphy, in which he deplores the limbo that will now occur until Blair's departure and Brown's succession, and goes on to explain the voting system for the deputy leadership. [4'.55"]

MP thanks Murphy and turns to the criticism of the Ministry of Defence for its decision not to send Prince Harry to Iraq. Cues former defence minister, Michael Portillo.

- Sound-bite from Michael Portillo, claiming that the Ministry has made a mess of this and previous matters concerning the war in Iraq.

MP then cues Conservative Member of Parliament and former territorial soldier, Desmond Swain.

- Sound-bite from Desmond Swain, alleging that the decision has handed a propaganda victory to the insurgents. [1'.00"]

MP: At least twenty-five people have been killed in factional violence in Gaza.

- Sound-bite from the political editor of an influential local newspaper. [1'.25"]

MP announces a development in the search for Madeleine McCann, the four-year-old who has disappeared while on a family holiday in Portugal. [0'.21"]

MP reviews the main stories in the daily newspapers and concludes:
'You're listening to *The Morning Report*. This is Channel 4 Radio News.' [0'.55"]

(Continued)

MP previews those stories that are still to come on the programme: the impending post office closures; the Amazon proposal to offer music downloads.
[REPEATED SOUND-GRAB FROM CNN REPORTER] Also money news, sport, and predictions of who will be our next great writers.
[MUSIC STAB] [0'.26"]

MP opens the story of the proposed closure of two and a half thousand post offices. 'Alan Burnett is a spokesperson for Help the Aged.'

- Sound-bite from Alan Burnett on the hardships that the closures will cause to the elderly.

MP announces that there will be an update on this story at twelve o'clock. [1'.00"]

MP delivers a brief news round-up:

1. The killing of a teenager in Newcastle.
2. The Food Standards Agency wants folic acid to be added to white and brown flour.

   - Sound-bite from Julian Hunt of the Food and Drink Federation

3. The NHS is suffering from problems with its computers.

   - Sound-bite from Jane Hendy, author of an article in the *British Medical Journal.*

4. The demise of the family dinner has been exaggerated.

   - Sound-bite from food writer, Sophie Grigson. [2'.00"]

MP: 'You're listening to *The Morning Report.* This is Channel 4 Radio News.'
[MUSIC STAB]

MP: 'On to foreign news now'.
The board of the World Bank is still unable to reach a decision over the conduct of its president, Paul Wolfowitz.

- Sound-bite from the former head of human relations at the World Bank.

'For other foreign news, here's Natasha Neguda.'
[MUSIC FADED IN UNDER] NN:

1. New French president, Nicolas Sarkozy, is expected to appoint a Prime Minister today.
2. Commuters in Argentina are angered by train delays:

   - Sound-actuality of shouting and rioting commuters.

3. A train has run between North and South Korea for the first time since the Korean War of fifty years ago.

4. A secret tunnel between the US and Mexico which was used by illegal immigrants has been filled with concrete by the US Border Patrol.

   • Sound-bite from Patrol spokesman.

5. An eighty year-old rift in the Russian Orthodox Church will be healed in Moscow today.

[MUSIC ENDS] [3'.00"]

Back-announcement from MP, who then begins a review of today's papers:

1. Scientists may have discovered the key to a cure for baldness (the *Daily Mirror*).
2. The Conservatives are embarrassed by a forum on David Cameron's website asking who is the sexiest female MP (the *Guardian*).
3. Municipal gardeners mistakenly mow a meadow full of rare wild flowers in Torbay (*The Times*).
4. An Oxford University student is fined for wrestling naked on the college croquet lawn (the *Daily Express*). [1'.00"]

[MUSIC STAB]

MP: 'On to money news now ... '

1. Amazon announces plans to introduce a music download store later this year. 'CNN's Maggie Lake has the details':

   • Recorded report from Maggie Lake.

2. Complaints against the water companies are at their highest level in thirteen years. 'I'm joined by our very own consumer watchdog, Kevin Murphy.' An informal interview with Kevin Murphy, who outlines the complaints and then says 'Let me bring in Dame Eve Buckland, who's chair of the Consumer Council for Water':

   • Sound-bite from Dame Eve Buckland.

   Murphy concludes his explanation.
   MP: 'OK, and what are the markets doing today?' Murphy gives a quick report on the stock markets and exchange rates. [3'.30"]

MP: The book industry has selected its list of twenty-five great British writers of the future. Cues an interview of John Howells of Waterstone's by *Morning Report*'s Kirsten Smith.

   • Interview with Howells (on a telephone acoustic) by Smith.

Back announcement by MP, then
[MUSIC STAB] [1'.50"]

(Continued)

MP introduces the sports news: 'It's Day 1 of the npower test between England and the West Indies ... Jules Warren joins me now from the sports desk.'

An informal interview with Warren, in which he observes that after a poor winter much is expected of the England team. The discussion then switches to the soccer championship play-offs and concludes with the story that just before the FA Cup Final against Manchester United, the dog of Chelsea manager, José Mourinho, seems to have gone missing.

MP (with a chuckle): 'Thank you, Jules, for joining us'. [2'.20"]

MP cues, 'before we go', a remark from *Donnie Darko* actor, Jake Gyllenhaal, who has arrived at the Cannes Film Festival.

- Sound-bite from Gyllenhaal observing that actors should lead tough lives instead of living it up at festivals.

A humorous back-announcement from MP, who signs off and is followed by a FINAL FLOURISH OF MUSIC [0'.38"]

TOTAL DURATION: 25'.35"

Language

In both programmes most of the words that are heard have been scripted, and broadcast script is neither conventional speech nor conventional writing. It is *spoken*, yet not – as speech commonly is – extemporised or addressed to people who are in the presence of the speaker. It is addressed to a distant and mass audience and is less colloquial, more premeditated and syntactically elaborate, than most conventional speech. It is *written*, yet not – as writing commonly is – addressed to readers but to listeners. It is premeditated and orderly, yet because (on radio) the listeners cannot see the speakers or their words, or what their words refer to, it is more colloquial and less syntactically elaborate than most conventional writing and may include redundancy in the form of repetition.

Many of these features are discernible in our samples. In both there are colloquial elisions – 'The government's going to confirm'; Prince Harry 'was told he couldn't serve in Iraq' (both TY); 'It's Thursday, the 17th of May, and I'm Melissa Preen'; 'the first test ... against the Windies' (both MR) – but not as many as we might hear in ordinary speech. For instance, 'senior officers've been ordered' is rendered more formally as 'senior officers have been ordered'. Because we can see neither the fixed, retrievable text of a newspaper nor even the words and numbers that can be flashed up on a television screen, statistics are made memorable by being expressed in round figures and repeated. In TY, the 'two and a half thousand post offices' are mentioned first in the headlines and then in the news bulletin, and overall the network has 'fourteen thousand branches' and is losing 'four million pounds a week'. It is highly unlikely that any of these figures is exact. MR also makes use of that phrase 'Coming up', which in seeking to surmount the limitations of media that exist in time rather than space, is peculiar to broadcasting. By running an eye down its preview column or flicking through its pages, the reader can see at a glance what her newspaper contains: in a news programme listeners, and to a large extent viewers, have to be told.

There are, nevertheless, some interesting differences between the language of MR and that of TY. MR's style is generally more vivid and punchy than TY's. The decision not to send Prince Harry to Iraq does not meet with mere 'criticism': there is a *backlash* against it. A large company which launches a new product becomes a *retail giant* that *weighs in*, and its routine competition with a rival is expressed as a *battle of the titans*. In all these expressions, which are typical of much news copy, there is a touch of hyperbole that makes one wonder for a moment why journalism has ever been thought of as the disinterested presentation of fact rather than a lucrative sale of half-truths.

The language of MR contains two features that can be found in writing, even if they are not wholly typical of it. First, it mimics the verbless headlines that the popular newspapers use in order to catch the eye of the potential buyer: 'No contest ...', 'Backlash against the decision ...' and 'Rising levels of water complaints', which is also something of a pun. (Puns are so widespread in journalistic copy as to suggest not so much careful inventiveness as a kind of subconscious verbal tic.) Since, as we shall see shortly, MR is offered to listeners as a programme that can also be consumed on a time-shift basis, this headlining is perhaps a hint that its aim is to challenge the press as well as TY – to persuade its listeners to stay with the convenient secondary medium of radio and skip the newspapers altogether.

The second feature of MR's language that is not unknown in writing is its use of the vivid present ('Post offices hear today'; 'Amazon weighs in') instead of either the future ('Post offices *will* hear') or the past ('Amazon *has* weighed in'). Yet it seems especially suited to speech, which can be heard only in a constantly-dissolving present, whereas the permanence of writing more rigidly defines its relation to those bygone or future events that it describes.

Unlike some of the headlines of MR, those of TY are all expressed in complete sentences. They are therefore longer and slightly more formal, and since extemporised speech is not easily divisible into conventional sentences, rather less colloquial than the headlines of MR. This gives TY a more leisurely and thoughtful approach to the news – one which seems closer than MR's to that of a broadsheet newspaper. It headlines only three stories compared to MR's six, plus weather forecast. It is true that MR's headlining is some 45 seconds longer than TY's, but even allowing for the fact that, unlike the latter's, many of them contain sound-grabs, this still represents a quicker delivery rate than TY's. On the other hand, the fully

(Continued)

rounded sentences of TY are elementary in structure and easily intelligible to the ear. Only one of them contains a subordinate clause and all the words are simple and concrete: 'The government's going to confirm ...'; 'Gordon Brown is going to take over ...'; senior officers 'have been ordered' after Prince Harry 'was told', and so on. The script is a well-crafted compromise of spoken and literary language.

Programme formats and styles of presentation

Perhaps the most striking difference between the two programmes is TY's recognition that many of its listeners are technologically conservative. It invites them to email if they wish and refers occasionally to blogs and websites, but its frequent time-checks, which serve as a kind of punctuation mechanism, rest on the assumption that most of its audience will be listening in real time and quite possibly in an intermittent fashion. This leads us to a paradox about TY: it is, as we have seen, in less of a hurry than its rival, yet much more sensitive to time as an organising principle and much more aware of the rate at which it passes.

MR, however, assumes an audience of technological sophisticates. It is delivered on a range of platforms and on the day of our sample was prefaced with what appears to be a routine announcement:

> This is Oneword Radio on D.A.B., Sky, Freeview and the Internet. ... We've thirty minutes of the latest news, courtesy of Channel 4 Radio, in *The Morning Report*. To download your own copy, visit the Channel 4 website at channel4radio.com

This raises a couple of paradoxes about MR. The first is an immediate tension between the up-to-dateness of its news and the possibility of its delayed consumption, which is doubtless the reason why there are no time-checks on the programme. And the second paradox is that if MR is downloaded and then played through ear-phones, there is perhaps a greater likelihood that it will be listened to closely and in its entirety – something of a reversion to pre-televisual habits after decades of distracted and intermittent listening to transistor sets and car radios.

The overall style of TY is more sedate than that of MR. Its format resembles a set of Chinese boxes. Between them the two presenters frame the entire programme: first the news bulletin, within which the newsreader in turn frames its different correspondents, then the various items featuring either the presenters' own interviewees or other correspondents, who in turn frame *their* interviewees and incorporate their own snatches of actuality. The format lends a sense of depth and perspective, suggests a careful process of mediation between the site of the news and its ultimate presentation to the listener. While the programme carries fewer stories than MR, they are more fully treated and posit an audience with more time and curiosity. On the other hand, intermittent listening is also allowed for by the fact that, as we mentioned earlier, certain of the items are repeated over its three-hour duration. From the top to the bottom of each hour the focus is on the 'harder' news, either the big and breaking stories or, like the piece on the Algerian elections, items of a certain import even if they are not included in the news bulletin. Then at the bottom of the hour and ascending back to the top, the programme turns towards the more routinised material: sport, financial news, some ongoing 'background' items, 'Yesterday in Parliament', 'Thought for the Day' and the weather forecast.

MR conveys its news with much more urgency, an awareness that many of its listeners are in a hurry. Indeed, it does so all at once: the headlines embrace all the big stories, and with their sound-grabs are in themselves a self-contained programme lasting a minute and a quarter. While the possibility of downloading MR for delayed consumption means that there are no time-checks, its implied listener is busy, energetic, technologically adept – and younger rather than older.

Thanks mainly to its single presenter, Melissa Preen, the programme also seems to be more homogeneous than TY. Preen reads the news, introduces all the items and conducts almost all the interviews, which means that although the programme features many other voices, we hear more of her than of anybody else. Even in an item like the factional violence in Gaza, with its colourful location report from a Palestinian journalist, some 40 per cent is taken up with Preen's contextualisation. In TY, John Humphrys and Carolyn Quinn create an overall continuity, but there are two of them, they are seldom heard at the same time, and there is also a sense that the news bulletin, read in our sample by Harriet Cass, is sharply demarcated from the rest of the programme. But in MR, Preen is a continuous, presiding presence who conveys a mixture of both authority and enthusiasm. It is noticeable, for instance, that she *speaks* her words of welcome at the beginning of the programme, but when the music plays in she *shouts* the news headlines.

As we have already suggested, MR is more pacey and informative, less discursive and reflective, than TY – and it is more compendious. In half an hour it contains over twice as many news items, however fleetingly some of them are treated. If TY bases its claim to be quality news on the way in which it mediates its material, MR's rests on the *amount* of material it provides. Its sound-bites from the people who are in the news are thrown straight at the listener without any audible questions from an interviewer, so that such perspective as is provided is mostly an implicit matter of careful editing. Yet this is not to suggest that there are *no* explicit attempts to create perspective, and here the comparison with TY is illuminating. TY relies heavily on 'correspondents' who 'report', and their reports are invariably read. Fewer correspondents are heard in MR, and they are never referred to by this name, nor do they read, but are interviewed by the presenter and reply in an extempore way.

This is apparent in two of the items from our sample, the Gordon Brown story and the story about complaints against the water companies. For the

(Continued)

former, 'our reporter in Westminster' is Peter Murphy, with a chatty and chuckly radio persona. Of the long period of transition between Tony Blair's leadership and Gordon Brown's he observes, 'I'm not sure how we're going to get through it without dying of boredom' – a remark which could not be imagined from a BBC correspondent – and he adds: 'It's democracy, Mel, but not as we know it.' He also offers the worldly, even cynical view that while the transition is a proper aspect of parliamentary democracy, it is well known that in practice people vote for leaders rather than parties, and that the system is in effect presidential. In an equally chatty way, he goes on to explain the rather different system for electing the deputy leader.

In the story about the water companies, Preen introduces 'our very own consumer watchdog, Kevin Murphy', who responds as follows: 'Morning, Mel. We're not very happy about our water, are we? [PAUSE] Or maybe that's a generalisation. This report comes from the Consumer Council for Water. What it says is, etc'. Again the tone is chatty and interpersonal, including a direct address to the presenter, who is 'Mel' not 'Melissa', and the phrase 'are we?', which, in inviting agreement, reflects a heightened consciousness of those who are listening. (Later, Jules Warren from the sports desk adopts the same style: 'a real winter of discontent, wasn't it?') Murphy's manner can perhaps be described as informally informative. He cues a sound-grab with the remark, 'To explain this, let me bring in Dame Eve Buckland, who's chair etc.', and characterises the consumers' complaints as 'moans and groans'. Then Preen asks him what's happening on the markets and he responds 'Let's have a look', as though improvising an answer to a question that was not wholly expected. Finally, it is worth reminding ourselves that Murphy is introduced as a consumer watchdog, not an economics correspondent, and his title is perhaps a further indication that his job is to represent the interests of the listener and not parade a kind of disinterested expertise.

What these interviews illustrate is a keenness on the part of the programme makers to avoid that didacticism that is still very much the hallmark of the public service-oriented BBC. They seem to be conscious of the modern orthodoxy that to be didactic is to be patronising, and the aim is therefore to teach by stealth. But in TY only the exchanges between the presenters and the sports correspondents approach this level of informality, perhaps because in the BBC, if not elsewhere, sport is not normally equated with 'serious' news.

Sound resources

While every news medium has its own means of providing variety and stimulus, radio's would appear to be more limited than those of its visual rivals (Crisell 1994: 104–6). Newspapers can offer typographical variations, a range of photographs, drawings and graphics and distinctive forms of layout. Television can match these pictorial resources and supply moving images as well as still ones – of any object, whether animate or inanimate, audible or silent. Radio only has forms of sound. These may afford considerable variety: different voices, different accents, different acoustics and non-verbal sound. But many phenomena are soundless and many sounds are not easily identifiable without words to accompany them (Crisell 1994: 47–8). Hence on the radio not only does the news copy itself consist of words, so, too, does most of the actuality that it frames. To put it another way, voices on the radio supply not only the *text* (those of the newsreaders, interviewers and correspondents) but much of the *illustration* (those of the people 'in the news': the interviewees, politicians, experts, eye-witnesses, and so on). We might therefore regard radio words as being both 'typographic' and 'photographic' (Crisell 1994: 106).

That said, sound is exploited very successfully in both our programmes and especially in MR. The sound-grabs in its headlines extend from the genteel Scots of Gordon Brown and the English accent of Prince Harry to the strident American twang of the CNN reporter and the gentler burr of Jake Gyllenhaal. Announced and back-announced by Melissa Preen in what is known as 'received pronunciation', the sequence could be described as an acoustic front page. It is at once a trailer for the rest of the programme and a complete bulletin in itself. The variety of voices, accents and acoustics, some heard for a minute or more and some just in sound-grabs, is maintained throughout the programme, but it is by no means lacking in TY. In a format which we described as resembling a nest of Chinese boxes, the presenter John Humphrys frames the newsreader Harriet Cass, who in the second news item, for instance, frames political correspondent Mark Sanders, who frames the recorded remarks of Labour leadership candidate John McDonnell. John Humphrys' interview with Major General Cordingley about Prince Harry is prefaced by five military blogs which are read out in five different voices, and in the following four-minute report on the Labour leadership issue, in which correspondent Ian Watson is framed by Carolyn Quinn, there are also five different sound-grabs. But another four-minute report, Ian Pannell's on the Algerian general election, contains even more atmosphere and variety. Beginning with a vivid description of central Algiers over a bed of actuality which includes the sound of electioneering, it contains sound-bites from members of two different Islamist political parties, a former Prime Minister and the US ambassador to Algeria, as well as the sound-track from an internet video and the noise of exploding bombs.

Yet there is a sense, however subtle, that sound in TY has a rather different role from that in MR. Its use is never gratuitous, it always exists to support or illustrate an endeavour which is primarily verbal and discursive. Even the considerable 'atmos' of the Algerian report – the street noises of the city and the video sound-track – is firmly contextualised by the reporter's account. In contrast, MR's minimal framing of many of the sound-grabs, however verbal they are in themselves, combines with the idents and music stabs to suggest something of a fascination with sound *per se*, a programme whose impulse is primarily iconic and illustrative.

(Continued)

Mention of music stabs brings us to that other great sound resource which we have so far ignored: music. We can describe music as abstract in the sense that unlike most other sounds it does not stand for something we can ordinarily see: it is non-representational and does not need, though it may benefit from, verbal identification. Nevertheless, there is a potential difficulty about using music in association with the news. Music is an organisation of sounds that is mainly intended both to express and appeal to the emotions, whereas news is regarded as an intellectual and dispassionate matter that requires balance and judgement. Hence such music as we hear in news programmes is likely to express emotion that will colour our judgement only in an oblique and fairly innocuous way. It will evoke not joy or sadness or yearning, but a state of portentousness or urgency – the latter often expressed in a 'busy' staccato melody that is probably intended to remind us of the sound of those traditional newsroom symbols, the typewriter and the teleprinter. Moreover, it still seems to be true that the more serious the news programme, the less likely it is to include music of any kind. This is true of TY, but MR's use of music is quite lavish. Its theme tune, taken from Channel 4's much lauded television news programme and thus an interesting example of cross-media branding, opens and closes the programme, and there are stabs and music-beds at frequent intervals throughout. The mood they evoke is a fairly typical one of bustle and importance, and the changes of rhythm and pace that they mark between one item and the next are expressed on TY by nothing more than presenters' time-checks.

Choice and prioritisation of news items

We asserted that MR covers twice as many news items as TY because its main preoccupation is to *report* while TY's is to *discuss*. But like many such assertions, its overall usefulness comes at the expense of particular truths. There are one or two important stories in TY that MR overlooks: the stem-cell research announcement, the policy report on Iraq, BT's plans to offer television via broadband internet connections. Nevertheless; there is a general agreement about what constitute the main stories of the day: TY's headlines are (1) the post offices (2) Gordon Brown (3) Prince Harry; MR's are (1) Gordon Brown (2) Prince Harry (3) the post offices. However, their respective subsequent treatments of these stories are illuminating. TY's news bulletin leads with the story about the post offices (which includes a correspondent's report), moves on to Gordon Brown (news copy, together with correspondent's report, a location sound-bite and some remarks on the related story of the contest for the deputy leadership), but then interpolates the story about Madeleine McCann before turning to Prince Harry (news copy plus correspondent's report). However, Prince Harry is the theme of the first major item after the bulletin, which consists of readings of the military blogs and then an interview with Major General Cordingley, and runs to a full five minutes. Having featured the Prince Harry story three times in 14 minutes, only then does the programme turn back to Gordon Brown.

After Melissa Preen delivers the headlines, MR turns straight to the Gordon Brown story (news copy, sound-bite from Brown and interview with Peter Murphy, including some discussion of the deputy leadership contest). Prince Harry comes next and with two sound-bites but runs for only a minute, and the story about the post offices is not heard of again until the trailer for up-coming items that occurs halfway through the programme. It is then featured immediately afterwards with a sound-bite, but also lasts only a minute.

What can be inferred from these differences? More importance seems to be attached to post offices and Prince Harry in TY than in MR: in the sequence that follows its news bulletin, the prince takes precedence even over the Prime Minister-in-waiting. But while importance is one factor in determining the sequence of stories in a time-based medium like radio, what might be termed 'listenability' is another. In the spatial medium of a newspaper, the reader can make her own selection of stories: she can decide not only which to read but in what order to read them. In a temporal medium the selection has to be made on the listener's behalf, and to make the experience more stimulating certain variations of mood and seriousness might be introduced (Crisell 1994: 85–6).

With this caveat in mind, we might nevertheless form the tentative conclusion that TY's focus on a story about the royalty implies a listenership that is older, or at least more conservative, than that of MR. We can perhaps be more confident in forming it with respect to the post office story. In MR it is only the third headline and is returned to well down the programme and long after all the other main stories have been covered. A further clue lies in the *way* it is covered – by means of an interview with a spokesperson from Help the Aged. Younger people send emails instead of letters and buy their stamps online rather than over a post office counter. They are more flexible and technologically more adept. Older people are less mobile, more technophobic, have to go out to collect their pensions and need personal service and the support of the wider community: the reduction in the number of post offices will affect them far more than it will affect the young.

There is other evidence that MR is pitching to a younger listenership. One of its big stories, which is not covered at all by TY, is the plan by Amazon to offer music downloads. The story is both headlined and trailed before being heard in full and its associated sound-grab is played no less than three times. The world of ambient music, downloads, MP3s and iPods is unmistakably the world of the young. Nevertheless, the other hi-tech story of the day, BT's plan to offer broadband television, is exclusive to TY and, as the subject of a three-minute package, is conceivably an effort to broaden its audience and counter the threat posed by its rival. But *Donnie Darko* provides further evidence of MR's youthful ambitions. Though headlined,

(Continued)

the story is little more than a 20-second sound-grab at the very end of the programme, and its inclusion will mystify anyone of middle years or older. *Donnie Darko* (2001) was a sci-fi film whose eponymous hero, played by Jake Gyllenhaal, is plagued by visions of a human-sized rabbit and embarks on a life of crime. Perhaps not surprisingly, the film was a flop on its release in the USA but found strong DVD sales and is now a cult classic. It seems fair to suggest that only the young would be generous and imaginative enough to make a cult out of anything involving a giant, humanoid rabbit.

Conclusions

It would be relatively easy to obtain demographic evidence about the character of the audiences for TY and MR: indeed, a great deal already exists in respect of the former and had it survived, would no doubt have been swiftly compiled for the latter. But here we have set ourselves a rather harder task. When broadcasters of any kind, whether journalists, dramatists or comedy writers, set out to make a programme they do so with a particular audience in mind, and in this analysis we have sought to infer, purely from 'what comes out of the loudspeaker', the kind of listeners these programmes were aiming at. Our purpose in doing so was to achieve a better understanding of radio journalism as a creative process, to explore the different ways in which a body of news and current affairs may be conveyed through a medium that is blind and evanescent and consumed (often distractedly) by a distant and atomised mass audience.

There is no doubt that the audiences for these programmes *are* different, but on the evidence to which we have restricted ourselves, their respective identities are quite hard to determine. It is possible to perceive the difference as *cultural* or *intellectual*. We have suggested that despite its acoustic variety and technical dexterities, TY is at heart verbal and analytical. The relative fewness of the items it covers suggests a programme that is even more concerned to reflect on what it perceives as significant news than to capture all the news there is. This is radio journalism which is as analogous as possible to the broadsheet newspaper. In contrast, the music stabs and IDs of MR, along with the bittier, more superficial treatment of its items, implies a more populist approach to the news. Yet to describe MR as populist in an era when much the greater part of radio news is heard only in the form of 90-second 'capsules' is, to say the least, severe: the overall length of the programme and the quantity and range of its items demand that it be characterised in another way. Indeed, MR could be seen as a programme that tries to take a populist or tabloid format and push it upmarket.

Another way of perceiving the difference, one which we have already inclined to, is *generational*. TY would appear to be targeting an older audience, MR a younger one. There is a certain ambiguity in TY's approach: its treatment of news stories is thoughtful and protracted, which might suggest listeners who are retired and have time on their hands, yet the frequency of its time-checks, the overall length of the programme and the repetition of many of the items also suggest busy and sometimes distracted listeners, many of whom will be driving to work. Perhaps the strongest evidence that its putative audience is older is the presumption, expressed in the time-checks, that it is listening in real time and therefore technologically conservative. Finally, TY affords rather more prominence to stories that seem to appeal to a rather older listenership.

In contrast, the number and brevity of news items on MR suggest a restless and energetic audience that is likely to be younger. The less formal, less didactic style will also appeal to more youthful listeners, as will the items on aspects of popular culture (the Amazon downloads and *Donnie Darko* both feature in the headlines) and the sprinkling of 'human interest' and lighter stories – family dinners, Argentinian commuters, the sexiest female MP, the errant municipal gardeners, future British writers and the naked student wrestler.

We might conclude by returning to Dorothy Byrne's attack on TY in order to assess how accurate it is and whether the faults she alleges against it are remedied by MR. However pejorative the terminology about middle-aged people from Bournemouth, cashmere twinsets and bowling clubs, the essence of her charge is that the programme appeals to the maturer and more reflective members of the community. The producers of TY might plead guilty but assert that the programme is none the worse for it. By suggesting that serious-mindedness is a characteristic of the older and white members of the middle class, Byrne risks offending other social, ethnic and generational groups, among whom this quality is not, apparently, to be found.

For Byrne's further charge that despite superficial hostilities both interviewers and interviewees are members of the same cosy oligarchy, we have little evidence either way. Humphrys' interview of Major General Cordingley is polite and restrained, but the questions are also incisive: he does not shrink from making the point that the Ministry of Defence appears to be setting a higher value on Prince Harry's life than on those of his colleagues. In reply, Cordingley observes that Harry's presence in Iraq would expose his close colleagues to even greater danger than they would otherwise encounter, and that in any case the media are largely responsible for the problem by constantly publicising the prince's whereabouts. Whether Humphrys and Cordingley are friends, enemies or strangers, it is difficult to envisage what other form or tone a professionally conducted interview could take.

Finally, Byrne affirms that in programmes like MR she wishes to 'appeal to everybody'. Does she succeed? Not, we would suggest, on the evidence of this edition of the programme. The number and range of stories it covers are far larger than those featured in the half-hour excerpt from TY, but they are not necessarily of more universal interest. There are certainly gestures towards younger enthusiasms than are catered for on TY, but there is nothing

(Continued)

on, for instance, race or gender issues that might widen the programme's social as well as generational appeal. Yet by showing the various capabilities of radio journalism even within two 'quality' news programmes that are aimed at broadly similar audiences, our analysis has illuminated an important purpose of this book.

As if to underline the uncertainties lying in wait for 4 Digital, when Oneword closed down, so did *The Morning Report*. On its website, a short statement promised more and better things to come. 'That's it from the *Morning Report* for the time being. We'll be working on the launch of three Channel 4 radio stations, so Channel 4 Radio News will be back next year'. (Channel 4, 2008).

Then, as if to prove correct our earlier point about the uncertainty of institutional study in a fast-moving industry, Channel Four announced in October 2008 that it was abandoning its ambition to launch into radio. Just as John Humphrys had suggested might be the case, another challenger to *Today* has come and gone.

8

READ ALL ABOUT IT: A CRITICAL BIBLIOGRAPHY

Making sense of the field

Since this book seeks to synthesise two distinct subjects, radio and journalism, our review of the critical literature, which is also in effect a recommendation of further reading, will progress along a spectrum from one subject to the other. We will begin with books that deal with radio in the broadest sense, then move to those that focus on radio journalism, and finally consider works whose scope is journalism in general. Their inclusion is justified by the fact that certain matters are of concern to all journalists, irrespective of whether they are working in radio, television, newspapers, magazines or the Internet. The bibliographical field could, of course, have been surveyed in a number of other ways, and we accept that our categories are to some extent arbitrary and distinguish between certain writings whose subjects at least partly overlap. But sense must be made of it somehow, and our aim is to give aspiring radio journalists a logical perspective on the relevant literature and a way of organising their studies.

We begin, then, with the radio medium – a phenomenon which must, however, be set in a number of contexts. One is its relationship to the other mass media, within which its fortunes, and to a large extent its institutions, are closely bound up with those of television. The two media are collectively characterised as 'broadcasting'. Then there are the social contexts – political, economic and cultural – of all the mass media. And finally, in order to understand radio more clearly, we need to have some knowledge of both its history and present situation. We begin this section of our critical review with some broad histories of the mass media, followed by a look at works that focus on contemporary themes, issues and debates that surround the media or are treated by them. We move to more specific histories first of broadcasting and then radio, followed by studies of individual radio programmes, and finally to writing that describes important contemporary developments within the medium.

Histories of the mass media, histories of broadcasting, histories of radio

Briggs and Burke (2002) provide a highly readable general history of the mass media from the invention of printing to the arrival of the internet. Williams (1998) writes another of similarly broad scope, though as suggested by his title – *Get Me a Murder a Day!* – he is mainly preoccupied with the journalistic aspects of the media. Chapman (2005) offers an ambitious comparative history which begins somewhat arbitrarily with the French Revolution in 1789. Though richly detailed, it includes particular insights into the historical evolution of journalism, not least in respect of radio. Curran and Seaton (2003) start their history even later, in the nineteenth century, and restrict themselves to a political approach to the press and broadcasting; while of a narrower scope still, though a luminous and stylish read, is Seymour-Ure (1996). Both Stokes and Reading (1999) and Briggs and Cobley (2002) provide near-contemporary surveys of the mass media, of their typical pre-occupations and of the debates that surround them.

Among the specialised histories of broadcasting, the standard work is by Asa Briggs (1995a, 1995b, 1970, 1979, 1995c). Briggs's role as the BBC's official historian gave him generous access to both internal documents and key personnel, and each of his volumes contains an astonishing wealth of detail. Yet the result is for the most part a history of the BBC; commercial broadcasting, especially before the 1970s, gets little attention and seems mostly to be viewed from the perspective of the corporation. An introductory account that seeks to embrace the whole field is Crisell (2002), while one that focuses on radio is Street (2002). Unusually, Regal (2005) traces a history of radio from an initially technological perspective, turning his attention in the second half of the book to other influences on radio programming in the United States, including politics and ideology. Histories of particular radio stations and networks are all too rare, especially of those that specialise in news and speech programming, but fortunately one now exists. Having availed himself of recently improved access to the BBC archives at Caversham Park, David Hendy, a former producer of *Analysis* and *The World Tonight*, has written *Life on Air* (2007), a fascinating and insightful history of Radio 4. Summaries of notable past news programmes can be found in Donovan (1992), who has also written a history of that flagship of BBC radio journalism, the *Today* programme (Donovan, 1997). A near-contemporary survey of radio institutions and practices can be found in

Hendy (2002b). This well-researched book, *Radio in the Global Age*, reviews a range of issues that confront the medium at the turn of the century.

Studies of the radio medium

Having reviewed those books that consider radio within its various contexts, we now move to those that seek to theorise the medium by approaching it in a more abstract way. What is fascinating is that many of the best of these focus not on radio news but radio *drama*, though some adopt a holistic view. In essence, they pose the question: What are the capabilities of a blind medium whose constantly dissolving messages are heard by distant listeners located within their own spaces and using it mostly as a background to other activities? Are its evident limitations in some sense also advantages? Most theorists have tried to show that they are. Aside from what he sees as its idiosyncratic sequences of talk-and-music, Crisell (1994) seeks to identify radio's distinctive character by comparing its genres with their counterparts in press, television and other media. His *Understanding Radio* was perhaps the first general academic study of the medium, but has since been followed by a wealth of material. Shingler and Wieringa (1998) tackle radio using a range of theoretical and critical methods, while Barnard (2000) focuses on 'fictive' forms of content – news, talk and music – as well as on industry practices.

McLuhan's trail-blazing discussion in 1964 of the 'global village' (2001) was an attempt to theorise the media that included radio in its analysis. Yet in comparison to the number of texts that discuss other mass media, we mentioned earlier the dearth of such inclusive approaches. An interesting example of the application of academic rigour to other media is Ferguson (2000), which considers the representation of race. Fortunately, though, mass media theory often lends itself to reinterpretation within radio contexts and many of the more general works are summarised and explained in McQuail's highly practical digest of *Mass Communication Theory* (2005). This book is regularly updated and the breadth and clarity of its discussion of media theory makes it an invaluable reference point. Even more accessible, although almost amounting to an encyclopaedia, is Watson and Hill's dictionary (2000) of the main terms and paradigms of media studies.

Among the most practical in their approach are those academic texts that concentrate on discourse analysis. Fairclough's work, including *Language and Power* (1989) and *Media Discourse* (1995), is a good example. Also worthy of note is Fowler (1991). Hutchby (2005, 2006) focuses more closely on radio, while the eminent scholar Paddy Scannell has adopted a number of distinctive approaches to the sound medium. In Scannell (1991) he analyses the peculiar features of talk that is shaped by the exigencies of broadcasting, and in Scannell (1996) he not only builds on this approach but explores radio and television in terms of the seriality of their content and the way that they synthesise the historical and public worlds, on the one hand, with the audience's a-historical, private worlds, on the other.

Studies of broadcast journalism, studies of radio journalism

From a theoretical consideration of radio in general, it is logical to move to a review of work that examines the kinds of *journalism* radio can do. We begin with a look at studies of its journalistic techniques and practices before moving to those that approach sound journalism through the various publics it seeks to address. Among the most compendious studies of *broadcast* journalism – not just radio but television – is Boyd (2001). This has long been a standard text and offers a pragmatic, businesslike approach to journalism in both media. *Radio Production*, by former BBC instructor Robert McLeish (2005), is the latest edition of what was among the earliest studies of *radio* journalism. But as the title indicates, it also covers other forms of radio expertise and thus contains much information that the aspiring journalist will find superfluous. Both Boyd and McLeish now face competition from *The Broadcast Journalism Handbook* (Hudson and Rowlands 2007), with its modern and attractive layout, its wealth of interviews and photographs of working journalists, and its tri-media approach. A DVD accompanies the book and a website promises to be a useful supplement to it. The foreword by BJTC Accreditations Secretary, Steve Harris, is a strong endorsement of the book, one which broadcast journalism courses across the land will need to take note of.

In *International Radio Journalism*, Tim Crook (1998) combines a number of historical and theoretical perspectives with solid practical instruction based on extensive first-hand experience. Crook was a respected IRN reporter, he is 'time-served' in the true sense of the cliché, and he knows his subject. As well as practical advice, he supplies a history of IRN and engages in detail with aspects of the international news agenda. He also makes comparisons between journalistic practices in various parts of the world, some of which differ considerably. Many studies of broadcast journalism techniques are written for specific markets and a good example is Phillips and Lindgren (2002), which focuses on Australia.

Significant among the manuals of its day was Chantler and Harris (1992), which grew from a highly respected book by the late Linda Gage and focused on journalism in *local* radio. An early radio handbook was Wilby and Conroy (1994), which was updated by Fleming (2002) with a wealth of new material, but unfortunately at the expense of some of the old.

Improving on an established work is sometimes only possible by increasing rather than decreasing the word count. Starkey (2004b) offers a synthesis of theoretical and practical perspectives on different radio forms, including the speech package, magazine and documentary genres. Though not intended to cover newsroom practice, it explains to students how they can subject both radio broadcasts and their own coursework to useful critical analysis. Providing valuable insights into a principal source of audio material, Bell and van Leeuwen (1994) concentrate on interviewing in radio and television, and Goody (1978) explores the often complex relationships between interviewer and interviewee. An interesting specialised guide to radio interviewing is provided by Beaman (2000). This has long been a favourite text for courses in both radio journalism and more general media production. There are several radio anthologies on the market which accommodate a range of material and perspectives. Among them, Crisell (2004a) explores the various social and ethnic groups that the medium targets in different parts of the world, while Mitchell (2001) focuses on the relationship between radio and women.

Broadcast journalism: personal memoirs and perspectives

Of considerable interest, if usually lacking the detailed referencing of more academic works, are the many accounts of their craft written by practitioners. Some of these are highly personalised, such as Kate Adie's autobiography (2002), which offers some interesting insight into national, local and World Service radio as well as the television context within which she later rose to fame. Jon Snow (2004) reflects at length on his career at LBC before he switched to television, and Greg Dyke (2004), while understandably not missing an opportunity to present his own uninterrupted account of the Gilligan Affair, provides an illuminating commentary on more general practices at the BBC during his tenure as Director General. Some personal accounts are not quite so egocentric as the conventional autobiography leads us to expect. Steve Wright's *Just Keep Talking* (1997) is an interesting survey of radio and television interviewers, while Pilger (1998) offers a diet of journalistic practice mixed with well-reasoned polemic. These personal accounts often lack the objectivity of academic studies since the authors have been encouraged to write from a personal perspective, but they act as very useful sources of recalled facts and first-hand impressions.

The big issues: books that theorise journalism

In our final category we move from journalism on the radio to journalism in general, to a consideration of a corpus of knowledge that all journalists ought to possess and issues that they should think about. The big, thorny problems of balance and bias in news reportage are addressed by Starkey (2007), while Franklin (1997) offers a critical appraisal of news and media in general and of the impact of populism in particular. Street (2001) explores the relationship between reportage and democracy and Kuhn and Neveu (2002) present a collection of articles on political journalism. The economic, political and regulatory environment of both press and broadcast journalism in the UK is explored by McNair (2008), and everything that journalists should know about media law can be found in Welsh, Greenwood and Banks (2005). Practitioner perspectives can be useful here, too. In *My Trade* (2004), the political journalist and radio and television presenter Andrew Marr provides another history of journalism, in a style described as 'rollicking' by the former *Times* editor, Sir Harold Evans.

There is no shortage of general academic theorising about journalistic practice, and in particular news, but it is most frequently contextualised within the print media. As we noted in Chapter 6 much of it focuses on ethical issues, and a range of perspectives can be found in Alia (2004), Belsey and Chadwick (1992), Fink (1988), Frost (2000), Goodwin and Smith (1994) and Sanders (2003). Some texts provide interesting, if now somewhat historical, ethnographic accounts of journalistic practice, such as Burns (1977), while others provide insights into institutional ways of working (Born 2005) and the assumptions made by practitioners when performing routine tasks (Schlesinger 1987).

Not all such theorisings have been well received by the practitioners. In the late 1970s and early 1980s, the *Bad News* series from the Glasgow University Media Group (1976, 1980, 1982) provoked a highly critical reaction, mostly from television journalists. For those struggling with competing perspectives on ethics, some clarity is afforded by the codes of conduct set out by such regulatory and self-regulatory bodies as the BBC (2005), Ofcom (2005) and the NUJ (2004).

A number of authors, such as Harrison (2006), have concerned themselves with the nature of news – what it is and how it is constructed. Among them are Sheridan Burns (2002) and Wilson (1996), who both use the title *Understanding Journalism*. In trying to define journalistic practice, Koch (1990) recognises the importance of commercial forces, a context within which journalism and journalists are not always perceived to be positive influences. Some academics rationalise news as entirely market-driven, which is considered by McManus (1994) to disadvantage the citizen, while Capella and Jamieson (1997) identify as equally damaging the 'spiral of cynicism' that some journalists create. Many years ago the celebrated media theorist, Stuart Hall (1974), raised a number of epistemological issues around journalistic representation, and the prolific Brian McNair (2000) has articulated an insightful review of the relationship between journalism and democracy.

Allan (2004) discusses several other issues in journalism, ranging from ideological influences and audiences, through gender, populism and racism, to the post-9/11 world and Iraq. His edited collection (2005a) presents a number of considered perspectives from a group of loosely-connected authors in a way that allows some quite distinctive issues and approaches to be included with the more mainstream ones. Finally, the compendious *Key Concepts in Journalism Studies*, by Franklin et al. (2005), includes a useful list of contents to aid structured reading for those who are not satisfied by a merely random acquaintance with the subject.

Academic journals about the mass media

There are a number of periodicals that are of relevance to students and practitioners of radio journalism. Perhaps the handiest and, on a day-to-day basis, the most useful is the *Media Guardian*, a weekly supplement of the *Guardian* newspaper that provides news and analysis of contemporary developments in all the mass media. Among academic journals, we can distinguish those that specialise in the mass media, those that specialise in radio, and those that specialise in journalism. Mass-media journals are of only sporadic relevance to the practitioner, but a look through the index of their articles can yield some nuggets. We will mention just four of the most notable journals.

Media, Culture and Society aims to provide a major international forum for the presentation of research and discussion on the media, including the newer information and communication technologies, and to do so within their political, economic, cultural and historical contexts. Of an international scope, the *European Journal of Communication* seeks to publish the best communication research and scholarship. It promotes dialogue on key issues across disciplinary and national boundaries, and offers a comprehensive diet of the best empirical and conceptual work. The *Historical Journal of Film, Radio and Television* is an interdisciplinary journal concerned with the evidence provided by the mass media for historians and social scientists, and with the impact of mass communications on the political and social history of the twentieth century. Finally, *Convergence* explores issues in the context of new media and some of these, such as the impact that new media will have on public service broadcasting, are of interest and relevance to students of journalism.

Academic journals about radio

The two leading scholarly journals which specialise in sound broadcasting are the *Journal of Radio Studies* and the *Radio Journal*, but as with those that cover all the mass media, not everything they contain is of interest to the journalist, and their article indexes will repay investigation. The former carries interdisciplinary inquiries into radio's historical and contemporary subject matter, though its focus has been almost wholly North American. The latter is of more recent origin, more consciously international in scope, and concerned with theory formation and research into the production, reception, texts and contexts of radio and other audio media.

Academic journals about journalism

Finally, there are four notable academic periodicals whose subject is journalism. The *British Journalism Review* monitors the media and is intended as a forum of analysis and debate. It is targeted at print, broadcast and online journalists, media academics and students, and 'anyone who cares about communication'. *Journalism Studies* provides an international forum for the critical discussion and study of journalism as a subject of academic inquiry, an arena of professional practice and an educational discipline. *Journalism Practice* is a new scholarly, international and multidisciplinary periodical that aims to afford opportunities for reflective, critical and research-based studies focused on the professional practice of journalism. *Journalism: Theory, Practice, Criticism* is also international and interdisciplinary in its approach. It seeks to develop social, economic, political and cultural understandings of journalism and to track current developments and historical changes in the field.

Journal articles about radio journalism

Let us briefly focus on the small but growing number of papers published in academic journals which concern themselves with radio journalism. As we noted in Chapter 6, the theorising of radio is itself a minority sport among academics and quite disproportionate to the importance of the medium in the everyday lives of many. Given its 100-year history, the relative neglect of radio by the academic community, and of radio journalism in particular, is all but incomprehensible. In 'The need for radio theory in the digital age', Jo Tacchi (2000) was among the first to argue for the development of the coherent field that was then emerging as 'radio studies', reviving interest in an old medium that had rarely been noticed by academics. Yet Tacchi also noted a number of new developments happening at the time, such as the formation of the Radio Studies Network, which has subsequently grown in size and importance.

Journal articles are often very specialised in focus, some giving detailed insights into the history of radio journalism. For example, Hogarth (2001) examines a number of radio documentaries in 'The other documentary tradition: early radio documentaries in Canada'. Some also offer insights into the development of specific genres. For instance, Madsen (2006: 189) compares the renaissance in the art of documentary and 'feature' production which occurred from the late 1960s, especially within the major public broadcasters of Europe, with other media forms, including *cinéma-vérité*. Other articles mark milestones in the development or decline of particular phenomena, some of them hugely significant in their own contexts. For example, McCleneghan (2006) marks the passing of local newscasts in the south-western states of the USA.

Certain papers provide an insight into the ways in which audiences access radio journalism. Mesbah (2006) considers 'The impact of linear versus non-linear listening to radio news on recall and comprehension'. Others foreground particular issues arising from quite specific contexts, offering conclusions which may or may not be generalisable to other contexts or to the radio industry as a whole. Brabazon (2002), for example, briefly considers the role of talk radio in Australian public controversies, including the 2000 Sydney Olympics – and the discussion is interesting in itself as well as a potential guide to how future policy decisions may impact on broadcasters and audiences alike.

A key focus within this modest but growing body of literature is Clayman (2004), which considers how public interaction through the media affects journalism, democratic processes and public discourse. The paper focuses on news interviews, news conferences and various media genres – including radio phone-in shows – which involve audience participation. Turner (2000: 247) argues that in the late 1980s deregulation in Australian commercial radio encouraged a narrowing of the range of programming formats and the rise of opinionated talk-show hosts paying scant regard to notions of objectivity, and in so doing failed to protect the public interest. Razafimbelo-Harisoa (2005) provides a detailed study of radio broadcasting in Madagascar, a country with 200 private local stations and more than 15 regional stations of Malagasy National Radio. There is an abundance of news coverage and news magazine programmes dealing with political affairs in the country, which is notable for the relative freedom of broadcasters, but also an increasing trend for religious broadcasters and a new generation of politicians to subvert radio for propaganda purposes. Finally, McCleneghan and Sean-Ragland (2002) examine the role of other media in determining the outcome of municipal elections in those Mexican communities that lack their own television stations.

Balance in political coverage is a prime concern. Each of the following examples has an obvious and direct relevance to current industry practice. Weza (2002) examines the operations of the Media Monitoring Project which, over a single week in 2002, recorded content, including radio, television and print journalism, in Zimbabwe. Hazel (2001) focuses on the findings of two key studies of coverage of the separatist debate in Quebec by the Canadian Broadcasting Corporation/Société Radio-Canada, and finds that long-standing perceptions of bias are ill-founded. Finally, Hall and Joseph (2002) discuss the impact of exposure on political talk radio on attributions about the outcome of the 1996 American presidential election.

Some useful websites

We conclude this chapter with a list of websites that are available at the time of going to press and in various ways of interest to the aspiring radio journalist:

BBC – home page of the BBC's domestic services. http://www.bbc.co.uk

BBC documentary series – hear examples broadcast by the World Service. http://www.bbc.co.uk/worldservice/programmes/archive/index.shtml

BBC Radio Five Live – the domestic news and sport service on AM and DAB, and via the Sky and Freeview digital platforms. http://www.bbc.co.k/fivelive/

BJTC – the Broadcast Journalism Training Council. http://www.bjtc.org.uk/

Campaign for Press and Broadcasting Freedom. http://www.cpbf.org.uk

CNN Radio News – live news coverage. http://www.cnn.com/audio/radio/winmedia.html

Digital radio – the BBC's digital radio website, with information on different digital platforms and further links. http://www.bbc.co.uk/digital/radio/

History of BBC and Independent Local Radio (ILR) – independent website with audio. http://www.transdiffusion.org/rmc/index.asp

Independent Local Radio – another history website. http://www.thisisilr.org.uk/

Independent Radio News – the IRN website. http://www.irn.co.uk/

London radio stations – informative guide with many useful links. http://homepages.enterprise.net/paulbaker/london_radio/

National Union of Journalists – advice and support from the journalists' trade union in the United Kingdom. http://www.nuj.org.uk/

NPR – National Public Radio in the United States. http://www.npr.org/

Ofcom – the UK media regulator, the Office for Communications. http://www.ofcom.org.uk/

Radio Academy – the United Kingdom forum for the radio industry and academia. http://www.radioacademy.org/

Radio documentaries – examples of documentary production in the United States, archived and available for free downloading. http://www.theamericaproject.org/documentaries/

Radio Studies Network – based in the UK, an international forum for academic studies of radio. http://www.radiostudiesnetwork.org.uk/

RAJAR – the official UK radio audience research organisation, recognised by most of the industry. www.rajar.co.uk

Reuters – news and company information. www.reuters.co.uk

Skillset – the UK's Sector Skills Council for the media industries. http://www.skillset.org/

Sky News Radio – access to the radio and audio news service of BSkyB. http://news.sky.com/skynews/fixed_article/0,,70004-1200025,00.html

Testbed Productions – an independent production company, producing documentaries for a number of BBC radio networks. http://www.testbed.co.uk/docarchive. html

You and Yours – BBC Radio 4's daily consumer magazine programme. http://www.bbc.co.uk/radio4/youandyours/

REFERENCES

ABC (2006) Average daily newspaper sales, 30 January to 26 February, London: Audit Bureau of Circulation.

Adie, K. (2002) *The Kindness of Strangers*, London: Headline.

Ala-Fossi, M. (2004) 'Digital reflections of Finnish speech journalism: YLE Radio Peili', in A. Crisell (ed.), *More than a Music Box: Radio Cultures and Communities in a Multi-Media World*, Oxford: Berghahn.

Alia, V. (2004) *Media Ethics and Social Change*, Edinburgh: Edinburgh University Press.

Allan, S. (2004) *News Culture*, Maidenhead: Open University Press.

Allan, S. (ed.) (2005a) *Journalism: Critical Issues*, Maidenhead: Open University Press.

Allan, S. (2005b) 'Hidden in plain sight – journalism's critical issues', in S. Allan (ed.), *Journalism: Critical Issues*, Maidenhead: Open University Press.

Anania, F. (1995) 'Italian public television in the 1970s: a predictable confusion', *Historical Journal of Film, Radio and Television*, 15 (3).

Barnard, S. (1989) *On the Radio: Music Radio in Britain*, Milton Keynes: Open University Press.

Barnard, S. (2000) *Studying Radio*, London: Arnold.

Barnett, S. (2005) 'Opportunity or threat? The BBC, investigative journalism and the Hutton Report', in S. Allan (ed.), *Journalism: Critical Issues*, Maidenhead: Open University Press.

BBC (1996) *Charter and Agreement*, London: British Broadcasting Corporation. http://www.bbc.co.uk/info/policies/charter

BBC (2004) *Annual Report and Accounts*, London: British Broadcasting Corporation.

BBC (2005) *Editorial Guidelines*, London: British Broadcasting Corporation. http://www.bbc.co.uk/guidelines/editorialguidelines/assets/guidelinedocs/Producersguidelines.pdf.

BBC (2007) 'BBC World Service: About Us', London: British Broadcasting Corporation. http://www.bbc.co.uk/worldservice/us/index.shtml (accessed 2/07/07).

Beaman, J. (2000) *Interviewing for Radio*, London: Routledge.

Bell, P. and van Leeuwen, T. (1994) *The Media Interview: Confession, Contest, Conversation*, Sydney: University of New South Wales Press.

Belsey, A. and Chadwick, R. (1992) *Ethical Issues in Journalism and the Media*, London: Routledge.

Bignell, J. (2005) *Big Brother: Reality TV in the Twenty-First Century*, Basingstoke: Palgrave.

Born, G. (2005) *Uncertain Vision: Birt, Dyke and the Reinvention of the BBC*, London: Vintage.

Boyd, A. (2001) *Broadcast Journalism* (5th edn), Oxford: Focal Press.

Boyle, A. (1972) *Only the Wind Will Listen: Reith of the BBC*, London: Hutchinson.

Brabazon, T. (2002) 'Australian popular culture and media studies', *Year's Work in Critical and Cultural Theory*, 9 (1).

Briggs, A. (1970) *The History of Broadcasting in the United Kingdom: Volume III – The War of Words*, London: Oxford University Press.

Briggs, A. (1979) *The History of Broadcasting in the United Kingdom: Volume IV – Sound and Vision*, Oxford: Oxford University Press.

Briggs, A. (1995a) *The History of Broadcasting in the United Kingdom: Volume I – The Birth of Broadcasting* (2nd edn), Oxford: Oxford University Press.

Briggs, A. (1995b) *The History of Broadcasting in the United Kingdom: Volume II – The Golden Age of Wireless* (2nd edn), Oxford: Oxford University Press.

Briggs, A. (1995c) *The History of Broadcasting in the United Kingdom: Volume V – Competition*, Oxford: Oxford University Press.

Briggs, A. and Burke, P. (2002) *A Social History of the Mass Media: From Gutenberg to the Internet,* Cambridge: Polity Press.

Briggs, A. and Cobley, P. (eds) (2002) *The Media: An Introduction* (2nd edn), Harlow: Longman.

Burns, T. (1977) *The BBC: Public Institution and Private World*, London: Macmillan.

Campbell, V. (2004) *Information Age Journalism: Journalism in an International Context*, London: Arnold.

Capella, J. and Jamieson, K. (1997) *Spiral of Cynicism: The Press and the Public Good*, New York: Oxford University Press.

Carey, J.W. (1988) *Communication as Culture*, Boston, MA: Unwin Hyman.

Carter, Jr., R.E. (1958) 'Newspaper gatekeepers and the sources of news', *Public Opinion Quarterly*, 22.

Channel 4 (2008) 'Morning Report', London: Channel Four Television Corporation http://www.channel4.com/news/watchlisten/morning-report.jsp

Chantler, P. and Harris, S. (1992) *Local Radio Journalism*, Oxford: Focal.

Chapman, J. (2005) *Comparative Media History*, Cambridge: Polity Press.

Chomsky, N. (1989) *Necessary Illusions*, London: Pluto.

Clayman, S.E. (2004) 'Arenas of interaction in the mediated public sphere', *Poetics*, 32 (29).

Cohen, S. (1973) *Folk Devils and Moral Panics: The Creation of the Mods and Rockers*, St Albans: Paladin.

Collett, P. and Lamb, R. (1986) *Watching People Watching Television: Final Report to the IBA*, Oxford: University of Oxford, Department of Experimental Psychology.

Cone, S. (1998) 'Presuming a right to deceive: Radio Free Europe, Radio Liberty, the CIA and the news media', *Journalism History* 24 (4).

Crawford Committee (1926) *Report of the Broadcasting Committee, 1925*, Cmd 2599, London: HMSO.

CRCA (2006) *Response to Draft BBC Charter and Agreement*, London: Commercial Radio Companies Association.

Crisell, A. (1994) *Understanding Radio* (2nd edn), London and New York: Routledge.

Crisell, A. (2002) *An Introductory History of British Broadcasting* (2nd edn), London: Routledge.

Crisell, A. (ed.) (2004a) *More than a Music Box: Radio Cultures and Communities in a Multi-Media World*, Oxford: Berghahn.

Crisell, A. (2004b) 'Look with thine ears: BBC Radio 4 and its significance in a multi-media age', in A. Crisell (ed.), *More than a Music Box: Radio Cultures and Communities in a Multi-Media World*, Oxford: Berghahn.

Crisell, A. (2006) *A Study of Modern Television: Thinking Inside the Box*, Basingstoke: Palgrave.

Crisell, A. and Starkey, G. (2006) 'News and local radio', in B. Franklin (ed.), *Making the Local News: Local Journalism in Context* (2nd edn), London: Routledge.

Crook, T. (1998) *International Radio Journalism*, London: Routledge.

Curran, J. (1990) 'The new revisionism in mass communication research: a reappraisal', *European Journal of Communication*, 5 (2).

Curran, J. and Seaton, J. (1997) *Power without Responsibility: The Press and Broadcasting in Britain* (5th edn), London: Routledge.

Curran, J. and Seaton, J. (2003) *Power without Responsibility: The Press and Broadcasting in Britain* (6th edn), London: Routledge.

Davies, H. (2006) '*Today* editor goes with a dig at Humphrys', *The Daily Telegraph*, 6 May.

DCMS (Department of Culture, Media and Sport) (2006) *A Public Service for All: The BBC in the Digital Age*, Cm 6763, London: HMSO.

Delano, A. (2000) 'No sign of a better job: 100 years of British journalism', *Journalism Studies*, 1 (2).

Donovan, P. (1992) *The Radio Companion*, London: Grafton.

Donovan, P. (1997) *All Our Todays: Forty Years of Radio 4's 'Today' Programme*, London: Cape.

Dyke, G. (2004) *Inside Story*, London: HarperCollins.

EBU (2004) *Radio: Public Radio in Europe 2004*, Geneva: European Broadcasting Union.

El-Nawawy, M. and Iskandar Farag, A. (2002) *Al-Jazeera: How the Free Arab News Network Scooped the World and Changed the Middle East*, Boulder, CO: Westview Press.

EU (2006) 'Success stories: BBC Somali Journalism Training Project', Brussels: European Union, Delegation of the European Commission to Kenya. http://www.delken.ec.europa.eu/en/information.asp? MenuID=3&SubMenuID=14&ThirdmenuID= 15 (accessed 1/9/06).

Everitt, A. (2003) *New Voices: An Evaluation of 15 Access Radio Projects*, London: Radio Authority.

Fairclough, N. (1989) *Language and Power*, Harlow: Longman.

Fairclough, N. (1995) *Media Discourse*, London: Arnold.

Ferguson, R. (2000) *Representing Race*, London: Arnold.

Fink, C. (1988) *Media Ethics*, New York: McGraw-Hill.

Fleming, C. (2002) *The Radio Handbook*, London: Routledge.

Flew, T. (2007) *Understanding Global Media*, Basingstoke: Palgrave.

Fowler, R. (1991) *Language in the News: Discourse and Ideology in the Press*, London: Routledge.

Franklin, B. (1997) *Newszac and News Media*, London: Arnold.

Franklin, B. (1998) 'McJournalism: the McDonalization thesis and the UK local press', in S. Allan (ed.), *Contemporary Journalism: Critical Essays*. Milton Keynes: Open University Press.

Franklin, B. (ed.) (2001) *British Television Policy: A Reader*, London: Routledge.

Franklin, B. (ed.) (2005) *British Television Policy: The MacTaggart Lectures*, Edinburgh: Edinburgh University Press.

Franklin, B., Hamer, M., Hanna, M., Kinsey, M. and Richardson, J.E. (2005) *Key Concepts in Journalism Studies*, London: Sage.

Frost, C. (2000) *Media Ethics and Self-Regulation*, Harlow: Pearson Education.

Galtung, J. and Ruge, M. (1965) 'The structure of foreign news: the presentation of the Congo, Cuba and Cyprus crises in four foreign newspapers', *Journal of International Peace Research*, 1.

Garfield, S. (1998) *The Nation's Favourite: The True Adventures of Radio 1*, London: Faber & Faber.

Gerbner, G., Gross, L., Morgan, M. and Signorielli, N. (2002) 'Growing up with television: cultivation processes', in J. Bryant, and D. Zillman (eds), *Media Effects*, Mahwah, NJ: Lawrence Erlbaum Associates.

Giddens, A. (1984) *The Constitution of Society: Outline of the Theory of Structuration*, Cambridge: Polity Press.

Glasgow University Media Group (1976) *Bad News*, London: Routledge and Kegan Paul.

Glasgow University Media Group (1980) *More Bad News*, London: Routledge and Kegan Paul.

Glasgow University Media Group (1982) *Really Bad News*, London: Writers and Readers Cooperative.

Golding, P. and Murdock, G. (1973) 'For a political economy of mass media', in R. Miliband and J. Saville (eds), *Socialist Register*, London: Merlin.

Golding, P. and Murdock, G. (2000) 'Culture, communications and political economy', in J. Curran and M. Gurevitch (eds), *Mass Media and Society* (3rd edn), London: Arnold.

Goodwin, G. and Smith, R. (1994) *Groping for Ethics in Journalism*, Ames, IA: Iowa State University Press.

Goody, E. (ed.) (1978) *Questions and Politeness*, Cambridge: Cambridge University Press.

Gordon, J. (2001) *The RSL: Ultra Local Radio*, Luton: University of Luton Press.

Gurevitch, M. (1996) 'The globalisation of electronic journalism', in J. Curran and M. Gurevitch (eds), *Mass Media and Society*, London: Methuen.

Habermas, J. (1989) *The Structural Transformation of the Public Sphere*, Cambridge: Polity Press.

Hall, A. and Joseph, N. (2002) 'The impact of political talk radio exposure on attributions about the outcome of the 1996 US presidential election', *Journal of Communication*, 52 (2).

Hall, S. (1974) 'Media power: the double bind', *Journal of Communication*, 24 (4).

Hall, S. (1981) 'The determinations of news photographs', in S. Cohen and J. Young (eds), *The Manufacture of News*, London: Constable.

Hansard (2003) 'Broadcasting (Wales)', in *Hansard Debates for 21 January* (part 33, column 274), London: HMSO.

Harcup, T. and O'Neill, D. (2001) 'What is news? Galtung and Ruge revisited', *Journalism Studies*, 2 (2).

Harris, S. (1991) 'Erasive Action: how politicians respond to questions in political interviews', in P. Scannell (ed.) *Broadcast Talk*, London: Sage.

Harrison, J. (2006) *News*, London: Routledge.

Hazel, K. (2001) 'The media and nationalism in Québec: a complex relationship', *Journalism Studies*, 2 (1).

Hendy, D. (2000a) 'A political economy of radio in the digital age', *Journal of Radio Studies*, 7 (1).

Hendy, D. (2000b) *Radio in the Global Age*, Cambridge: Polity Press.

Hendy, D. (2007) *Life on Air: A History of Radio Four*, Oxford: Oxford University Press.

Herman, E. and Chomsky, N. (1994) *Manufacturing Consent: The Political Economy of Mass Media*, New York: Pantheon.

Hogarth, D. (2001) 'The other documentary tradition: early radio documentaries in Canada', *Historical Journal of Film, Radio and Television'*, 21 (2).

Hood, S. and O'Leary, G. (1990) *Questions of Broadcasting*, London: Methuen.

Hudson, G. and Rowlands, S. (2007) *The Broadcast Journalism Handbook*, Harlow: Pearson.

Hutchby, I. (2005) *Media Talk: Conversation Analysis and the Study of Broadcasting*, Maidenhead: Open University Press.

Hutchby, I. (2006) *Confrontation Talk: Arguments, Asymmetries, and Power on Talk Radio*, Mahwah, NJ: Lawrence Erlbaum Associates.

Hutton, Lord (2004) *Report of the Inquiry into the Circumstances Surrounding the Death of Dr David Kelly C.M.G.*, London: HMSO.

Jackson, K. (2003) *Media Ownership Regulation in Australia*, Canberra: Parliament of Australia. http://www.aph.gov.au/library/intguide/sp/media_regulations.htm (accessed 10/03/05).

Katz, E., Blumler, J. and Gurevitch, M. (1974) 'Utilization of mass communication by the individual', in J. Blumler and E. Katz (eds), *The Uses of Mass Communication*, London: Sage.

Koch, T. (1990) *The News as Myth: Fact and Context in Journalism*, New York: Greenwood Press.

Kuhn, R. (1995) *The Media in France*, London: Routledge.

Kuhn, R. and Neveu, E. (eds) (2002) *Political Journalism: New Challenges, New Practices*, London: Routledge.

Lasswell, H. (1927) *Propaganda Techniques in the First World War*, New York: Knopf.

Leavis, F.R. and Thompson, D. (1933) *Culture and Environment: The Training of Critical Awareness* (reprinted 1977), London: Greenwood Press.

Lewis, J., Inthorn, S. and Wahl-Jorgensen, K. (2005) *Citizens or Consumers? What the Media Tell Us about Political Participation*, Maidenhead: Open University Press.

Lewis, P.M. and Booth, J. (1989) *The Invisible Medium: Public, Commercial and Community Radio*, Basingstoke: Palgrave Macmillan.

Livingstone, S. (1990) *Making Sense of Television: The Psychology of Audience Interpretation*, Oxford: Pergamon.

MacGregor, B. (1997) *Live, Direct and Biased? Making Television News in the Satellite Age*, London: Arnold.

MacKenzie, K. (2000) 'Let's lose the tea leaves', the *Guardian*, 4 September.

Mackenzie, K. (2002) 'RAJAR accuracy questioned by MacKenzie', *The Radio Magazine*, 520 (30 March).

Madsen, V. (2006) 'Radio and the documentary imagination: thirty years of experiment, innovation, and revelation', *Radio Journal*, 3 (3).

Marr, A. (2004) *My Trade*, Basingstoke: Macmillan.

McCauley, M. (2005) *NPR: The Trials and Triumphs of National Public Radio*, New York: Columbia University Press.

McChesney, R. (2000) *Rich Media, Poor Democracy: Communication Politics in Difficult Times*, New York: New Press.

McCleneghan, J. (2006) 'FM local newscasts in the Southwest: a disappearing service', *Social Science Journal*, 43 (3).

McCleneghan, J. and Sean-Ragland, R. (2002) 'Municipal elections and community media', *Social Science Journal*, 39 (2).

McCombs, M. and Shaw, D. (1972) 'The agenda-setting function of the mass media', *Public Opinion Quarterly*, 36 (2).

McCombs, M. and Shaw, D. (1993) 'The evolution of agenda-setting research: twenty-five years in the marketplace of ideas', *Journal of Communication*, 43 (2).

McLeish, R. (2005) *Radio Production* (5th edn), Oxford: Focal Press.

McLuhan, M. (2001) *Understanding Media*, London: Routledge.

McManus, J. (1994) *Market-driven Journalism: Let the Citizen Beware*, Thousand Oaks, CA: Sage.

McManus, J. (2002) 'Does serving the market conflict with serving the public?', in D. McQuail (ed.), *McQuail's Reader in Mass Communication Theory*, London: Sage.

McNair, B. (2000) *Journalism and Democracy: An Evaluation of the Political Public Sphere*, London: Routledge.

McNair, B. (2003) *News and Journalism in the UK* (4th edn), London: Routledge.

McNair, B. (2005) 'The emerging chaos of global news culture', in S. Allan (ed.) *Journalism: Critical Issues*, Maidenhead: Open University Press.

McQuail, D. (2005) *McQuail's Mass Communication Theory*, London: Sage.

McQuail, D., Blumler, J. and Brown, J. (1972) 'The television audience: a revised perspective', in D. McQuail (ed.), *Sociology of the Mass Media*, London: Penguin.

Mesbah, H.M. (2006) 'The impact of linear versus nonlinear listening to radio news on recall and comprehension', *Journal of Radio Studies*, 13 (2).

Mitchell, C. (ed.) (2001) *Women and Radio: Airing Differences*, London: Routledge.

Monteleone, F. (2003) *Storia della radio e della televisione in Italia*, Venice: Marsilio.

Neil, R., Benson, G., Boaden, H., Tait, R., van Klaveren, A. and Whittles, S. (2004) *The BBC's Journalism after Hutton: The Report of the Neil Review Team*, London: BBC. http://www.bbc.co.uk/info/policies/pdf/neil_report.pdf.

Nelson, M. (1997) *War of the Black Heavens: The Battles of Western Broadcasting in the Cold War*, Syracuse, NY: Syracuse University Press.

NUJ (2004) *Code of Conduct*, London: National Union of Journalists. http://www.nuj.org.uk/inner.php?docid=59.

Ofcom (2005) *Broadcasting Code*, London: Office of Communications. www.ofcom.org.uk

Ofcom (2006) *Future of Radio*, London: Office of Communications.

Peacock Committee (1986) *Report of the Committee on Financing the BBC, 1986*, Cmd 9824, London: HMSO.

Peirce, C.S. (1960) *Collected Papers* (vols I and II), edited by C. Hartshorne and P. Weiss, Cambridge, MA: Harvard University Press.

Pew Research Center (1999) *Striking the Balance: Audience Interests, Business Pressures and Journalists' Values*, Washington, DC: Pew Research Center for the People and the Press. http://people-press.org/reports/display.php3?PageID=316.

Pew Research Center (2004) *News Audiences Increasingly Polarised*, Washington, DC: Pew Research Center for the People and the Press. http://people-press.org/reports/display.php3?ReportID=215

Phillips, G. and Lindgren, M. (2002) *The Australian Broadcast Journalism Manual*, Melbourne: Oxford University Press.

Pilger, J. (1998) *Hidden Agendas*, London: Vintage.

Radio Advertising Bureau (2007) *Radio Marketplace Charts*, London: Radio Advertising Bureau.

Radio Authority (1995) *Media Ownership: The Government's Proposals (CM2072) – A Response by the Radio Authority*, London: The Radio Authority.

Radio Magazine (2006) 'City Talk will be "closer to the edge"', *Radio Magazine*, 763 accessed 22/11/07.

RAJAR (1997) *Quarterly Summary First to Fourth Quarters*, London: Radio Joint Audience Research Ltd.

RAJAR (1998) *Quarterly Summary First to Fourth Quarters*, London: Radio Joint Audience Research Ltd.

RAJAR (1999) *Quarterly Summary First to Fourth Quarters*, London: Radio Joint Audience Research Ltd.

RAJAR (2005) *Quarterly Summary, First Quarter*, London: Radio Joint Audience Research Ltd.

RAJAR (2006) *Quarterly Summary, First and Third Quarters*, London: Radio Joint Audience Research Ltd.

RAJAR (2007) *Quarterly Summary, First Quarter*, London: Radio Joint Audience Research Ltd. http://www.rajar.co.uk/QuarterlySummary/

Razafimbelo-Harisoa, M.S. (2005) 'Radio in Madagascar: roles and missions', *Radio Journal*, 3 (1).

Regal, B. (2005) *Radio: The Life Story of a Technology*, Westport, CT: Greenwood Press.

Ritzer, G. (1998) *The McDonaldization Thesis*, London: Sage.

Roberts, B. (2003) *Drinking in the Last Chance Saloon: Individual Privacy, Media Intrusion and the Press Complaints Commission*, Manchester: University of Manchester Press.

Roncarolo, F. (2002) 'A crisis in the mirror: old and new elements in Italian political communication', in R. Kuhn and E. Neveu (eds), *Political Journalism: New Challenges, New Practices*, London: Routledge.

Ross, K. (2001) 'Women at work: journalism as en-gendered practice', *Journalism Studies*, 2 (4).

Ross, K. (2005) 'Women in the boyzone: gender, news and *her*story', in S. Allan (ed.), *Journalism: Critical Issues*, Maidenhead: Open University Press.

Sanders, K. (2003) *Ethics and Journalism*, London: Sage.

de Saussure, F. (1983 [1916]) *Cours de linguistique générale* (trans. as *Course in General Linguistics*), London: Duckworth.

Scannell, P. (1991) 'Introduction: the relevance of talk', in P. Scannell (ed.), *Broadcast Talk*, London: Sage.

Scannell, P. (1996) *Radio, Television and Modern Life*, Oxford: Blackwell.

Schlesinger, P. (1987) *Putting 'Reality' Together*, London: Methuen.

Seymour-Ure, C. (1974) *The Political Impact of Mass Media*, London: Constable.

Seymour-Ure, C. (1996) *The British Press and Broadcasting since 1945* (2nd edn), Oxford: Blackwell.

Shanahan, M. and Neill, K. (2005) *The Great New Zealand Radio Experiment*, Wellington: Dunmore Press.

Sharp, R. (2006) 'Humphrys bites back at "Today" jibes', *The Observer*, 5 June.

Sheridan Burns, L. (2002) *Understanding Journalism*, London: Sage.

Shingler, M. and Wieringa, C. (1998) *On Air: Methods and Meanings of Radio*, London: Arnold.

Skillset (2002) *Journalists at Work: Independent Survey by the Journalism Training Forum*. www.skillset/org/research/workforce

Skillset (2003) *Skillset Workforce Survey 2003*. www.skillset/org/research/workforce

Snow, J. (2004) *Shooting History: A Personal Journey*, London: HarperCollins.

Starkey, G. (2003) 'Radio audience research: challenging the "gold standard"', *Cultural Trends*, 45, London: Policy Studies Institute.

Starkey, G. (2004a) 'BBC Radio 5 Live: extending choice through "Radio Bloke"?', in A. Crisell (ed.), *More than a Music Box: Radio Cultures and Communities in a Multi-Media World*, Oxford: Berghahn.

Starkey, G. (2004b) *Radio in Context*, Basingstoke: Palgrave.

Starkey, G. (2004c) 'Estimating audiences: sampling in television and radio audience research', *Cultural Trends*, 13 (1).

Starkey, G. (2007) *Balance and Bias in Journalism: Representation, Regulation and Democracy*, Basingstoke: Palgrave Macmillan.

Stokes, J. and Reading, A. (eds) (1999) *The Media in Britain: Current Debates and Developments*, Basingstoke: Macmillan.

Street, J. (2001) *Mass Media, Politics and Democracy*, Basingstoke: Palgrave.

Street, S. (2002) *A Concise History of British Radio*, Tiverton: Kelly.

Stuart, C. (ed.) (1975) *The Reith Diaries*, London: Collins.

Sutter, D. (2001) 'Can the media be so liberal? The economics of media bias', *Cato Journal* 20 (3) http://www.cato.org/pubs/journal/cj20n3/cj20n3-7.pdf

Tacchi, J. (2000) 'The need for radio theory in the digital age', *International Journal of Cultural Studies*, 3 (2).

Thompson, J.B. (1990) *Ideology and Modern Culture*, Cambridge: Polity Press.

Tunstall, J. (1971) *Journalists at Work*, London: Constable.

Turner, G. (2000) 'Talkback, advertising and journalism: a cautionary tale of self-regulated commercial radio', *International Journal of Cultural Studies*, 3 (2).

Underwood, D. (1993) *When MBAs Rule the Newsroom: How Markets and Managers Are Shaping Today's Media*, New York: Columbia University Press.

Watson, J. and Hill, A. (2000) *Dictionary of Media and Communication Studies*, London: Arnold.

Weaver, D.H. (2005) 'Who are journalists?', in H. de Burgh (ed.), *Making Journalists: Diverse Models, Global Issues*, London: Routledge.

Welsh, T., Greenwood, W. and Banks, D. (2005) *McNae's Essential Law for Journalists* (18th edn), Oxford University Press.

Welsh, T., Greenwood, W. and Banks, D. (2007) *McNae's Essential Law for Journalists* (19th edn), Oxford: Oxford University Press.

Weza, S. (2002) 'Zimbabwe's media under scrutiny: the work of the Media Monitoring Project in Zimbabwe', *Round Table*, 91 (366).

White, D.M. (1950) 'The "Gatekeeper": a case study in the selection of news', in D. Berkowitz (ed.), *Social Meanings of News: A Reader*, Thousand Oaks, CA: Sage.

Wilby, P. and Conroy, A. (1994) *The Radio Handbook*, London: Routledge.

Williams, K. (1998) *Get Me a Murder a Day! A History of Mass Communication in Britain*, London: Arnold.

Wilson, J. (1996) *Understanding Journalism*, London: Routledge.

Winston, B. (1998) *Media Technology and Society*, London: Routledge.

Wright, S. (1997) *Just Keep Talking*, London: Simon & Schuster.

INDEX

Weaver, D. 35, 36, 38
Welles, Orson 118
Welsh, T. 71, 154
Weza, S. 157
White, D.M. 106
Wieringa, C. 151
Wilby, P. 152
Williams, K. 150
Wilson, J. 154
Wiltshire Radio 32, 39

Winston, B. 3
Wireless Group 32, 33, 78, 115
World at One 14, 63
World Tonight 14, 63, 150
Wright, Steve 153

Xfm 127

YLE Radio Peili 125
You and Yours 63, 64, 159